THE Yellow Star HOUSE

THE REMARKABLE STORY OF ONE BOY'S SURVIVAL IN A PROTECTED HOUSE IN HUNGARY

PAUL V. REGELBRUGGE

ISBN: 978-1-4834-7594-3 (sc)
ISBN: 978-1-4834-7593-6 (e)

Lulu Publishing Services rev. date: 08/13/2019

Contents

Part I

Part IV

Dedication

This book is dedicated to all my students – past, present and future. You inspire and motivate me every day to be the best person and teacher for you as possible. Thank you for teaching me.

The book is additionally dedicated to the memory and honor of Robert Holczer, Ara Jeretzian, and their respective families. You will never be forgotten!

Acknowledgements

I wrote *The Yellow Star House* for two primary reasons. First, I was a friend of Robert until he died on August 28, 2017. I met him when I, a teacher then in Spokane, Washington, asked him to come speak to my 6th grade students as a culmination to their lessons about the Holocaust and the mandate that "change begins with me." My students and I were enthralled by the truly unique story of Robert, who transported the amputated limbs of wounded patients during the Siege of Budapest during World War II, and the motivations of his rescuer, Ara Jeretzian. Consequently, because we became friends over the last decade of his life, I wrote this to honor him, his family, and what Jeretzian, who was recognized by *Yad Vashem* in 1981 as Righteous Among the Nations, did to save him and 400 others. Second, the story of the Jews in Budapest has never been told in a context such as this, hopefully accessible to readers of all kinds and, more importantly, one which affords readers both the perspectives of victim and rescuer.

In addition, honoring my commitment to the United States Holocaust Memorial Museum as a Museum Teacher Fellow, writing this book has helped preserve the memory of Robert, a Holocaust survivor, Ara Jeretzian, a rescuer, and the countless others who were victims of the Holocaust, the essence of which was hatred. I sincerely hope that this book provides lessons about the senselessness of hate, where hate leads, and how love, kindness and seeking understanding are the best antidotes to hatred.

I owe thanks to so many people. This would never have come to fruition without any of the following: Kristin Thompson of the USHMM, as my then MTF Director, both encouraged and supported this "outreach project," ultimately helping to get Mr. Jeretzian's memoir translated into English. The USHMM funded the translation, which was ultimately and skillfully completed by Mr. Adam T. Bogar of Link Translations, courtesy of Halil Yigit. Fellow MTF Taylor Beal volunteered endless hours to help edit and provide elucidating feedback for the original draft. My entire MTF cohort 2017 has been supportive and integral to my motivation for this project. Thank you, Lisa Reardon, for meaningfully editing two chapters, my proposal, and offering me great insights, and Ben Jones, for patiently reading the first draft and offering invaluable comments and questions.

Thanks also to Ilana Cone Kennedy, Julia Thompson, Dee Simon and all at Seattle's Holocaust Center for Humanity, without whom I would never have met Robert nor would I be the teacher and person I am. Thanks to Joanna Millick of Mir Corporation for putting so much heart into the importance of this learning, Mir's Dmitry Rudich for organizing my 2018 Budapest trip and Adrienne Krizsevszky for being my guide in Budapest.

Thank you to Jan Holczer, Mary De La Fontaine and the entire Holczer family for being so supportive and encouraging even though this project has often been such a painfully sad reminder of your loss. Your photos, stories and family background information were indispensable. I also sincerely appreciate the Hungarian cookbook, Jan! Thanks, Ara Jeretzian, for supporting my efforts to bring your father's story into greater prominence. Your messages and words enabled and inspired me to show your father as accurately as possible. It was a privilege and honor to meet you in Budapest.

Thank you so much, Dr. Danny Berg, for your incredible interest, passion, excitement, encouragement and overwhelming support for this book. You helped me, among other ways, to show and introduce others to your incredible mum, Eva, the girl with laughing eyes. You also helped me appreciate even more wholeheartedly the incredible nature of the story of what happened at 1 Zichy Jeno utca.

Thanks to my mom, Angela, and stepfather, Michael Kenyon, for your love and support. You are awesome, and I love you immeasurably! Thank you brothers David, virtuoso guitarist, and Daniel, mega-talented writer, for always pushing the envelope.

Last, thank you to my wife, Marla, and my sons, Adrien and Gabe. You've supported and encouraged me along this journey in every way, and I'll never forget it. I love you all so very much!

PART I

1

1935
Marbles in the Gutter

If he lay perfectly still -- not a sound, not a breath, nothing -- he wouldn't be caught. The boy had been training for this moment. He and his parents had moved to this small apartment in the 5th District of Budapest on Rottenbiller utca just nine days ago. Since then, he had practiced sliding under the giant walnut china cabinet without his mother noticing. There was just enough space for him to fit. Unless a person got down on all fours, there was no way – he was positive – that he could be detected. And now that his mother's Steinway piano was delivered, the time to hide was upon him! He may be little; he may be just six, but Robert knew, of course, what would happen if he was apprehended.

"Robi!" His mother called, "Robi, it's time for your lessons, darling. Robi, where did you go? How else will you become Hungary's Mozart if you don't practice?"

Robert held his breath. His mother's high black heels announced her every step on the immaculate wooden floor. She was coming closer, and now she stopped – directly beside the cabinet … HIS cabinet!

Wait, Robert thought to himself, *How…?* Suddenly Robert felt firm pressure around both ankles and realized he was being dragged from beneath the cabinet. Away from his dark, safe cover, and into the bright light of his inescapable fate: It was time to practice the piano.

"Ha, ha, now look what we have here -- a dirty, lazy boy!"

"I won't do it, *Anu*, I won't. I'm not yours to make and do." Robert squirmed free of his mother's grasp and tried to run. "I hate the piano," he exclaimed. Realizing there was truly no place to run in the small apartment, he started to wind around the piano – the object of his torment – when, to his great surprise, his mother began to give chase!

"I'll get you, little devil!" On her way around the piano, his mother grabbed the dreaded wooden spoon she sometimes used to spank him and -- was she smiling?

Robert stuck out his tongue. "Devils don't play the piano, *Anu*," he taunted.

Just as he turned again around the corner to see which direction his mother was coming, he heard the front door open, and then felt a giant arm lift him into the air.

"Devils don't dare talk back to their mothers, if they know what's good for them!"

"*Apu!*"

The arrival of Robert's father spared the boy from capture. He hugged his father with all his might.

"Can we go now, *Apu*, to *Nagymama's* -- grandmother's house, please?" Robert pleaded.

"Not so fast, Robi. You two were making such a racket I could hear you all the way from the stairs. Now --" he said, winking at Robert, "seems to me you owe your mother an apology, *and* an hour of lessons!"

"But—"

"Don't you 'but' me- now *do* it. Your mother knows what's best for you far more than I do."

"But when can –"

Robert's father didn't need to say anything further. He gave "the look," and Robert understood that this meant the end of the conversation. His mother, half smiling and half glaring, stood beside the piano bench. She put down the wooden spoon and raised her right index finger, motioning, "Come here."

Robert's father set down his things beside the cabinet, kicked off his shoes, dutifully placed them beside the entry door, and then resumed the custom to which he had adhered for as long as Robert could remember. After tenderly kissing *Anu* on her lips, he walked over to the radio and turned on BBC Europe. He poured himself a fresh cup of black coffee from the percolator, and sat beside the radio to listen to the world news.

"Why do you listen to this news, *Apu?*" Robert would ask. "It hardly ever talks about Hungary; what's happening around *us*."

"It is necessary to consider things from many points of view, Robi," his father often told him. "Always remember this: If we look with only one eye, we are blind to things and people that we might have seen had we looked with two eyes. We must take care not to place our trust only in whom or what is most popular at the time…."

Little of this made much sense to Robert at his tender age, but the boy knew this: He worshipped his sandy haired, blue-eyed father, and if his *Apu* did or said something, it must be right. Though he lacked the formal education of Robert's mother, his father always seemed to have all the answers. When his father would take him along to his favorite café, the luxurious New York *Kavehaz* on Erzsebet krt., Robert gaped in awe at how one person after another would approach his father to greet him, ask for advice, wish him well, and even offer to pay for his coffee or a biscuit (he always refused). Lajos Holczer was, in business, a salesman of colognes and perfumes. But he was, to Robert, a god whose gentle but firm demeanor and respect and concern for others – especially his enormous family of 12 brothers and sisters – were … amazing.

Of course, Robert also loved his mother. But whereas *Apu* represented freedom, discovery, and the pursuit of knowing things – important things that seemed to matter like life and death -- his *Anu* was a closed door. Rules, duties, unjust impositions … and the piano! Unlike his father, who didn't seek out others but was too polite to refuse them or treat them with anything less than respect, Robert's pretty, industrious mother was a social butterfly who lived for endless, tiresome conversation with anyone and everyone. It always bored Robert so.

Plus, Robert resented visits to the home of *Anu*'s Orthodox parents in Vac, 40 kilometers north of Budapest, and the way his mother's family treated him like a problem to be solved or cured. To them, he wasn't "Jewish" enough. He would often sneak his way around eating kosher, he showed no enthusiasm for his religious lessons, and he never wanted to wear his yarmulke. Worse, Robert despised how they were condescending toward his father, often snidely belittling his lack of education. No, a visit to his mother's parents was quite the opposite of time spent with his father's Jewish, though non-practicing family, most of whom thankfully lived much nearer to Robert's new home on Rottenbiller utca.

When Robert finally finished practicing the piano, he raced to his father. "Now, *Apu*? Now can we go visit *Nagymama*?"

Just then, there was a soft knock at the door. Robert's father exhaled; then rose to open it. Robert was a step behind him, peering around his right hip.

It was Bela, Bela's little brother, Sandor, and a taller, pudgy boy whose arms were too long for his light, knit sweater. The bigger boy was probably eight or nine. Robert went to school with Bela, and though he wouldn't say they were friends, it turned out that Bela lived in the same apartment house, three doors down.

"Hello, Mr. Holczer. Hello, Robert," Bela courteously said. "This is our cousin, Gabor. He's here visiting us for the weekend from the town of God. Is it okay if Robert comes to play marbles with us outside?"

"Please, *Anu*," Robert begged his mother. He knew whose permission he needed for matters like these. "Please?"

"You'll be right outside by the corner, yes, Bela?" His mother didn't wait for his reply. "If I come out and see you in the street, I'll tell your mother, and this will be the last of your games, you hear?"

Gabor wiped his nose on his sweater sleeve. Bela replied, almost frightened, "Of course, and we won't be more than an hour, Madam."

"No, you won't, will you…?" His mother smiled wryly, now turning to her son and handing him his jacket. "Robi, dinner will be waiting when you return in an hour, so listen for the chime of the church bells. When they ring six times, you come inside, understood? Don't make me come for you...."

Robert ran excitedly into his room to retrieve his sack of marbles. He had not fared very well the last two times he played with Bela and Sandor, and so his stock of marbles was diminishing. He hoped maybe he would have better luck with Gabor here, though this giant's frequent sneezes and coughs sounded worrisome, if not gross. Immediately after they left the apartment, Gabor sneezed directly at Robert's new tan jacket -- without covering his mouth.

"Sorry," he laughed, looking to his younger cousins for approval. Bela simply nodded his head, while Sandor, who was not yet in the nearby school run by an orphanage that his brother and Robert attended, looked on in wonder, as though he were accustomed to his cousin's barbaric behavior.

"Never mind," Robert tersely replied, "Bela, you have the chalk, right?"

Without answering, Bela held up the stub of chalk as he led the troupe down the common stairs, three flights down to the building's exit. The Rottenbiller apartment house was a four-story building with five apartments per floor. Each apartment consisted of four or five rooms, including a living room, kitchen, dining room, bedroom, and bath. Robert slept on the couch in the living room, unless they entertained guests, in which case he would join his parents in the bedroom and sleep on the floor. The corridors were elaborately styled with marble columns, and there were wrought iron railings in the staircase. At the building's entrance, there was a marble paneled archway leading to the stairs.

It was now late afternoon on this brisk autumn day. The boys proceeded to the sidewalk near the street corner, beneath the tallest of a row of maple trees, the leaves of which were just beginning to take on yellow and red. One advantage to living here, in addition to their proximity to the school – which was, according to his mother, the main reason they moved so near the city center- was that there was ample room for Robert to play.

Bela got down on his knees and drew a circle, about a meter, or three feet across. He then drew another straight line several feet away from the base of the circle. He called 'red,' and so placed six of his red marbles into the center of the circle. Robert followed with six pristine blue marbles, Sandor with green and Gabor, again shoving his nose into his sweater, dropped six black marbles in a heap near the others.

"What are your rules?" Gabor challenged.

"For keeps again, right?" Robert asked. Bela and Sandor nodded, and Gabor shrugged. Bela then took out the 2 *pengo* coin to determine the throwing order. After a round robin of heads or tails, it was decided that Gabor would go first, then Bela, Robert, and Sandor.

Bela explained: "Right, Gabor, we all have our shooter marbles. We take turns trying to knock each others' marbles out of the circle by throwing behind this here line," he said, pointing. "You get a point for every marble you knock out until all the marbles are out. Then, we tally them all to figure out who wins. The player who knocks out the most marbles wins everyone else's marbles – 'for keeps!'"

Gabor spat beyond the grass and onto the red cobblestone street as a small truck passed by. "Let's get on with it, already."

"Oh, another thing, if your shooter marble – your bigger, heavier marble comes to rest inside the circle after you throw it, it's fair game until your next turn. So, if anyone knocks out your shooter marble, you automatically lose and must give all your marbles to that player, got it?"

Gabor didn't wait for Bela's question, but instead awkwardly flicked his shooter marble. Not only did it fail to even touch another player's marbles, but his shooter came to rest just inside the circle, slightly beyond where most of the regular marbles were scattered. Gabor fumed: "Anyone knocks me out, and I'll knock you out!"

Either Bela feared his cousin's threat, or simply saw the bounty of marbles he could knock out. In any event, his flick was excellent, knocking out three marbles at once: Two of Robert's, and one that belonged to Sandor. He fist-pumped in excitement, and his little brother sighed dismissively. Bela's red shooter landed safely outside of the circle after doing its impressive damage.

"Haw, nice one," snorted Gabor.

Next up was Robert. There it was. He knew he could get a quick strike to atone for the loss of his two marbles and his overall recent spot of bad luck if he could just knock out Gabor's big, black shooter marble. He knelt beside the line, gently caressed his blue shooter, took a deep breath, and flicked … it landed squarely on top of Gabor's shooter, and successfully knocked it out of the circle before his own came to a rest beside it.

"Wow, that was awesome!" Robert jumped. Sandor beamed and raised his hand to congratulate him, as Bela turned to Gabor.

"You lose, Cousin," Bela tried to suppress a smile. "You must give over your black marbles to Robert."

Gabor's head, topped with carrot orange hair and adorned with four or five freckles all curiously strewn across the left side of his face, looked like it was going to explode. He grabbed his six marbles and shooter abruptly, indifferent to knocking others from their place. Gabor stood taller than he already was, glaring at Robert.

"I know who you are. My uncle told me all about your family," he fumed. "And I'll have you know I'd rather throw my marbles down in the gutter than to give them over to a filthy Jew!"

As Gabor snarled these words just inches from Robert's puzzled, horrified face, he flung all his marbles forcefully into the red cobbled street. Robert stepped to the edge of the street to watch the black marbles he could still see bounce, then roll, then follow the pitch of the street toward the edge, and then slowly down the gutter. Down, as far as Robert's eyes could see. Away.

2

October 1941
Oranges

When Robert went to visit the small, overcrowded tenement of his grandparents in Kobanya, hours felt like minutes, minutes like seconds. Time meant nothing there in the poor section of an area primarily known for its stone quarry in District X. Because this home in the southeast section of Budapest -- the same in which his father and his 12 siblings were born and raised -- was so near to his Rottenbiller apartment, Robert was fortunate that his visits there were frequent.

Usually, laughter permeated the air there like mountain mist at dawn. There were his *Nagymama* Julia's homemade pickles and coffee cake, spicy goulash, endless heaps of beans or, on special occasions, wiener schnitzel. No, this was not a kosher household, and Robert loved every minute of it. But most of all, there was the thrill of mischief and surprise with every visit. The fact that several of Robert's father's siblings were relatively close in age to Robert afforded him the "brothers" and "sisters" he always wished to have.

Despite neither running water nor electricity in the unavoidably cluttered apartment, no one ever complained about what they lacked. To the contrary, one of the things Robert loved so much about most of his aunts and uncles was how they could always make something from nothing. They always seemed to know ways to gain access to places even though they did not have money. They never looked at challenges, including a lack of formal education, as obstacles, but rather as problems to solve – by whatever means necessary. It was as if the Holczer family extended their collective middle fingers to the Hungarian scales of class and entitlement and simply worked harder, or more often more cleverly, to enjoy fruits beyond their actual means. Sneaking into skating rinks and musical and theatrical performances, taking discarded fruits and vegetables from street vendors while they weren't looking…. This life of seemingly harmless crime and mischief was Robert's definition of freedom, of life itself in his younger days.

His father, the eldest boy, played life's game more by the rules than his siblings, serving both as primary information-gatherer and arbiter; judge and jury in disputes well beyond the walls of his parents' family and Robert's own. He did not so much seek this role as much as it came to him by virtue of the man he was. He was serious, but full of heart. Law abiding, but always asking why. Indifferent, like his entire side of the family, to God and their Jewishness, but fully supportive of Robert's mother's more Orthodox upbringing and her wishes to raise Robert to be more observant than he ever wanted to be.

Today, however, 12-year-old Robert sensed immediately that there was a tenseness in his father's family's house that weighed upon his arrival with his parents like an ample blanket of December snow atop the playgrounds in Varosliget Park near his apartment.

Robert's father had just returned two nights ago from his second eight week-long Jewish forced labor detail working to help improve and build railroad tracks in and around Budapest. So far, from what Robert knew, this was the worst it had gotten for the Jews in Hungary. Apparently, in order to help further Hungary's alliance with the Nazis, Hungary had agreed to provide able-bodied Jewish men to serve their respective purposes by doing labor. According to his father, the work was very hard and long, but they were not treated that badly. His father's increasingly gaunt appearance, however, betrayed his words. His eyes seemed more distant; his speech was slower, and his laugh became increasingly more difficult to conjure.

Even Robert and his Jewish middle school classmates were not impervious to the Nazi war cause, as they were required once a week to submit to seemingly ridiculous work in the guise of "labor battalion practice," chopping at stones, digging ditches and trenches, and being too often the objects of derision and insults by their Hungarian commanders and other onlookers. Shouts of "Dirty Jews," "Jewish scum," and "Can't you get the message yet, Jews – Just leave Europe and we'll all be better off!" rang throughout the streets often. Robert endured these and other anti-Semitic insults the way his parents told him he must: He swallowed them, growing angrier and resentful all the while.

"Robi, my dear," exhaled his *nagymama*, his grandmother, as she trudged around the oversized rectangular dining room table to kiss him. To do so, she had to navigate her ample frame beyond the protruded chair of his Aunt Aranka, who was seated staring strangely away from everyone with an empty cup of coffee in front of her. His grandmother's arms were extended for a hug, a dish towel strewn across her left shoulder, and a dripping wooden spatula in her right hand. She smothered Robert, more than hugged him. "Your uncles, Dezu and Bobby, are across the street playing football with others. Why don't you join them – there are things we must discuss with your parents. Dinner will be ready in a couple of hours."

Robert readied to object that he was old and wise enough but thought better. The lure of playing with his uncles was more tempting than the increasingly bleak news of the day. "Fine, *Nagymama*, it's great to see you too," he smiled, and promptly headed out the door to make the most of this Sunday. "Hi, bye, Auntie!"

The door closed loudly, and suddenly, up sprang Aranka to refill her coffee cup. Robert's father demanded, "What's the matter, sister?" He pulled back a chair first for his wife and then gingerly sat down himself.

"Her husband, Tamas, is dead, Lajos," blurted Robert's grandmother, waving her spatula.

"What? How?"

Aranka, whose eyes were noticeably red with dried tears, fumed as she put down her cup. "It was on his forced labor work, Lajos. I just learned this earlier this morning from Marton, Marton Gedenczi, his old friend that served with him. Where did you just get back from?" Without waiting for an answer, she continued. "Their unit was called to the Eastern Front to support the German offensive against the Russians. Do you know what the *German* version of Jewish support means?"

"Go on," said Robert's father, visibly disturbed as his hands were clenched on top of the table.

"Tamas' entire Jewish unit were given Hungarian military uniforms, if you can believe it – Marton gave me this picture of him here," she exclaimed, throwing the picture in front of her brother. "You know, Lajos, Admiral Horthy, Hungary's fearless leader, is no friend of the Jews – he has forbidden Jews to wear the uniform yet uses us to suit their purposes. And so, the Nazis, Hungarians, whatever, ordered Tamas' unit to sweep an area for land mines. Lajos, they were never even trained!" She broke. "Tamas and most others were killed the very first day!"

Robert's father stared blankly, first ahead as his wife placed her hands on his hands and whimpered, then at the picture. Staring back at him was the striking face of Tamas, whose blond hair and blue eyes in a Hungarian uniform betrayed the fact that he was a Jew. "He actually looks like them," he sighed. "They don't give proper uniforms to labor details, I should know…. Why…?" It was only then that Lajos noticed his father, both hands over his head, lying down on the couch in the dark of the living room.

"This is bad, Lajos. I told your sister, these are the worst times to be a Jew," Lajos' father said without expression.

"Exactly," agreed Aranka. "This is why I'm thinking we can't live like this. You hear the news on BBC more than any of us, Lajos. You hear how it is outside of Hungary, and now you can see it will be the same here, if not now, then soon enough."

"Well, what did you have in mind, Aranka? We've already sent inquiries to America and England about taking some, if not all of us, but who has the money for that? Even if we did, have we heard any interest from anyone about taking Europe's Jews? I don't see anyone lining up to take us," Robert's father exclaimed, frustrated, as he extended his own cup to receive coffee poured by his mother. "Besides, I just don't see that it will be as bad for us here in Hungary. Sure, we Jews are constantly reminded that we are Jews in Hungary, but so long as Hungary is allied to Germany, how do we pose a problem to anyone? It would be beneath Hungary's "dignity" to let Germans dispose of our Jews to God knows where they're sending them…."

"The question isn't how or why do we pose a problem, brother, it's more the fact that, for them, we ARE a problem. So, listen, this picture got me thinking. Why the devil did they give Tamas' unit Hungarian military uniforms, only to then offer them up as bait for landmines? I intend to take this photo in and use it as evidence that, given my own golden hair and smaller nose, I'm not a Jew. That way, as one of *them*, I can help the family as necessary. What do you think?"

"How would a picture alone solve your Jewish *problem*?"

"Leave the rest to me. I have a plan for that, with our mother's cooperation," glancing at her mother, nervously stirring her fragrant sauce on the stove. "But rest assured, you'll have a sister who is *not* a Jew, and you'll see what I can do…."

"Aranka, I love you, but let's let time run its course; do nothing rash. We are so very sorry for your loss – *our* loss. You know we all loved Tamas; let us help you with the arrangements…."

Aranka sipped her coffee as their mother turned again to place a hand on her shoulder. "You'll see, Lajos. Don't trust them. Today they send you just several kilometers from here for your forced labor, tomorrow to the front as a sacrificial lamb. You'll see…."

***

The clock on the wall exclaimed it was not yet half past noon. None of the hands on the clock on the wall of Mr. Gera's middle school art classroom were moving fast enough for Robert's burning desire to return home to talk more of yesterday's devastating news that his Uncle Tamas was killed. More particularly, Robert was struggling to discern what this meant for his own father.

Up until now, his father's forced labor stints seemed harmless enough-just things to do that one didn't want to do, like going to school. Robert and his mother could visit his father and bring him pastries and cookies, talk about their days. He generally seemed to be in good spirits on these scheduled days of visitation, permitted by their commanders whom Robert never actually saw.

Of course, it was difficult to be without his father at home during these labor assignments. The worst part, for Robert, was that in his father's absence there was no buffer between him and his mother's insistence that he continue to practice the piano. How he dreaded playing! He knew, despite his piano instructor insistence how well he was playing, that he would not grow up to become "Hungary's Mozart," as his mother dreamed. He knew he would quit the first chance he could.

The second worst part of his father's absences were his father's absences. When *Apu* was home, there was life; there was conversation; there was laughter. There was BBC Europe, or else the classical music of Liszt and Chopin was always playing. There was discussion about the news, the war, the best composers and why. Like a lawyer, *Apu* would always prove his points with evidence. He would never just opine; he would play a piece of music to demonstrate why one crescendo was more powerful than another. Why one soprano was superior to another. How the latest news of Nazi excesses and Hungarian permissiveness -- if not willingness, perplexed him more than the last.

The final worst part of being without his father was that he was obviously unable to perform his regular duties as a salesman and earn his regular salary. Gratefully, however, Robert's father was held in such high regard that his non-Jewish employer agreed to continue to pay a decent percentage of his salary to Robert's mother while her husband was off on forced labor. Robert and his mother had already been discussing that, should these stints continue, Robert might need to use his bike to start doing some odd jobs to earn some money to help.

But now that Uncle Tamas was killed, and Robert learned that "forced labor" for Jews could include front line duties and other such hazardous assignments, Robert and his mother were understandably terrified. What was next? Why would Hungary allow the Nazis to essentially dispose of its Jews? Yes, he couldn't wait to get home to talk further and see what his father was thinking after his first day back to his regular job in several weeks.

These questions and concerns weighed heavily on Robert's head and heart as Mr. Gera stood at the front of the classroom, drawing what he claimed was a maple tree on the blackboard. He was using different colored chalks for different parts of the tree that didn't seem to follow logical rhyme or reason to Robert, but then, what did Robert know? Like the piano, he had no aspirations for a career in the Arts.

The assignment given to Robert and his classmates in this secular middle school next door to Robert's Rottenbiller apartment was to do exactly what Mr. Gera was doing. Nothing more, nothing less. Just copy what he was drawing, using the exact same colors in the exact same places.

Robert thought this was stupid. Nevertheless, he was doing the best he could, deciding, however, that he should put in traces of yellow and red in some of the leaves, as it was, after all, the beginning of autumn. He thought that the predominance of green for the leaves was unrealistic. He thought these things in between his thoughts of the clock on the wall and all that the clock implied when, to his dismay, he inhaled a revolting concoction of foul breath and excessive cologne. It was Mr. Gera, leaning in closely behind him and eyeing his paper.

"You Jew, Holczer! What did I tell you?" Indifferent to any answer Robert was yet to even conjure, Mr. Gera raised his mahogany walking cane and began to strike Robert. First across the back, then when Robert cowered and moved to try and block the blows, Mr. Gera hit his neck, hands, and arms repeatedly. "When I say do as I do, I mean do as I do," the raging old man seethed and heavily gasped at once. Not one of Robert's classmates, at least a few also Jews, dared to even look up, let alone move.

Robert managed to duck away from one final blow destined for the side of his head and stood up and ran for the door. He was delirious and smoldering with hurt and rage. He felt and tasted blood trickling down from his nose and onto his lips.

"I hope you go to Palestine to sell oranges, Jew," Mr. Gera maniacally panted and frothed. "You'll find your Jewish homeland there – that's where you all belong!"

Robert ran out the door, out of the school and, gratefully, just next door to his home. Once inside, his mother turned in shock from the dining room table where she seemed to be having a serious conversation with a woman Robert didn't know.

"Robi, what…? You're hurt! What are you--"

"I hate being a Jew!"

After his mother's guest politely departed without being asked to do so, indicating that they would talk again soon, Robert calmed down enough to explain what had occurred. As he did so, his mother dressed his wounds with a bag of ice on the back of his neck, a wet cloth for his bloody nose, and a tissue for his tears. Once his superficial wounds were addressed, she told Robert to change his shirt and comb his hair.

"Why, *Anu?*"

"We must go back to your school at once, Robi," she calmly explained. "Now do as I say and let's go."

Robert was alarmed. Surely, he wanted vengeance and consequences to be levied against Mr. Gera, but he anticipated it would be his father, not his mother, to achieve his desired retribution. He anxiously did as his mother asked and followed nervously, in reserved awe.

Upon returning to the scene of the crime, Robert's group of classmates had already exited, and in their place was another group of students, apparently being compelled to do the identical maple tree drawing and coloring exercise. There was Mr. Gera, and upon hearing his mother's knock on the door and seeing Robert peering in the classroom door window, he turned and smiled arrogantly.

Putting his piece of chalk down as the students in the room looked on in wonder, he took hold of his weapon – his cane, and walked slowly toward the door to open it.

"You must be Mrs. Holczer. I am Mr. Gera – your son, Robert, has committed a grave offense, Madam."

"I know this, Mr. Gera. Robert has told me. We are here to apologize for his actions and assure you he will never disobey you again."

Robert's nervous smile and sense of awe suddenly vanished. In their place, his jaw dropped, and he looked first to his mother, then to Mr. Gera in disbelief. Was he imagining this? How could his mother betray him like this?

"Isn't that right, Robert?" His mother turned toward him. "Now tell the good Mr. Gera that you are sorry and will always do as he says."

Mr. Gera grinned victoriously as Robert mumbled a first apology, and then gutted out a second with "feeling" as demanded by his mother.

"I will see to it, Mrs. Holczer, that Robert does as he must."

Robert's mother left him to complete his school day, though Robert was entirely oblivious to the remainder of the day. When the final bell rang and he re-entered his home in a zombie state, he hung up the jacket he originally wore to school on a hook by the door and walked directly over to the couch that was his bed. He walked right past his mother, who was peeling potatoes by the sink in the kitchen.

"How could you, *Anu?*" He finally spoke after sitting for some moments.

"Now you must understand, Robi," she replied without looking up from her potatoes. "A lot of things that you cannot understand now…. I could not go in and do anything *except* apologize for your behavior."

But Robert heard nothing. He tried to imagine his father's reaction. He tried to imagine that his father would react as he predicted and hoped, but somehow began to realize he might be disappointed; he might be mistaken. There appeared to be forces at play that eluded Robert, which frustration led to even more anger.

3

February 1943
For Absent Brothers (Or Sisters)

The Jewish question was becoming a problem of deepening scope and heft. The Nazis and their Hungarian cronies were exhausting and sacrificing Jewish labor forces and many others in the East, culminating with Germany's disastrous and decisive defeat in Stalingrad. Now, Robert's father, who had only recently come back from a fourth forced labor stint which he refused to talk about, was informed that he and several thousand other Hungarian Jews were to report to the Bor copper mines in the Serbian part of Yugoslavia in less than two weeks. There, they would work indefinitely under Nazi supervision as a labor force to replace the Yugoslavian Jews whom the Nazis had already annihilated. As devastating as this news was for Robert, this morning, Robert's mother told him to put on his best clothes and yarmulke. Today, she said, they were taking the train north to Vac to visit her parents.

The thing that Robert detested most about his visits to his mother's side of the family, the Oestreichers – well, there was not just one thing; there were so many things. But really, it all started and would end with his Grandmother Joszefa. Grandmother Joszefa was angry, judgmental, and condescending, even to her husband, Grandfather Jonas, and she imposed her Jewish piety on all who entered her home, especially Robert.

In stark contrast to the freedom he enjoyed with his comparatively poor father's side of the family in Kobanya, Robert felt that time spent with the Oestreichers was like a prison term, both spiritually and physically.

"Robert, it's time to go to synagogue; Robert, you must wear your yarmulke at all times; Robert, you are not reciting your prayers with the right inflection and sincerity; Robert, you are a *shaygetz*, unclean, dirty, and a disgrace to Jews…."

These and a myriad of other insults and barbs typified the *warmth* of his *dea*r Grandmother Joszefa, whose black hair tightly pulled back from her forehead exacerbated her large, circular glasses, tiny brown eyes, and permanently frowning mouth. Such putdowns and orders, however, Robert could endure, especially because, as a born rebel, he always plotted ways to assert his own nonconforming wishes. He'd remove his hat whenever he thought she wasn't looking, and sometimes, for good measure, when she was. He'd *accidentally* let slip that he'd eaten unkosher food with his other grandparents…. Sure, he went along and obeyed his mother's – but mostly his grandmother's demand that he perform his Bar Mitzvah before he had even turned 13 ("It is time you become a man, *shaygetz."),* though he couldn't even remember any of his chosen Torah readings within days of the event. What irked Robert more than anything, however, was the way his mother's side of the family treated his father.

Of course, Robert's father never complained, and, unlike Robert, he was too polite to talk back or otherwise resist. But, to Robert, it was clear even at a young age that the upper middle class Oestreichers did not approve of their older daughter Cornelia's marriage to Robert's father. He was, in Grandmother Joszefa's eyes, beneath her daughter. Not only in social class, but in manners, education, and in his lack of religious devotion. Robert's father's Jewishness may have been an inherent part of his identity, but in practice, he only observed as necessary for the sake of Robert's mother and her family. Indeed, Robert noticed on more than one occasion his father mouthing the words of prayers and scripture that were all wrong. He was only *pretending* he knew such Jewish rituals for the love and respect he held for his wife. Robert said nothing but added this secret to the admiration he would always bear for his father.

"Lajos, two of the legs on the dining room table are loose," barked Grandmother Joszefa immediately upon their arrival in Vac. "This good for nothing, my lazy husband, doesn't know what to do, and I refuse to pay money for such a thing. I don't suppose you learned anything with *all* of your education," she paused disdainfully to ensure that her words got her point across, "to know how to do it?"

Robert's father hesitated.

"Mother!" Robert's mother snapped. She hadn't been feeling well for what seemed to be the past several weeks, and she excused herself to go to the washroom. She had likewise spent much of the train trip to Vac in the cramped restroom.

"Of course, I will try."

"I'm going outside," Robert declared. "I have things to do. Hello Grandfather! Hello Uncle and Aunt! So nice seeing you again!" Robert's mother's younger sister and brother were seated dutifully at the broken table with their father. Chopin's Nocturnes were playing on the Victrola, which was the only welcoming thing about this lavishly decorated, immaculate but soulless home. None of them motioned back to Robert. They were both married, though Robert didn't immediately see their spouses or children, and didn't much care. They were all far too old or far too young for Robert, and all of them boring.

Robert had decided before their arrival in Vac that these Vac visits had to end. One way or another, he would see to it that he would no longer be welcome there. He could no longer endure the insults, the requirements, the interminable prayers at the synagogue. If there was one thing he knew about his grandmother, it was that she became enraged to the point of hyperventilation whenever she learned that Robert was permitted to eat unkosher meals with that *shaygetz* Holczer side of the family. It was even worse, Robert knew, that her closest friends – all of whom were likewise Orthodox, deeply observant Jews – would ever have anything *on* her to disparage her reputation as a fellow pious Jew.

Drawing from funds he'd been saving from his weekly allowance, Robert brought with him the sufficient *pengo,* Hungary's currency, and headed for the local butcher shop. "I'll have one of those ham hocks, please," Robert smiled to the butcher. "Can you get me one of the boiled ones; cooked?" Noticing Robert's yarmulke, the silver-haired butcher, with a moustache whose tips curled up to nearly touch his respective nostrils, raised his lengthy, connected eyebrows but said nothing. He handed over an ample, obvious ham hock, took the exact *pengo* from the 13-year-old Robert, and glanced over to a smiling, pretty woman wearing a similar, bloodied, white smock. Robert assumed this was the man's wife. "Thank you," Robert grinned widely as he beheld the pig part like a trophy.

Robert knew exactly where he was going. This was the exact time scores of Jews would be converging upon Vac's major synagogue for their evening prayers. Likely not his grandmother – she, no doubt, had already been there today, but … she would know.…

Fully adorned in his best clothes underneath his winter coat, yarmulke firmly positioned on his head, Robert arrived at the grand, colorful synagogue with the 10 commandments at its peak and sat on the highest brick step right before the entrance door. It was cold, but not too cold today. Robert sat down. He blew warm air onto his hands and then removed the ham hock from its white paper bag. Smiling and waving as he took one sizeable bite after another from the prominent remains of a pig – most definitely unkosher -- he reveled in the mutterings and shouts of disgust, displeasure, and disapproval from his fellow Jews, far more Orthodox than him.

"That's Joszefa – Joszefa Oestreicher's grandson. From Budapest, isn't that right?" Robert heard one woman whisper loudly to her husband as they walked past smiling Robert, oily pig meat all over his face and hands.

"Wait until she hears of this blasphemy, this outrage," said the husband, more audibly.

Mission accomplished, thought Robert. "Hello, good people!" Robert cried out nearly laughing while chewing, open-mouthed. "May God be with you all!"

Two days later, safely back at home, the call came from Vac. Robert's mother answered the telephone. It was her mother. "What! He did what? You never want to see him again? Robert!"

Little did Robert know that his grandmother's wish, curse – whatever, would come true. She never did see him again, nor Robert any of his mother's family. Any.

***

Robert's father was ordered to depart for Bor in just under a week. He had been going in to continue to work, selling supplies, colognes, and perfumes, and filling orders in and around Budapest. Miraculously, his Christian employer, who had been continuing to pay a fair amount of his salary, agreed to continue to do so while he was able. "I don't like the direction this war is going, Lajos," his boss told him. "Not that I care for the Nazis to win, certainly, but so long as Hungary is aligned with their fate, what will become of any of us, let alone Jews? What of the Russians? It's only a matter of time before the Americans enter. What will Horthy do?"

"All good questions, friend," Robert's father replied. "Your kindness can never be repaid. What you are doing for my family…."

"Nothing you wouldn't do if the situation was reversed, Lajos. This Jewish issue … I don't understand. What did any Jew do to deserve what is happening? And Hungary … I'm ashamed, my friend."

But this morning when Robert woke up to go to school, his father was still there. He was seated beside his mother, listening to one of his favorite concertos by Brahms on the phonograph. The volume was turned down low, and they were talking softly.

"Ah, sleepy head Robi! Just the young man we were waiting for," smiled his father. "Come, before you get your jam and bread to go to school. There is something we wish to briefly discuss with you."

"Are you feeling any better, *Anu?*"

Robert's mother exchanged a brief glance with her husband. "I'm fine, dear."

"I *am* sorry about offending Grandmother Joszefa. Well … the point is, I will apologize to her the next time we visit."

"It's not that, Robi," his father interrupted. "Robi," he paused, "I know you have been listening as anxiously as me to the news of the day. Things are bad and getting worse. This will be very difficult for all of us, while I am in Bor. For you, for your mother, there are things...."

"Yes, *Apu*. We already talked about that. I know, yes, I will talk to your friend at the architectural firm in the city to see if I can run errands for them on my bike, as we discussed. And, of course, I will help take care of mother. Nothing will happen...."

"It's not that, son. I'm proud of you and know you will do what you must. It's something else entirely." He took the last sip of his coffee and then stood up to turn over the record to play the other side. "The surviving Jews from other parts of Europe are on the run and need help. We have an opportunity, Robi, through my friends at the New York *Kavehaz* in the city center, to be a kind of interim house for two refugee families, one from Poland, and the other from Czechoslovakia. They should only be here a couple of days each as they make their way to more permanent destinations, but that is out of our hands. They should all be here and gone before I even leave next Monday. Are you willing to help and keep the matter quiet?"

Robert beamed. "Why, yes, *Apu*. How exciting! Do they speak Hungarian, or even German at least? Any kids my age?"

Again, Robert's parents exchanged a rapid glance. "I believe the Czech family has a little girl," his father smiled. "Quite a bit younger than you. Then it is settled. Life will go on as usual these last few days. You will come sleep in our room, and we will be good hosts to our guests. Now, get going on your way to school!"

"Don't forget your breakfast, Robi. And here...." His mother got up and walked to the counter to get his lunch sack. "Here is your lunch." She kissed him on the forehead and deftly wiped away her soft red lipstick as he tried to pull away. His father reached over to turn up the volume of the concerto and returned to his place on the couch. The sun was shining outside on the freshly fallen snow, making everything seem so bright through the windows of the apartment.

When Robert closed the door and hastened on his way to school, he somehow felt there was something else. *What was it,* he wondered as he descended the marble staircase to exit the Rottenbiller house. *Why is father still at home – they could have told me all of this after school. Why did they keep looking at each other?*

***

After the door closed and Robert's father was sure his son was gone, he stood up again, but this time to elevate the arm of the phonograph to usher in silence where before there was the dazzling poetry of music- the fire of life. He felt compelled to cry but didn't. How he wished to honor Robert's pleas that they run away to avoid his looming departure for Bor, but he had no place to go and no money to pay for it.

Cornelia looked at her husband with loving eyes, tears starting to form, causing her brown eyes to shine like the sun through the windows. "It's time, Husband. We're sure of this, then…."

"I see no other way. We've been through all of this a dozen times. Everything is too uncertain with the war, with me having to go away…. Who knows? This is no world in which to raise a baby, my love…."

The Holczers retraced their son's footsteps down the stairs and out of Rottenbiller utca 39. Lajos held his wife's hand, like love. They had been striving to finally give Robert the brother or sister he so desired for as long as they could remember. They had been to doctors, counselors, to friends of friends…. And then, well after they had already resigned themselves to the fate that their Robert would remain an only child, they had miraculously succeeded. However, the world outside the walls of their apartment had meanwhile betrayed them. Or maybe it was Hungary. Or the Germans….

They walked, it seemed, forever, when in reality it was just three blocks to the residence of this friend of a friend of a friend who indicated he could perform the requisite procedure for next to nothing. And next to nothing, in these times, was what Lajos Holczer had in his pocket and even in his savings. He was about to go to a place called Bor and knew, by all accounts of what was happening to the rest of Europe's Jews, he might never return. His wife knew this too. Deep down, he knew that Robert knew this too. All he could hope for was the survival and safety of his family, and he knew there was no place in this world of uncertainty, for a newborn, potentially fatherless child.

They knocked on the door and were greeted warmly. His wife had never looked so beautiful to him. She was his dream, his "cutest thing," his everything. He could even endure her family to treasure every moment he could with her.

"If Robi ever finds out...." His mother turned to her husband. "How will we … how can we…?"

"He won't, darling. At least until a day should come when perhaps he ought to know…. If you need to recover further after all of this, I'll still be home to take care of our incoming guests. We'll tell him I brought you to a physician today, and he ordered you to rest. Don't worry about anything." He paused, squeezing her hand warmly, doing all he could to prevent his own tears, but obviously failing. "*Szeretlek*, I love you. I am here for you." He embraced her and didn't want to let go.

"It's time," said the man. "Everything will be fine."

"Thank you. Thank you so much." Robert's father turned to him, trying in vain to prevent the man from seeing the tears in his eyes. "Take care of her, sir. I'll be waiting right outside." He did everything he could to keep from crying aloud.

"Goodbye, my love," Cornelia told him. "I'll see you on the other side…."

"Darling, I must ask." He took in a deep breath of the warm air of the anteroom to the dimly lit room into which his wife had already entered. "Do you know if our Robi was going to have a brother … or sister?"

"Does it matter?" She smiled, never taking her brown eyes from those of the love of her life. She sobbed. She motioned goodbye as the man closed the door.

4

Shovels and Stars
March 1944

It was not yet spring, but Robert needed no calendar to announce this obvious truth. The tall oaks and elms that lined his bicycle paths, parks, and cobblestone streets remained steadfast in their refusal to offer hope – a panacea to another seemingly eternal Budapest winter – in the shape of spring blooms, let alone buds.

And the cold was ever more stark- the darkness more profound in his father's absence. In the months since his father was in Bor, the percentage of the wage his father's employer agreed to pay continued to wane.

War cast an increasingly ominous cloud over Europe. After the Soviet Red Army had outlasted and overwhelmed the German 6th Army at Stalingrad, they were approaching Hungary's doorstep in their murderous, vengeful rampage to expel the Germans back from whence they came. The cost to Hungary had been substantial. Eighty-four percent of Hungary's Second Army was annihilated fighting alongside their Nazi allies. Meanwhile, the Americans had joined the Allied operations and were similarly succeeding to help push the Nazis back from Sicily and then on the mainland. There were rumors of an imminent, broader Allied invasion.

Hungary, as a member of Germany's Axis, remained bound to the fate of the Nazis. This was true despite recent BBC radio chatter that Admiral Horthy and Prime Minister Miklos Kallay were mulling options to extricate Hungary from the Axis. To most, it now seemed there was little doubt that the Nazis would lose the war. The question was how to reach an accord with the British and other Allies, dramatically fortified by the Americans, considering the rapid advance of the Soviets. Once the Soviets took over, it was clear that the country would be overtaken by Communism.

Fourteen-year-old Robert, of course, could do nothing about the war, apart from continuing the ritual he and his father so relished: To listen to the news of the world on BBC Europe radio whenever he could. The trouble with this was that whenever his mother would catch Robert sitting to listen and, in her eyes, doing nothing, she perpetually suggested that he practice the dreaded piano.

As Robert's father's income continued to dwindle steadily on account of his indefinite absence and the toll of war on the Hungarian economy, Robert did what he could to help his mother and him manage. Chiefly, he served as a courier for an architectural firm near the city center in Budapest. He would ride his beloved bold, blue Hercules Model QD, double top tube two-speed bicycle that was the envy of most of his friends all over the city to make deliveries, pick up documents, and make deliveries again. Since he so loved to ride his bike, he would have blushed to be paid for such a "job" that was fun to him if it weren't for two things: He and his mother needed the money, and since the winter was eternally long and cold, they weren't always joy rides.

Nevertheless, Robert would have loved to ride his bike for money all day long, every day, were it not for his 8th grade school year and the obligatory weekly labor battalion details which continued to occupy hours of every weekend. At first, such brainless but imposing tasks were an inconvenience, though demeaning and physically exhausting. As the war progressed, however, it seemed that Jews were increasingly bearing the brunt of Hungary's frustrations. And so, as the supply of Jewish men, like Robert's father, was being expended for the sake of forced labor abroad, the Jewish youth were being punished in kind with redundant, inane verbal humiliation and more frequent beatings.

On the 18th of March, Robert and five others, including his closest friend, fellow secret "Boy Scout" Matyas, were ordered after lunch to "dig a trench here, three feet deep, six feet long, and two feet wide. When you Jewish scum are finished, signal for me and I will inspect it," spat a stumpy Hungarian captain – Behrentz. The bullish Behrentz bore a square face and a missing front tooth through which he whistled every time he uttered words bearing the letter 's'. He was the kind of man who deserved a derogatory nickname, but the boys were too frightened to call him what they all thought (*Szarhazi*, "Shithead") for fear of the consequences.

Robert's crew did their best to disguise their contempt for both the man and the task. With hands so blistered they had long callused, they completed the trench. On any day this would be an exceedingly difficult assignment. Today it was even much more harrowing on account of the top layer of the ground being nearly frozen solid. When done, Robert raised his weary, chafed shovel for the captain to come. Upon his arrival, with darkness enveloping the day, he turned to the two dozen or so other labor battalion members and dismissed them curtly. As Robert, Matyas, and their four fellow trench diggers readied to leave themselves, the captain squealed. "Not so fast, you worthless kikes! This trench is no better to suit its purpose than you are to humanity!"

"Excuse me, Captain Behrentz, sir," Matyas suddenly interrupted as Robert elbowed him to shut up. He continued, "Perhaps if you'd told us the purpose…."

The narrow-eyed captain leaped like a tiger onto its prey and punched Matyas across the left side of his face. Matyas suddenly fell backward into the senseless trench. Before Robert could take two steps to the pit to tend to his friend, the captain, frothing and smiling wildly, whistled. "Now you kikes don't go home until you refill this trench. I order you to put all this dirt back where you found it in such a way that no one could ever tell you dug here in the first place," he gasped, either for effect or more likely from the energy expended for his tiger imitation. "I don't care if

27

you bury your friend here or pull him up; it makes no difference to me. Next week, you will re-dig this trench in exactly the same spot! We need it. We need it done right."

When Captain Behrentz smiled even more maniacally while whistling these witless words, Robert could have sworn he observed a gnat depart its swarm and fly into the black hole between the sad captain's front teeth. As Robert reached to lift his friend from the hellacious, pseudo-trench, the captain turned away; laughing at first, then suddenly coughing. Then coughing some more and so on until all Robert could hear, against the backdrop of the swelling dusk was the cacophony of shovels into dirt, coughing, and cursing like he had never heard before.

"*Szarhazi,*" Robert muttered. "Shithead."

***

Until March 19th, 1944, despite the taunts, occasional beatings and forced labor for the men and, to a lesser extent, the weekly labor battalion "practice" for younger men of Robert's age, being a Jew in Hungary was far less egregious than in most other European countries. By March 19th, thanks to the BBC News on the radio, Robert and most others in Budapest were already painfully aware of Jews being made to wear the Star of David prominently on all of their clothing to identify them. The price for not wearing one was immediate imprisonment, after which they were typically rounded up into ghettos, and then deported to concentration camps where they were most often killed in one way or another in Poland, in particular. He was unaware of the *Einsatzgruppen*, the mobile killing squads which had been rounding up Jews to shoot them in forests and bury them in pits in too many Eastern European forests. He, like most Hungarians, was also unaware of how Hungary deported over 18,000 Jews without Hungarian citizenship to Kamenets-Podolsk, an area in southwestern Ukraine. These foreign Jews, and at least 1,000 others in the Bacska area, were then similarly massacred in August 1941 and early 1942, respectively by German and Ukrainian troops. As was later revealed, these were attempts on Hungary's part to demonstrate their allegiance to the Nazi cause – anything to help Hungary gain back lands it, like Germany, lost after World War I.

Until March 19th, 1944, Robert believed the counsel of his father that killing Jews was somehow "beneath the dignity" of Admiral Horthy and the aristocracy, particularly in Budapest where so many Jews were enmeshed in the very essence of the city. This belief, naive or not, even empowered Robert to keep faith that his father, several months into God only knows whatever he was being made to do in Bor with so many other Hungarian Jews, would be alright. Buoyed by a postcard they received from him weeks ago which simply said, "I am well. I love you," Robert kept emphasizing this fact to his mother, prone already to so many nights of crying herself to sleep.

"Keep faith, *Anu. Apu* needs us to be as strong as him so that he can do what he must to come home to us."

On Sunday, March 19th, 1944, Robert's belief that Jews in Hungary would remain relatively safe was shattered like one of the delicate porcelain dolls that once fell from his mother's fine china cabinet when Robert bounced a rubber ball rather too zealously, knocking the doll onto the hard wooden floor. He would receive consequences for his recklessness that day, but nothing compared to the torment that lay ahead for the Jews of Hungary.

The day started harmlessly enough. But it worsened the way a sore throat typically signals more grave ailments in the days ahead.

Robert awakened to the sound of his mother playing Chopin's *12 Etudes* on the phonograph. It was his father's favorite recording. Or was it the smell of the bread she had baked, or the coffee that prompted him awake? Regardless, as he tried in vain to keep in the darkness by pulling the covers over his head, Robert knew that the music was his mother's invocation to him to practice the piano. What mattered more to him, devouring the sweet bread and coffee … or prolonging the inevitable that he would have to play piano for his mother by remaining shrouded by his blanket? *Ah, the devil with it*, he thought to himself.

He played, rather beautifully, for nearly an hour before Matyas and two other Jewish school friends, Aron and Adam, arrived to save the day with a knock on the door.

"Did you hear what happened to Mr. Dobler, Robert? Aron demanded breathlessly. "Oh, sorry, hello Madam Holczer."

"Mr. Dobler, Robi," his mother interrupted. "Isn't he that teacher of yours who told your class to tear apart that terrible, racist propaganda book…? Matyas -- what is that bruise across your face? How…?"

"Yes, *Anu*. Mr. Dobler's the only one of our 8ᵗʰ grade teachers who's not useless. He actually cares about us Jews even though he's not one himself. He teaches us that hate, and the Nazi and current Hungarian thinking that certain races and ethnicities are superior to others, spells the death of humanity. He is like George, the Scout leader. He says we must…."

"He's gone, Robert," Matyas finally interrupted. "They've taken him away."

"What? Who? They took him … where?"

"Who knows where? My father's friend – you know him, Karoly, one of the custodians at the school, told my father last night he saw the gendarmerie come into Mr. Dobler's classroom after school Friday, and they hit him many times before basically dragging him outside. They got into a car and…."

"How could this…? How are we only finding this out now? Come on, let's go!"

"Where?" asked Matyas. "What can we do?"

"You're not going anywhere, Robi," his mother intervened. "You must…."

"*Anu*, I will be back shortly. I need to run over to the school and see what I can find out. Mr. Dobler is … our friend."

Robert grabbed his coat from the hook as he ran out, letting the door close harshly behind him. His mother yelled something about being back in an hour or something as Matyas and the others followed.

Over two hours had passed, and the boys had discovered next to nothing. A couple of people indicated they heard something about someone being dragged out of the school, but no one saw or knew anything. Two 8th grade schoolmates only laughed, one shouting, "He was a Jew-lover. They'll come for you next!"

Before Robert could summon the necessary calm to return home, he implored his friends to ride their bikes with him through the park. In truth, Robert would not have minded – he may even have preferred -- to ride alone on this day He needed to process the apparent capture of the only teacher who inspired Robert to imagine and to dare to make a future in which people would not hate others for their race, religion, or ethnic backgrounds. Although Robert was already too cynical for that, he recognized the importance of hope. He vowed to himself to maintain a sense of hope for as long as he would live. And Mr. Dobler, like his father and George, his "underground Boy Scout" leader, was indispensable to his evolving world view. Through these mentors, Robert understood how hope should never be such an abstract concept. Instead, each person must do his part to make a difference; to help the thing he hopes to become reality.

"We'll ride with you, Rob. But didn't your mother tell you…," Matyas warned.

"She'll understand. She knows how much Mr. Dobler means to us. Besides, let's race to the candy store across the park. You know I have the best bike and will win!"

"Your legs are too short, Robert," teased Aron. "I'll win, anyway, Matyas is still sore from the beating he took at labor battalion! Oh, is it true about the gnat that got into the shithead captain's mouth? Matyas was telling--"

"Wanna bet? You're all talk, the lot of you!" Matyas raced to the bicycle rack beside the school where the boys left their bikes and was already dodging traffic to cross the street into the park before Robert and the others joined the race. This was what Robert needed, a good, old-fashioned bicycle race!

***

When Robert finally returned home in the middle of the afternoon, he heard the BBC shouting at him down the hall. He warily approached the door, hearing the frantic voices of news reporters, but he could not yet make out what was making them so expressive. He opened the door to see his mother sitting, pale as a ghost, on the white sofa in his father's favorite corner.

"*Anu*, I am sorry. You know…."

"It's not that, Robi, that's alright," said his mother, coldly, a monotone ghost of herself. She produced and simultaneously wiped tears from her eyes. "The Nazis are here! They have entered Hungary. They were dissatisfied with Hungary's handling of the 'Jewish question,' and believe that our Regent Horthy was trying to broker deals with the Russians or the British and Americans."

Robert stood frozen at the door. He still had one sleeve of his coat off, dangling beside him as he stood in place.

"The Germans are here? In Hungary?

"Eichmann. *Obersturmbannführer* Adolf Eichmann is in charge, but with the apparent full cooperation now of Horthy and, get this – Budapest's Jewish Council!"

"Our Jewish Council?" Robert suddenly lunged forward, stilling himself against the great piano, which provided solace now instead of its usual menace. He disregarded his coat on the floor.

"They must think that if they cooperate that things will be better for us."

"*Apu?* What will become of him now in Bor if Hungary is not quite Germany's willing ally? What of my grandparents? Your mother and father also?"

"I've phoned my mother, Robi -- And they are also your grandparents, dear. She's worried but won't admit it. I also spoke with your Aunt Aranka, your father's sister. She's telling you and me not to worry." Robert's mother stood to approach and embrace her son, but Robert did not reciprocate. He was dizzy with this information, layered atop news of Mr. Dobler's disappearance with all the subtle grace of an avalanche.

"Robi," his mother continued to weep.

"I know, *Anu*, we will be okay," he interrupted, unconvincingly.

"Robi, dear. You haven't heard the worst part," she gasped. "The radio said we Jews are ordered to … we are required to wear yellow Stars of David on our clothes within one week, or we'll be jailed on the spot."

As Robert was being embraced by his mother, he stood, limply, staring through the thin, see-through curtains, across the street and into the high maples of the park through which he and his friends had just been racing. As Robert was being embraced, he imagined a night sky of stars on a perfectly clear, cool winter night. And then he tried to imagine a night sky of *yellow* stars, far above hundreds of thousands of Jewish Hungarian people, all wearing yellow stars. He briefly imagined what such uniformity, such solidarity could achieve, but then remembered himself and laughed.

"Stars," he finally said. "Yellow stars … then ghettos … deportations.… Oh, *Anu*.…" Robert exhaled, suddenly dizzy. He finally placed his arms around his mother stronger than he could ever remember, at least up until then.

5

Summer 1944
The Road to God Knows Where

Had Robert only known that cycling with his friends through Varosliget Park on the 19th of March would be his last such ride, he might have swooped by to collect his mother in order to honor the promise he made his father. But he also might otherwise have kept riding until borders became superfluous. In a Europe with no borders, perhaps time could become imaginary. Perhaps he could imagine his father right back into moving pictures, with his mother and him in them. They might be laughing about the piano or arguing about the piano – it no longer mattered which. Perhaps he could send word to his father's family, begging them to join them with haste, so that Robert could again cause mischief, feel free, feel … alive, and cling to the remains of a childhood that seemed to have set somewhere on the horizon too many days, weeks, months ago. When was it that his father went away…? Everything seemed to be frozen, and yet it was all moving too fast. Is that possible? Yes … it was happening.

Several days after the Nazis entered Hungary, the Jews of Hungary helplessly watched their freedoms dissipate. Like a fly caught in a web, horrified as the spider slowly approaches, the Hungarian Jews could only convulse as the beginnings of deportations, which they had heard were happening in Poland, now prevailed upon them.

First came the yellow stars. A badge of faith subjugated to mark all Jews; tell everyone, "Not one of us." Next came the surrender of radios- then cars and bicycles, no Jew could operate any business, no Jew could attend secular schools, and no telephones: No way to communicate. Like flies in a web became the Jews of Hungary.

The Nazis had insisted that the conservative aristocratic Prime Minister Kallay – too hesitant to handle the Hungarian Jewish "question" to their liking – was replaced with Dome Sztojay, who promised to continue Hungary's war on the Axis side. Consequently, in early April, Allied bombs fell on Budapest for a stunning, terrifying, but gratefully brief while. And with the bombs came, at long last, the loss of *naivete*, the loss of the increasingly delusional dream that Hungary, let alone its Jews, could somehow be immune from the horrors occurring elsewhere on European soil. And with the bombs came citizens displaced from their homes.

New Prime Minister Sztojay then ordered the confiscation of over 1,500 Jewish apartments in Budapest. These apartments were simply handed to Christians whose own apartments had sustained bomb damage, while their previous Jewish inhabitants were relocated to other districts. Apparently satisfied with this allocation of resources since it simultaneously impressed their Nazi overlords, Sztojay issued a new decree on April 28th. All apartments occupied by Jews were being confiscated and assigned to non-Jews, while all Jews must move to designated "yellow star houses," apartments in which there already lived a majority of Jews, or any modern apartments with low maintenance costs.

Rumors swelled so loudly that they nearly drowned out the sound of Jewish hearts pounding to the beat of the very fear generated by the rumors. There were rumors that Jews were already in ghettos in the countryside and provinces surrounding Budapest. Rumors that the "yellow star houses" were one step from the same fate: Ghettos. Then deportations to God knows where. Only God, so many Jews were saying, was nowhere to be seen. In his place, Adolf Eichmann, the notorious Nazi in charge of mass deportation in other parts of Europe, was now in Hungary, wasn't he? The devil in God's place? In Hungary?

The inability to confirm facts was driving Robert's mother crazy. No telephone, no transportation. No way of knowing what was happening in Vac, where her parents and the families of her brother and sister lived. No way of knowing the fate of her husband – was he even still alive? Yes, she had to believe he was still alive because the alternative was simply unbearable. No way of knowing where to go. The Rottenbiller apartment was her home- her family's home. Where could they go? Where would they be forced to go?

No longer able to use his bike to continue to make money as a courier, and now forced with the reality of having to vacate his home, Robert made inquiries where he could. Many families considered trying to move in with family in the provinces, but the lack of transportation, communication, and still unconfirmed rumors occurring rendered such option futile. Matyas and his family, like most of his Jewish friends, were going to one of the nearby yellow star houses, but Robert was reluctant.

"*Anu*, I know this isn't easy." Robert sat on the couch beside his mother and took her hands into his. He knew that the uncertainty of everything was becoming too much for her, and so she was saying and doing less and less. She was frightened to leave the apartment to visit friends and ashamed to wear the yellow Star of David, to be so obviously branded and identified by the religion that had informed the very fabric of her life: "*Zsido* … Jew." He clenched her hands firmly and looked into her soft brown eyes about which his father always raved. "We have to raise money now. I have gathered some of my books and other valuables to sell. You're going to have to give me some of your jewelry, *Anu*."

"Of course, Robi," she said blankly. Then, as if suddenly aroused from her reverie, "How was your visit with your father's family in Kobanya? Is everything okay? Your journey was safe?"

"Yes, but you know they have no room there for us."

"That's not what I meant. I meant are they safe there? They don't have to move, do they?"

"Not yet, anyway. They live just outside the districts forced to move. Aunt Aranka laughed that they have never lived as Jews, so why should they be treated as Jews."

"I'm sure your grandparents weren't laughing."

"No, they weren't. They all seem to think that because they live in the poor section where some Communist leaders live and have offices, they are somehow immune. I'm not sure I understand this logic -- I thought the Nazis hated the Communists also -- but I was too tired from my long walk to argue, and I knew I still needed to walk back before curfew."

"Yes, God only knows what would happen if a Jew is on the streets after 6:00." She looked down, sighed, and then slowly stood up to walk to the stove, on which she had been boiling water for tea. "Would you like some, Robi?"

"No, thank you. Anyway, Aranka has made connections to get herself into an apartment in the District VI, 1 Zichy Jeno. It's near the Opera House, right across the street from St. Istvan's Basilica. She says she may be able to get us and some other family there once she gets settled. She can't be certain that staying in Kobanya is safe. She's trying to anticipate what might happen next. She seems to think that this apartment will be safer for all of us."

"How did she get it? If it's not a Jewish house … and besides, no Jew can acquire anything now that isn't assigned to them, right?"

"The way she told me, *Anu*, it *is* a designated Jewish Yellow Star house in which there already live several prominent Jewish people … doctors, businessmen and their families. But you are correct; she couldn't get a unit of her own unless she was a Gentile, which she somehow made herself."

"What are you talking about?" His mother quickly placed her steaming cup of tea onto the table and sat down on the piano bench. The room seemed naked without the radio, which they were already forced to turn in to the gendarmerie, the Hungarian police. Naked, and silent.

Robert stood to select a record to play on the phonograph as he finally turned to answer his mother's question.

"Speaking of valuables to sell, any chance you'll let me sell the piano? Even in these times I'm sure I can get us a lot for it."

Robert's mother shot him a cool glare that answered his question.

"I had to try," he smiled sheepishly. "Anyway, you remember how her husband died in a minefield in Russia, and she had that picture of him wearing the Hungarian army uniform, right? Well, Aranka took that picture, and then brought her mother –- my *nagymama* -- with her to the city hall office to have her lie and swear under oath that she had Aranka illegitimately- with a Gentile lawyer who is now conveniently dead and cannot be brought in to deny the report."

"What?"

"I kid you not, *Anu*," Robert grinned widely. "So, then they pronounced that Aranka does not qualify, under our own Nuremberg laws, as a Jew – she is a Gentile, a Christian, and it is official. Can you believe it? So, she can now move about freely, and she wants to help us and my uncles and aunts…."

"That woman … how could she? And your grandmother went along with it – confessed to adultery for Aranka's sake?"

"I know, right? Aranka's a bloody genius! So, I was thinking. I know we have no way of gaining such 'official' means of becoming Christians, but I hear that, for a price, I can get us blank birth certificate papers that we can falsify. They might help us in case things get worse for Jews."

"Okay, I won't ask questions about that. Just be careful, you hear? I just worry so much. I have no idea what is happening to my mother and family in Vac, and I am…. And what about *Apu*? If – I mean, when he returns and we move somewhere, how will he find us?"

"You know *Apu* expects us to survive and to find a way. You know that, so we will deal with that *when* he returns. As for your parents –"

"I know," she interrupted, as if instantly energized by her son's confident air. She looked at him now, dark hair stylishly and slickly combed with a stark part to the right side of his beautiful face, with such pride. He had the confidence and looks of his father, for certain, but the stubbornness and outspoken nature of her mother – the one whom he so resented. *How could he be only 14 years old,* she wondered. "Your favorite people in the world!"

Robert briefly smiled. "It's nothing. They are your family, so of course I still love them, I just don't have to *like* them." He stepped away from the phonograph, finally, pleased by the sounds emitting from the grooves of his father's most prized possession. He chose Tchaikovsky's *Capriccio Italien,* and his mother tacitly approved of the stirring piece. "Let me sell things. I will make inquiries and find somewhere for us to go until the place with Aunt Aranka perhaps works out in our favor. If we must go, better to be with family, right?"

"See what you can learn, Robi. This uncertainty...."

Robert hugged his mother, uncertain what he would learn, but certain that doing nothing was not an option. He too had heard the rumors. He too feared what might be happening in the provinces, and what was in fact already happening in Budapest. The music steeled him. "Please give me all you can to sell. Matyas said he will do the same, and he is going with me to get the papers."

"I love you, Robi."

***

Selling the jewelry and other valuables was not a problem for either Matyas or Robert, once they were amenable to accepting significantly less than what the items were worth. Figuring that they had no leverage and even fewer options, they resigned to accept something rather than nothing. Even so, they were both able to obtain the papers necessary to make false birth certificates to hopefully help them in one way or another. The boys, who had been neighbors, schoolmates until they were told there was no more school for Jews, Scouts until … and, above all, friends for the past several years, embraced each other and bade their farewells. At least, they said, they would still see each other at the forced labor battalion practices each weekend. Hardly a pleasure cruise, but at least they had each other to endure them.

"Do you think, Robi, there will come a day?"

"What, Matyas?"

"A day when we can return to our lives? Our homes, school, our Scout group, riding our bikes again and chasing girls?"

"You know I am much better looking than you, Matyas, so although I'm confident there will soon come a time when girls will again chase me, it is you, I'm afraid, who must be resigned only to chase them!"

They both laughed and patted each other on the backs. In their laughter, they forgot, if only for a moment, everything that was happening. But it was in that moment they saw one another's yellow stars on their shirts, and they remembered. Seeing this recognition in each others' eyes, Robert offered Matyas, "Soon enough, my good friend. Soon enough."

But soon did not come fast enough for Matyas.

In May, Robert's Grandfather Geza, his father's father, went, as every year to the National Central Alien Control Office in Budapest. He did so in order to have his citizenship papers stamped. Even though Geza and every member of his family had been Hungarians for as many generations as anyone could remember, Geza's own father was, as best as Robert could understand, born in a part of Hungary that was Hungarian at the time, but now was a part of Yugoslavia, thanks to land allocations made after World War I.

Consequently, Aranka later told Robert and his mother, when Grandfather Geza reported to the office in May for the first time since the Nazis had occupied Hungary, his papers were scrutinized more than ever. He was officially proclaimed a "foreign Jew," not Hungarian. This was not a new accusation made against him, but it had never amounted to an actual offense until now. If there was ever any Hungarian tolerance for their Jews, there was none for foreign Jews, as evidenced by the massacre of nearly 20,000 "foreign" Hungarian Jews in late 1941 and early 1942. And now that the Nazis were overseeing everything, Hungarian anti-Semitism and intolerance gained its most passionate advocates. According to an officer at the office who knew Aranka, he reluctantly told her that Grandfather Geza was deported by train to a place in Poland -- Auschwitz. Auschwitz. Aranka was already aware of Auschwitz. Aranka understood that, particularly for the elderly or weak, like her father, Geza, this was not a labor camp; this was a death camp. Even then, she had no idea what was to come, and what plans were already in place.

Aranka had gone to the naturalization office at her mother's request to find out why Geza hadn't yet come back home. Upon her return to her parents' Kobanya home, the sorrow and anger in her face betrayed her golden hair. Her mother, who was in her normal position by the kitchen sink washing dishes, briefly looked back and registered that Aranka was alone. She immediately turned to continue washing the dishes, towel over her left shoulder.

"What next, Aranka?"

"He is gone, *Anuka*. Gone."

Unflinching, her mother was steadfast in her refusal to look back at her strong, clever beyond belief daughter, who always seemed to have an answer for everything. She knew that if she were to look into her daughter's eyes, she would lose it. Her husband may have been a lazy, "good for nothing" at home, but he was her life. The father, at least in name, of their 13 children -- regardless of her "white lie" to the bureaucrats about Aranka's Christian father. "That's not what I asked," she raised her voice an octave or two. "What next, Aranka?"

"We will survive this, *Anuka*. I will keep us all safe; I promise. From this day on … I am so sorry I wasn't here to go with my *Apu*." She broke, but through clenched teeth, continued. "From this day on … I will make them pay. We will live through this, I swear."

Unknown to the Jews of Hungary, when the Nazis occupied Hungary on the 19th of March, Regent Horthy agreed to deliver to Hitler 300,000 of Hungary's Jews from the provinces outside of Budapest to be "deployed" for the German war effort. This number was immediately increased beyond that, at Horthy's agreeance, to include entire families, since laborers would be more content if they had their families with them.

The Nazis, Hitler, and Eichmann were told they would have the full cooperation of the Hungarian military and gendarmerie.

By the middle of July, Robert and his mother had already been staying for some weeks with Seventh Day Adventist Christian friends of his father, the Guzmics. They had only brought clothes, entrusting some of their easily movable valuables to Christian neighbors -- the Slivacs -- who swore they would protect the valuable possessions that the Holczers had not already sold. It was awful to leave their home, their furniture, their memories behind to another family, but there was no alternative. They hoped against hope that they would soon return, all of them.

Staying with the Guzmics was a temporary situation, but Robert was already discerning that they would again have to move because he felt it was no longer safe. It was safe neither for his father's kind friends, nor Robert and his mother. Budapest Jews, they knew, were already supposed to be in yellow star houses. To be caught living outside of such a house could have dire consequences, and any person caught hiding Jews would be imprisoned, or worse. On his way one afternoon to see his Aunt Aranka, in order to find out if it was still safe to move in with her, Robert recognized a boy his age with whom he used to play in Vac when he needed to escape the wrath of his grandmother. Robert had to do a double take to make sure it was in fact the same young man he knew. It had been two or three years since he had seen this boy.

"Daniel? It's me, Holczer, Robert. Do you remember?"

The boy, walking with his parents and perhaps his sister, stopped and stared at him, at first confused. "Oh yes, of course, Robi ... Robi Holczer. Father, Mother ... this is ... this is the Oestreichers' grandson, do you remember?"

Daniel stared at Robert strangely, as if he were seeing a ghost. But when Robert looked at his parents, both holding their maybe 12-year-old girl's hands, they looked like they were seeing death itself.

Hesitating at first, then stepping in front of his son, Daniel's father released the now nervous grip of his daughter and looked around the street anxiously. When he finally decided it was apparently safe to speak, the father at first muttered, then said calmly, "I am sorry, Robert. I assume you have heard the news, yes?" He looked back again to his wife. Robert was watching the exchange of glances like table tennis volleys.

"No, sir. What news? I was going to ask if...."

Again, there was the rapid eye contact that seemed to avoid contact altogether. This time Robert saw Daniel, his mother and sister, simply look down. Other pedestrians walked by this busy Budapest intersection at Andrassy and Jokai utca in the heart of the city, more than a few looking at this increasingly strange exchange between a Jew and a Gentile family.

The tall father, balding with a dark, bushy mustache that seemed to bear enough hair to patch his baldness, leaned down, closely. "Robert, you don't know about your grandparents?" He went on, "They ... Hungarian gendarmerie took all of the Jews of Vac from their homes. At first...." The man placed his hand on Robert's shoulder as his family, standing now squarely beside him, all began to cry, as if on cue. "At first, they had all the Jews crowded into, I don't know, several houses in a small section of Vac by the synagogue. Then, just a couple of days later they sent them all away. All of them. Close to 2,000. On a train...."

All around Robert there was life. The intoxicating aroma of paprika-laden dishes from too many kitchens overhead, a baby's cry, the laughter of lovers, violent words exchanged from one driver to another.... But in a moment, it seemed everything had died. He heard every word above the din of passing traffic, passing conversations and squeals. He heard them as if in slow motion, and now that the words were in the air, there was a part of him that was jumping from his body here, there, anywhere to catch each and every single floating word. He would put them in a bottle, run to the Danube, and throw it down the river. *If the words go away,* he thought, *the deed never happened.*

"Sir ... thank you." Robert turned and walked ... anywhere.

Hours later, just minutes before curfew, he stealthily returned to the home of the Guzmics to see his mother reading a book under the lamp light on a chair in the main living room. There was a plate of food waiting for him beside a nub of a candle at the center of a wooden kitchen table.

The Guzmics may have been there, but if they were, Robert only saw his mother. She closed her book and smiled. Smiled, until she saw Robert's tears. He had sworn to himself he wouldn't cry; he had to be strong. He could only imagine the effect this would have on his mother. In truth, he was already crying for her. *Don't cry, mother,* he thought to himself. *Don't cry,* he begged, for her sake. For his mother's sake. For … *his* sake.

"Oh, *Anu*…."

***

A few days later, Robert and his mother moved in with Aranka at 1 Zichy Jeno Utca in District VI, a five story, light gray brick apartment building with a large porcelain store, among others, on the main floor. When they arrived, there was a conspicuous yellow star over the entrance to designate the building as a yellow star house. It is doubtful that his mother registered anything of her new surroundings, her vision so obscured by seemingly perpetual bouts of crying spells that her tears could have formed at least a tributary into the vast Danube. They were all suffering, but only Robert and his Aunt Aranka were bent, by necessity, on forging ahead in the wake of these tragedies. In the two room, sparse but clean apartment, already lived Grandmother Julia, Uncle Laszlo and his wife and small daughter, Uncle Bobby and Uncle Bela. There were more bodies in the room than walking space, but, now that Grandfather Geza was gone and everything that was occurring in the provinces, no one felt safe anywhere. And so, they were all together. Like packed sardines, but together.

The following Saturday, in early July, Robert was again to report for labor battalion practice, but this time just northeast of the Budapest limits. The last few sessions had been successively more exhausting- to the point of collapse, for some. They had been digging, endlessly digging, so that adult labor crews after them could lay additional railroad tracks leading out of the city. Not a good omen at all, the boys all thought, but to refuse to report could mean imprisonment.

On this particular Saturday, Robert awakened early, and, of course, found that Aranka and *Nagymama* Julia were already awake and boiling water for tea or coffee. His mother was still sleeping on a thin mattress on the floor in the living room beside all the others. No one else had a mattress, including Robert, but apparently everyone was most concerned about Robert's mother, still missing her husband, and having lost her *entire* family to Auschwitz. Conversations in the apartment were not light.

"Hey, Robi," Aranka whispered so as not to wake anyone unnecessarily. "Where did you say you have to report for labor today?" Her breath already reeked of coffee.

"In Dunakeszi, or Mogyorod, I forget which," yawned Robert. "A bus is supposed to take us there from Andrassy Utca, that's all I know. I'm to meet Matyas there in 15 minutes. Can I have a cup, please?" Robert asked, still rubbing the sleep from his eyes.

"Dunakeszi, Mogyorod … suburbs of Budapest. No, you are sick. You won't go today."

Her mother stopped in her tracks before handing Robert a cup of steaming black coffee. "Aranka?"

"What do you mean, I'm sick? I'm fine, Aunt. If I don't go in…."

"*When* you don't go in, then I'll deal with it. I will go now in your place to inform them you have a high fever and are seeing the doctor today. I have a bad feeling about this," Aranka informed Robert. There was stirring from the rest of the family as a soft morning light meandered its way through the shutters in the living room. That and the smell of the coffee….

"What about Matyas and the others? Most are my schoolmates."

"I can't very well go to them and say, 'go home, boys. I am Robert's aunt and I have a sixth sense about this labor business today. Go home.' I can only say you aren't coming. If I see this Matyas…."

Aranka noted Robert's description of Matyas but did not see him. There were so many boys with yellow stars there at the platform. She did succeed, however, in telling the Hungarian military officer that Holczer

Robert could not go due to a terrible illness. The man, clearly agitated, frowned. Without ever looking up, he told her to move along. She obeyed.

The next afternoon, Robert went to find Matyas. He knew that he now lived in one of the yellow star houses closer to Rottenbiller, still in the fifth district, and he wanted to ascertain the latest developments with their labor battalion. Mostly, he was worried that "Shithead" Captain Behrentz might have his way with Matyas and his other friends, and he wouldn't be there to do or say anything about it. In reality, of course, he couldn't do or say much about anything in response to the idiotic and harsh treatment inflicted upon them. Yet, when he was there with his friends, their experiences were shared, and they united them far beyond, he supposed, what more typical adolescent experiences could ever afford. He would never wish them upon anyone, for certain. However, particularly as an only child, he felt that the inane, abusive labor details somehow rendered him and his friends, several of whom were also Scouts with Robert and Matyas, brothers. United.

When he finally found the apartment in which Matyas and his family were staying, he wanted to immediately turn around and run as fast as he could back to 1 Zichy Jeno. Matyas' mother, hair disheveled, tears dried along her cheeks, suddenly began screaming when she opened the door to see her son's friend, Robert.

"You?" She both croaked and screamed simultaneously upon recognizing Robert. "You? How can this be possible?" she cried, turning at once to her husband.

"What … yes, hello Madam. Is Matyas…?"

Her husband, spared forced labor assignments due to a crippling leg injury he sustained fighting in the first world war, staggered from god only knows where in their darkened room to take hold of his wife and literally pull her back into the black. "Why wasn't he there … with our Matyas?" beckoned his wife to her husband, or perhaps anyone. He emerged again, limping into the yellow hallway light as Robert backed up as far as he could against the pale wall of the sagging hallway. Zichy Jeno was a far better maintained house than this place. The stark smell of must seemed to pervade the entire building. He saw more than a few heads emerge from other doors in the hall to spy upon what was occurring.

"Robert," exhaled Matyas' father, almost unrecognizable absent his suit and tie he wore as a lawyer. In their place he was obviously unshaven and wearing a robe over pajama bottoms. At this afternoon hour. "Robert, you weren't there? You weren't with them?"

"No, sir. Yesterday? Why do you ask? I am here to see your son, is he okay?" Robert heard only wailing from the dark of the apartment. He now knew this sound far too well, and he was terrified. He turned to leave. "I'm sorry, I...."

"Wait, Robert. I am happy to see you are okay, truly," he paused. "They sent them all away. The whole youth labor detail." He was now borderline hysterical. "There was a train car that was empty, the man told us, and they ordered Matyas ... and all the others onto it. They sent them to ... they deported them to...."

"No!"

Robert did not know how or when he returned to Zichy Jeno. When he did, he hugged Aranka. He did not hear anything she said or asked, kissed his mother on the cheek, and, like his childhood game of trying to hide to avoid playing the piano, he pulled a thin blanket over his body and tried to wish the world away. He knew he could not succeed in this endeavor, and then he cried beneath the blanket. Not because he couldn't wish the world away, but because of everything. He would be 15 in just a few weeks, but for the first time in his life, days, weeks, months, and years never mattered more. Or maybe less. He felt like he was losing everything ... everyone ... himself.

6

October 1944
Us and Them

Robert leaned over his Uncle Joszef, still sleeping on the couch, to open the window to another day. So many people inside the apartment made Robert feel like he was suffocating. The air was stagnant and the days increasingly, mind-numbingly boring and filled with doubt, worry, and fear. Card games and conversation did not disinterest Robert, but when each passing day repeated every preceding day, well, Robert felt like he was losing his mind. He felt like every day they were waiting- waiting for who knows what. A life in limbo. He had no recourse, no bike rides, no radio, *Apu,* no more friends … no more friends.

There were several Jewish children of the many physicians in 1 Zichy Jeno, including some very beautiful girls. However, they all belonged to a higher social class, a higher world even as they were all bound to live as the Jews they were under the same dire circumstances. He tried speaking with some of them, and though no one was deliberately condescending, he was able to get no further than polite conversation about nothing in particular. Perhaps it was something in the way they looked or spoke to him, beautiful eyes quickly glancing away. Or perhaps it was the look of their parents as the short, but strikingly handsome Robert so obviously was flirting with their daughters. Perhaps instead it was Robert's own perceptions, his seemingly lifelong history of being made to feel as an 'other,' an outsider.

He turned around to silently nod to Aranka and his grandmother, who was whispering something to his mother. His mother held up an empty cup of coffee. Did he want some? Of course, he wanted some. This was now their morning ritual. Trying in vain to pretend life was okay. Soldier on. Talk about the weather. Don't dare talk about what and who was already lost, or what worse things may lay ahead of them still. This all might be manageable if it was just confined to morning time, but the truth is there was really no escape from the monotony, the anxiety-ridden repetition of these days.

Robert's attention was again drawn to the window. It sounded like marching outside. He awkwardly reached over Uncle Joszef and, this time, climbed over the couch to look straight down to the street below. And there they were … several black-clad Nazi officers with a dozen or so *Wehrmacht,* soldiers in their gray uniforms and heavy, black jackboots, stomping as loud as thunder. There were also as many as 30, maybe 50, Hungarians wearing their gray Arrow Cross uniforms with green emblems, some of which seemed far too big and baggy for the size of many of them. There were random shouts and cheers, some in German, others similarly incomprehensible. To Robert's dismay, many of the Arrow Cross members appeared to be no older than him! Yet, perched like a bird on a ledge from their third story apartment window, the spectacle of black and gray uniforms below was dazzling despite the overcast, gray day that perfectly suited how he was feeling. How he would have loved to even be allowed to wear a uniform, almost any uniform!

"Thank you, Aunt," he whispered louder than he wanted as Aranka gently placed the cup of coffee into his hands.

"What are you looking at out there," she asked, either incapable or insufficiently tempted to join her nephew and somehow hurdle Uncle Joszef and the couch.

"Nothing, Aunt," he smiled, eyes not so much looking into the street as they were perhaps a thousand miles, or days, away.

Although he had been a kind of Boy Scout since he was nine years old, Robert had never been allowed to wear a uniform. From as far back as his childhood marbles incident, Robert learned very early that one man is hardly equal to another if he was not born into the right family, religion, race, or social class, or if his parents' way of thinking differed too much from others. Very early he learned that words such as 'Jew' or 'Gypsy,' for example, were not merely nouns to define a people or religion. Instead, they were too often either deliberately or implicitly accompanied with adjectives such as filthy, rotten or scum. As such, Robert already felt even by the age of 15 that he and too many others were indelibly branded -- as if the Star of David was even necessary -- to live the life of an outlaw from birth.

Because he was both a Jew and -- thanks to the citizenship issue that concerned his Grandfather Geza that further called into question his entire family's *Magyar*, Hungarian roots -- not purely Hungarian, Robert discovered early on that he was not counted among the authentic, real, blue-blooded citizens of his country. He discovered early on in life that hatred and being looked down upon as something below human by others were as much a part of life as the weather. These lessons were reinforced even in school textbooks and by teachers. "We true Hungarians are better than them; be brave soldiers, and one day we will rise. Our enemies, our neighbors will fall!" Like Nazi Germany, many Hungarians, and particularly its rising fascist Arrow Cross Party and their leader, Ferenc Szalasi, sought a return to ethnic pride, nationalism, and purity following the debacle that was World War I for both countries. They were looking for someone to blame in order to feel better about themselves.

It was against this childhood backdrop that, at the age of nine, Robert once noticed a group of shiny, impeccably dressed Hungarian Boy Scouts marching on Rottenbiller utca past his school. How they seemed so important, so distinguished, so … powerful. He raced home to tell his mother, begging her to let him join. After initial protestations and skepticism, and with her husband gone on business as much as he was, she agreed that Robert should have a hobby beyond school and piano.

He needed structured time, time to make new friends. She walked him over to the nearest Boy Scout office to register him. At first, he was well-received, and he participated in the various initiation activities with great relish. He was finally feeling a sense of belonging, of stature.

Just before the day on which he was to be sworn into the Scouts and finally be given a uniform, someone in the office began asking questions about his home, religion, family, income, and political affiliation. On the morning of the day he was to become a Scout, Robert and his mother were called in to the office, which was located just down the street, beside his school. Robert was told to remain in the lobby of the building while his mother was curtly escorted in by two men. Not long after, she emerged alone, pressing a tissue to her cheek to dry apparent tears. We were going home, she said, as Robert, in utter confusion, watched other families and their boys, already in their uniforms, excitedly take their seats in the auditorium for the ceremony. The ceremony was apparently rescheduled to an earlier time, and no one had told Robert. Ah, now he understood.... One or two of the boys waved, but Robert saw their parents look at him with incredible contempt, pulling their sons away from Robert and his mother, walking the opposite direction.

The next day, Robert was coming home from school when a man he thought he recognized from somewhere motioned to him. Was he a teacher there? He introduced himself as George Belyasz, a friend of Robert's parents, inquiring about the Scout disaster. He stated his mother asked him to speak with Robert, explaining that he too experienced a similar situation. Robert agreed to speak with him, and they sat on a bench across the street from his home. Robert could see his mother's shadow looking down at them from their Rottenbiller apartment. A former Scoutmaster, George was kicked out not because of his citizenship, race, or religion, but for his beliefs that, contrary to the Hungarian Scout ideal at the time, peace is better than war, and every person, regardless of background, should have the right to live in dignity.

George explained that he had formed a kind of "underground" group of Scouts that believed in these principles of the true Boy Scout spirit, describing their activities and adventures. Would Robert like to join? George explained that there were other boys, Jews and non-Jews, who already belonged to this group, including a boy Robert's age named Matyas who had recently moved into a nearby apartment house. Had Robert already met him at school or in their labor requirements?

At the first meeting Robert attended, he could not wipe the smile from his face. They met in the basement of a nearby apartment, and had to act covertly, keeping as quiet as possible so as not to give the slightest hint of their group's existence. They discussed what it really meant to be an actual Boy Scout, to value all people, to love all neighbors, to give and never belittle. George also explained, to Robert's initial dismay, that since their group would be disbanded if discovered, and perhaps he would even be jailed for operating such an illegal group, they could not wear a uniform, bear membership cards, or even talk about the group outside of the group meetings and functions.

For a clandestine group of children aged nine to 14, Robert's underground Scout group fared rather well. They met once or twice a week, went on hikes as often as they could, and even went camping together when possible in the summer. From time to time they did various things to avoid suspicion, such as changing their meeting places to athletic clubs, apartment house basements, and synagogues. Over the past few years, the boys formed a great bond, far in excess of what Robert thought even possible from the first day he laid eyes on the so-called real Boy Scouts marching by his school when he was nine. He, Matyas, and the others felt a great deal of bitterness and envy toward the legitimate Boy Scouts and, even more, for not being permitted to be recognized by the outside world for the scope of their deeds, let alone existence. Nevertheless, no amount of recognition or even uniforms could ever compensate for the deep friendship and camaraderie these boys felt for each other. They all realized, in time, how ultimately fortunate they all were to have such sincere, honest leaders among their group, and, above all, each other.

Of course, this all came to an end. Hopefully, Robert wished, not permanently. Since the Nazis came, and, with them, the increased anti-Jewish laws and decrees, everything became far too dangerous. And more recently, since all the group's Jews were scattered in different yellow star houses, or, like Matyas and undoubtedly others, gone forever, there was no group. Robert neither had the will nor the ability to look. He wondered where George even was. The older group members and other group leaders who were Jewish had already been sent to forced labor, like his father, so who knows where they might be? As for George, Robert lost track of him earlier in the summer. Had he been arrested? No one knew.

In the absence of a radio, by which they could listen to international news from several countries, neutral information was now virtually impossible to access. There were now only the State-controlled newspapers, which only told facts from the German perspective. This would have driven Robert's father crazy, so insistent he was on learning multiple points of view before formulating his own opinions.

Nevertheless, the facts presented in the newspapers were soul-numbing. Between May 15 and July 8, 1944, 437,402 Jews were deported from the Hungarian provinces, most to Auschwitz, almost all to their immediate deaths. In just 54 days, the Hungarian military, gendarmerie, and police had zealously obliged the Nazis' wishes and rendered Hungary *Judenrein*, entirely Jew-free, only with the exception of the approximately 160,000 Jews in Budapest and those who might still be alive in forced labor camps.

To try and stave off boredom, Robert was always the one who insisted on going out to buy the newspapers during these weeks. Not only that, but he was the self-appointed reader of news to others after dinner each night. One-sided as the news may have been, he asserted that reading aloud was "good practice" for him, good enough to compliment the tutoring his mother had initiated for him since schools had been closed to Jews. Plus, although Robert could not answer whether bad news was better than no news, he felt that reading aloud even one-sided news kept his mind active, allowing him to pose questions and think of everything around him more critically. He knew this was what his father would have wanted.

Robert learned and shared with his family the news that Regent

Horthy ordered that the deportations of Hungary's Jews cease on July 7th. He did this due to rising international pressure, as world leaders could no longer pretend they did not know what Hitler was doing to Europe's Jews, particularly Hungary's Jews.

"Can this be," asked Robert's *nagymama*, covering her mouth. "Does this mean we will be spared? In Budapest?"

Not so fast. Eichmann was outraged by Horthy's order. He first deported to Auschwitz all Jews currently imprisoned in labor camps, and then drafted more Budapest Jews into work camps to take their place. But then, Robert shared, Romania broke their alliance with the Nazis and joined with the Soviets, who were now on the verge of entering Hungary. This caused the Nazis to divert their attention elsewhere, and so Eichmann begrudgingly returned to Germany, for the moment. Reading about the changing tides of both the war itself and the Nazis war on Jews was like watching tennis volleys: One moment there was optimism, the next skepticism; heads turning left, right, hopes going up, down and so on.

Meanwhile, Robert's Aunt Aranka had learned through her many contacts that Swiss, Swedish and other international help to Jews was arriving in Budapest. Carl Lutz, for Switzerland, and Raoul Wallenberg, on behalf of Sweden and the War Refugee Board, were issuing passes of safe conduct to as many Jews as possible. In theory, Aranka discerned, these passes would protect their holders – Jewish or not – as citizens of those respective countries. Both the Swiss and Swedes were even making arrangements for their newly "protected" citizens to stay in protected houses in Budapest's 5th and 13th Districts.

"Would it be safer to go there, than to remain here?" asked Robert's Uncle Joszef.

"Of course, you are welcome to go, brother," Aranka sighed over a post-dinner cup of coffee. "But I, myself, wish to remain here. At least for now, I prefer what I know, rather than what may or not be…."

Neither Aranka, Robert, nor anyone in their apartment knew for certain whether, for how long, or to what extent the passes might work, but they all agreed to secure Swedish "Schutz Passes" for all living with them in 1 Zichy Jeno. They opted not to move into the protected houses, still unsure what, if anything, was worse to come. Perhaps these passes, in addition to their falsified birth certificates, could keep them safe. Even though Aranka had the initial protection of being considered a Christian, she never separated herself from the interests of her family members. To the contrary, she always hoped she could use that yet additional protection to help save the lives of her remaining family. This resolution was made firmer in the wake of what happened to her father, and the fact that she wasn't there to somehow save him.

On October 15th, the day Robert had been looking outside his window at the passing Nazis and Arrow Cross party officers, Horthy addressed the Hungarian people on the radio. All remaining radios in Budapest in non-Jewish coffee houses, taverns and shops were turned on as loud as they could go. Everyone everywhere was listening. Rumors had been swirling around like autumn leaves on a crisp, windy day that Horthy had reached a deal with the Soviets to switch sides, as Romania had done earlier. Robert and the others -- seemingly every Jew in his building and people as far as he could see -- were now outside the open coffee houses and drinking establishments to listen:

"Today, every sober-minded individual will recognize beyond a doubt that the German (Reich) has lost this war. (Hungary) cannot sacrifice itself on the altar of loyalty to an alliance.

***

(D)espite my wishes and will … the Gestapo employed the methods that it had followed elsewhere and began dealing with the Jewish question in the familiar way, one that goes against what humane behavior demands." Horthy concluded his radio address indicating that he had informed the Nazis of his intent to sign a ceasefire against the Allied forces. Additionally, he instructed the Hungarian military to stand down, calling on "every

Hungarian with a sense of honor to follow me on the sacrifice-filled road to salvaging the Hungarian people."

Despite Horthy's attempt to significantly downplay Hungary's own role in the ghettoizations and deportations by blaming everything on the Gestapo, the Nazi secret police, rather than revealing the truth that such acts were perpetrated by Hungarians, Budapest's Jews who received word of this cease-fire were jubilant. Robert enjoyed every moment. He must have been hugged, even kissed by all the pretty girls from 1 Zichy Jeno. Even his mother was smiling, though Aranka remained stoic, arms folded tightly. She was wearing her glasses more often nowadays, but now she seemed to be staring *into* them rather than through them to actually see anything.

Such celebrations and premature visions that they had or would now survive were remarkably short-lived. Contrary to Horthy's myopic belief that this *coup* would catch the Germans and those Hungarians loyal to them off guard, the opposite was true. The Nazis had not only anticipated this action, but they had already drawn up plans to force Horthy's immediate resignation. Horthy and his son were arrested, and the Nazis transferred leadership to the Jew-hating Arrow Cross Party leader, Ferenc Szalasi. At long last, the *true* meaning of terror had arrived for the Jews of Budapest.

7
October 1944, Part 2
Laugh or Cry

The girl with laughing eyes sung when she spoke. She must have been Robert's age, maybe a year or two older, but such confidence ... such beauty. When Robert first noticed her, laughing arm in arm with an almost equally gorgeous friend, he realized he wasn't the first to notice her. Far from it. There must have been a trail of eight teenage boys -- some older than he. These young men were so obviously pursuing her, flexing imaginary muscles, "accidentally on purpose" cutting in front of her, and doing anything they could to grab her attention in the lobby of 1 Zichy Jeno. Where on earth did this girl come from?

Robert had been downstairs asking Theo, the building's superintendent, if he knew where to safely get some milk. The 'super' curtly replied that there was no longer a place safe for Jews outside in all of Budapest. Just then, both he -- easily in his 40s -- and Robert turned suddenly to behold a girl with laughing eyes and her friend descend the narrow, white stone staircase and seemingly glide toward them. There was a train of boys and young men in their wake and darting all around, dizzy like moths around a streetlamp. Catcalls and whistles created utter cacophony above the din of too many increasingly anxious tenants carrying on to each other about the worsening news.

She was wearing a red hat and scarf that framed her dark brown hair, laughing green eyes and high cheekbones. She was a painting, yet her eyes were luminous, so she was surely three-dimensional. She seemed to perfume the lobby, if not the whole of a Budapest that was in as much need of such a vision as sunflowers seeking the sun.

"Excuse me," she seemed to sing to the super as her eyes mischievously glinted because of, or despite her stalkers. "Do you know where we can get a liter of milk, we just…."

"Arrived yesterday, yes, of c-c-course my lady," blurted the slack-jawed super. "It's … it's … w-w-w-we have some right here in the lobby bar for our s-s-s-special guests, thank you."

Robert surely heard this confession that there was milk on the premises, but he continued to stand there, feet cemented to the gaudily patterned carpet that led from the entry door throughout the lobby and up to the base of the stairs and steel-caged elevator. His eyes never left the girl with laughing eyes.

"Um, you're welcome," she simultaneously laughed and sung, her sparkling, green eyes seeming to penetrate the skin and bones of the now blushing, profusely sweating super. Her friend, giggling and stepping up to place her head on her taller companion's shoulder, squeezed her arm to go, surveying the veritable horde now surrounding them to take in this beauteous vision. "So, can I get some, then? How much do I owe you?"

"I'm sorry, f-f-f-follow me." He left his post near the entrance, leaving Robert among the gawking group of tongue-tied young men. He cut through the crowd with surprising ease and reached under the bar where there must have been a refrigerator, because he then magically raised a small glass container of milk. "W-w-will that be enough? Would you like me to help you w-w-w-with it?"

The beautiful girl laughed, then left. "Thank you," she and her girlfriend called out, as if in continuous song. They were laughing, of course, all the way back up the stairs. The horde groaned, sighed, exhaled; each one of them daring each other that they would be the one….

Robert groaned, sighed, exhaled…. Then, eyes unwavering from the staircase, "W-wh … ahem, who is that?"

Toweling off his brow, the super, Theo, suddenly rediscovered his fluency. "Kadar, Eva. She is the granddaughter of Dr. Zahler, a very important man who lives on the first floor next to Dr. Volgyesi, the famous psychiatrist."

Robert had heard people talking about how many famous Jewish physicians were in this building, but this was the first he had heard specific names. "And the other one … her sister?"

"No, Marika – Hoenig, Marika, I think. A friend of hers. She came here with her physician father yesterday at Eva's invitation, and Eva two days before with her mother, Erzsi, and her great grandmother, Dr. Zahler's mother, to stay with Dr. Zahler and his wife. I know that Erzsi had operated an upscale hotel at 12 Vaci Utca until the Germans ordered them out. Erzsi, Eva and the great grandmother finally came here the day of Horthy's speech and the Arrow Cross -- Holy Sabbath, did you see that Eva?"

"Easy, Theo, mind your age!"

"Young Holczer, I may be getting up there in years but my eyes cannot deny the truth of beauty, no matter the age." Still wiping down his nearly bald scalp, Theo smiled from ear to ear. "I can still dream, can't I?"

"So, about that milk…?"

Robert was halfway up the stairs with his own liter bottle of cold milk when he realized he couldn't stop grinning. *What a vision*, he thought. Even though he didn't dare presume he could contend to win the hand of the girl with laughing eyes, *I can still dream, can't I?* He laughed. Then, upon seeing the door to his Aunt's apartment, he stopped, finally and immediately sobered. So much had happened in these past couple of days. The Arrow Cross was out there, supposedly rounding up Jews all over Budapest. There were rumors of beatings, and worse. There were rumors that Eichmann had returned to Budapest and that deportations of the Jews of Budapest would now begin. Where was there to go? What to do?

Could their passes help them? No one seemed to know anything specific, and that was almost more distressing than the actual rumors.

He opened the door, still lost in thought. There was his mother, nervously sewing at the table with other relatives playing cards. Were they just goldfish in a fishbowl? Pawns on a chess board? Was there a move available to them?

"It's about time, Robi," announced Aranka, removing her glasses. His mother smiled without looking up as his grandmother deftly dealt another hand. "Want to play, Robi?" his mother asked. She raised one eye in his direction as he continued to stand at the door. How much older, or was it sadder, she looked. The worry was taking such a toll on everyone. But in her case, having lost her entire family and with her husband gone, everyone continued to give her whatever extra space they could. One cannot measure, weigh or compare loss, but that didn't mean that Robert's family didn't attempt to at least acknowledge her predicament, her grief. Robert had run out of things to say, so he just tried to be as useful as he could and simply pretend his father was away on another business trip. To think otherwise was unbearable, so, he didn't.

Just then, there was a loud pounding, then screams and shouts. They seemed to come from down the three flights of stairs, in the lobby. Robert opened the door as soon as it had just closed. In the corridor, he saw a number of other heads similarly breaching their respective doorways to ascertain the source of the startling commotion below.

"Out! Everyone out of their rooms!" yelled a series of competing voices growing rapidly nearer. "All you Jews come down to the courtyard at once!"

As every other door immediately slammed shut, Robert remained, now flanked by Aranka and his Uncle Joszef, crammed inside the doorway, trying to ascertain what was happening. Voices called out behind them, and seemingly everywhere, more muffled behind the closed doors of the third floor.

"Robi, Aranka, what is it? Do we go down?" cried Robert's mother, wild-eyed.

Before anyone could answer, the voices and shouts came louder. Then, Robert could see two young Arrow Cross members in their light gray uniforms, green shirts and red and white-striped armbands with intersecting green arrows step onto their floor. "Out, you Jews! If we find that any Jew is still inside after we get down to the courtyard, you'll be sorry. Now come out! Everyone out!"

"But I'm not Jewish," called a voice behind a closed door next to Aranka's apartment. "Nor I," called another. This was undoubtedly true, as Robert understood that several non-Jewish residents of the apartment house refused to move out despite it being recently marked as a "yellow star house."

"We don't care, we want to see everyone down in two minutes, or else!" the shorter of the two Arrow Cross men yelled. He raised his rifle high, even though, as far as Robert could tell, he and his uncle and aunt were the only three whose door was still open to see this apparent show of force. "Two minutes!"

Aranka hastened her brother and Robert inside and abruptly closed the door before the men got any closer. Everyone huddled closer to the door and surrounded Aranka. Robert and Joszef joined the huddle.

"Listen," Aranka paused, looking first at her mother, then everyone else. "I have my Christian papers, and everyone in this room has the Swiss Schutz Pass. That should count for something. These Arrow Cross buffoons -- traitors to our country -- will only want Jews, and only those without papers. You'll see."

"What about the Jews in the provinces, Aranka?" called out one of Robert's uncles. "They've -- the Nazis, our so-called fellow Hungarians killed all of the Jews there, so why not us now?"

Robert's mother immediately bellowed.

"Then you stay here, Bela, with our *anuka*, mother, and the rest. If they want us all, so they'll come for us all," She somehow remained calm. "I'll go down with my papers to find out what the hell is going on."

"I'm going too, Aranka." The sound of his own voice startled Robert.

"Me too," muttered a few others.

"Robi, no! I can't lose you too," Robert's mother squealed, silencing everyone at once.

"No one's getting lost, Cornelia." Aranka finally put her hand on Robert's mother. "I won't let them."

The shouts were growing louder in the hallway, and Robert heard doors open and close briskly. "Come out, now, you Jews! Time's up!"

"Let's go, then," Robert's mother conceded. "I'm going with you. We'll be together." Robert smiled as his mother took his hand and pressed it to her lips. A tear streamed down her cheek and onto his hand.

"The rest of you, keep quiet and stay back," Aranka ordered. "Don't open the door for anyone."

Theo the super had told Robert yesterday there must be more than 300 people now living in the 1 Zichy Jeno apartments. There were so many Jews coming in to stay with relatives and friends that it was hard to keep track, Theo said. "Not everyone here is a Jew, you know, but by far most of them – and that includes all the Jews here with Christian papers!"

As Robert surveyed the courtyard upon their entry, there were nowhere near 300 people outside. Maybe half that number, at most. The courtyard consisted of a small, rectangular concrete slab that contained a trash receptacle and open area, attached to which was an entry to the building's basement. Beyond this slab was a more open, relatively more inviting, round gathering area framing a few rusty tables and some potted flowers. From here, looking up, one could see the four-story terraces and porches of those units with this view, and access to see the courtyard. Aranka's apartment did not bear this view; it faced out onto the street, able to easily see St. Istvan's Basilica.

The sky was gray, an endless cloud cover to such an extent that it was impossible to distinguish a single cloud among what appeared to be a ceiling of one giant cloud that enveloped the whole world. It was lightly drizzling, but everyone had hurried out so fast that Robert saw very few people wearing jackets. He clung closely to Aranka's side, holding his mother's hand on his other side. There were six uniformed Arrow Cross members there, each of them holding a rifle, and each of them no older than 20. "Don't they know there are many more of us still inside the apartments?" Robert whispered aloud.

"Shush," Aranka instructed.

"Against the wall. Everyone against this wall in a single line," ordered the same shorter man Robert had seen upstairs. With the stub of a cigarette between his fingers on the hand not holding his gun, he was motioning to one of the two longer walls in the unconventionally shaped courtyard. The group had to navigate around the tables and plants in the middle of the yard, and it didn't take long before the Arrow Cross men kicked them over and aside. The potted ferns and other plants were likewise kicked over, spilling their contents all around. There were pigeons observing the scene from the rails of respective terraces, trails of their feces streaking the yellow walls of the courtyard randomly.

The other Arrow Cross members disbursed to corral the residents more quickly. Finally, one man called out: "What do you want with us? We all have protection, so why don't you go on your way and let us do our work. Many of us here are physicians…." As Robert scanned around him to locate the voice, he suddenly recognized that this distinguished, older man was standing beside Eva Kadar, the girl with laughing eyes. She was holding the hand of her friend, shuffling almost imperceptibly behind what must be her grandfather, Dr. Zahler.

"Physicians, you say? That's good to hear. Where you'll all be going, I'm sure physicians will be needed," laughed the short Arrow Cross man. In his gray uniform and oversized cap, he looked more like a train official than a soldier, except for his gun. The other members laughed but appeared more nervous. He took a final drag from the stub of his cigarette, then flicked it to the wet, shiny pavement and stomped on it. "Today is only a preliminary inspection. We are ordered to bring with us any person over the age of 60 for registration on Andrassy Street, the Arrow Cross headquarters. We will return these people," he glanced at his comrades, "as soon as we process them."

There was immediate commotion among the residents in the courtyard. Robert noticed that there was a woman standing beside Dr.

Zahler and his granddaughter who was clearly more than 60 years old. This must be the great grandmother whom Theo had mentioned. His mother squeezed his hand tighter, and Aranka whispered to Robert and the others in the family group there, "Be prepared to run upstairs to protect Mother. If necessary, I will create a distraction."

Before Robert could formulate a response to his aunt, he heard Dr. Zahler again call out. "Let me go with them. My mother is with me, and she will need my care even if she is gone for a short period of time, as you say. She cannot walk without difficulty."

The man-child again stomped his foot, this time against nothing. The young man's fuse for patience was apparently as short as his stature. "That's it! Men, take out anyone who looks as old as your own grandparents. We can come back later to sweep the apartments and root out the rest. Shut your mouth, Doctor. I assure you they will be back, and that is all."

Sure enough, as the residents against the wall braced themselves and pushed closer together, the Arrow Cross young men and their guns pulled out as many as 15, maybe 20 older people. There were no shots fired, but he saw one Arrow Cross smack a man across the head with the butt of his rifle. The man had been trying to prevent two elderly people beside him from being taken. The man fell, and many in the crowd of residents screamed and uttered various derogatory slurs against their oppressors while a few others tended to the fallen man.

Once the elderly people were in a loose approximation of a line, the man-child instructed his comrades to march them out of the courtyard and away from the building. Robert saw Dr. Zahler's mother standing there with the others. She looked, strangely enough, at ease. She was calm, and managed a quiet smile toward Eva, her beautiful great granddaughter, whose face was now obstructed from Robert's view by many people taller than him. The great grandmother, whose silver hair shined despite the grayness of the day, raised her left arm with some effort and waved as she and the others were finally coaxed forward. It was surely less a march than a procession, slower and more labored.

"We will be back, I assure you. Time's up, Jews!"

"What is that supposed to mean?" cried various residents. "When will our elderly return?" Dr. Zahler stood forward again, just as the short man-child was turning away to join the procession. "What is your name?"

"My name, you ask?" he turned back and smiled. "My name is the last thing you need to know. Unlike you filthy Jews, our names mean nothing. We work together and don't try to screw each other over for our own profit! Now you hear me, we *will* be back. With or without them, *we* will be back!"

"Your name!" Dr. Zahler insisted.

The man-child smiled as the rest of the procession departed the courtyard, painstakingly slow on account of the elderly among them. He reached into his breast pocket for another cigarette, apparently, but couldn't seem to find one -- or at least grasp one in the drizzle of the gray afternoon. "Ivan," he said at last. "Call me Ivan … the Terrible!" He snorted as he laughed, the snort abruptly cutting short the laughter. "And I know you … Dr. Zahler, yes? The pediatrician. You were my brother's doctor a few years ago until our mother … which is the only reason I don't shoot you now." He smiled again and held up his rifle.

The crowd again cried out in agony and protest as the man called "Ivan," aiming his gun and feigning shots, mouthed, "Phh … phh … bang bang … you'll all be dead!" He turned and finally ran out, leaving the residents to turn to each other and instantly become braver: What they would have done if they had the chance; what they will do the next time…. "We will make them pay," Robert heard several say.

As his mother pulled his hand to get back to their room immediately, Robert turned his attention again to where he saw Dr. Zahler and Eva, his granddaughter. "Wait, *Anu*," he said, pulling back his hand as Aranka looked at him crossly. There they were: Dr. Zahler and the woman who must be his wife; Eva's friend Marika; Eva's mother Erzsi, and Eva herself, the girl whose eyes were no longer laughing. In place of her laughter was a veritable pool on the verge of overflowing with tears. Sadness, despite her mother's firm embrace. There she was, crying. Robert was looking right at her, maybe 15 meters away. Helpless, like the rest of them. Robert could not tell whether Dr. Zahler looked angry, or whether he was simply in despair. Helpless.

"Helpless," Robert mouthed to himself.

***

The procession trudged ahead, merging at seemingly every city block with one new procession after another. The groups were seamlessly unified not only by their relatively advanced ages and accompanying Arrow Cross men wielding batons, sticks and rifles, but by the yellow stars on the outer garments of those being marched.

Occasionally, there were shots fired along the way. More often, there were screams; hateful, disgusting screams from those in charge and screams that tethered on cries from those tormented. "Move … march … you lazy, useless Jews…!" Laughter. These shouts, cries and desperate pleas for mercy served as the soundtrack for this procession heading west from Pest and onto the Margit Bridge toward Buda. Of course, the soundtrack gained volume as more and more elderly Jews begrudgingly joined this chorus of the damned.

"Where are we going?" was heard again and again, like children begging parents when their destination would be reached. "Where are you taking us?" "Can we have some water?" "Please, have mercy!"

By the time more than half of the group had trekked across the start of the Margit Bridge from Pest, more and more marchers fell, unable to go forward. Some cars and trucks slowed to get a closer look, their passengers gawking at this spectacle and some even encouraging the Arrow Cross members to "finish them off!" Others rolled up the window and tried to find a way to speed up so they would not have to look at what was transpiring. Random gunshots were audible.

One black car heading east into Pest suddenly pulled over to the opposite, west bound side as far as it could go without striking the marchers, far enough over so that eastbound traffic could safely proceed. The car stopped as close as it could to where a short, stout, teenage-looking

Arrow Cross man was striking an old man lying on the wet road beside the edge of the bridge. Other walkers necessarily kept walking forward, around this scene which was already commonplace to them. The Arrow Cross man kept shouting; hitting the man across his back and sides with the butt of his rifle. "Keep moving, dirty Jew! Get up right now, you are slowing us down!"

Just as the Arrow Cross man was about to strike the old man again, he heard a loud voice from a man who emerged suddenly from the back of the stopped black car. The tall man, in his mid-20s, was dressed in an Arrow Cross uniform the younger man had never seen. In addition, he held his head high and exuded leadership. *He must have been a high-ranking officer,* the younger Arrow Cross man thought.

"Stop at once," the apparent officer called out. "What do you think you are doing?"

"This dirty Jew doesn't want to go on, no matter how much I beat him. We have orders to get these old Jews to the Austrian border, one way or another. From there, I can only assume…." He paused to wipe his brow, propping his rifle against his left hip and setting his right foot on top of the old man on the ground, wondering if he could dare to look up yet. "This pile of dung lay down in the middle of the street where you can see him now. He doesn't want to move. May I throw him now into the Danube?"

The apparent officer felt an unexpected chill. The rain seemed to have stopped, but he felt a sudden, almost violent wind sweep into his face, blowing from west to east. He loathed the volatility of the air above the river, every time. The grayish Danube continued its relentless journey southeast below. He surveyed the old, Jewish man on the ground, badly beaten, and the discolored Danube, seemingly without taking his eyes off the younger, shorter thug. To the apparent officer, what they shared in common – relatively matching uniforms and moustaches – could not possibly unite them in any conceivable way, could it? As members of the same Hungarian nation? As human beings?

In the eyes of this younger man, the apparent officer could only see contempt. In the eyes of the old, beaten Jewish man on the ground, desperation; surrender. To the apparent officer, it seemed that in this question – whether a man can hurl another into the Danube as if he had no greater value than an old, dirty paper bag, and in this scenario of elderly, dignified Jewish men and women being marched toward their inevitable deaths, the value of human life and emotion had been rendered obsolete. *These Arrow Cross thugs will stop at nothing*, the apparent officer thought to himself as he looked around him once more at the marchers and thugs. *Now I know what is surely waiting for the rest of the Hungarian Jews. This is the end of the line for all of them.*

"Hey, brother," the apparent officer finally conjured, motioning to the man on the ground. "We are not murderers. If our great commander, Szalasi, knew how you are treating these people it would be the end of you. Just do what you were ordered and take them where you were told. It is not like Hungarians to treat fellow citizens in this way in the meantime. Do you understand?"

The younger man reached for a cigarette but remembered he didn't have one. He looked as if his favorite toy had just been taken from him. He eyed the apparent officer, envious of the pack of cigarettes he plainly saw in his breast pocket and suspicious now of the uniform. He had never seen this combination of clothes on the Arrow Cross uniform. And why didn't he bear any weapons?

The apparent officer spoke again, louder this time. "I said, do you understand, brother!"

"I understand, brother," he smiled. "What is your name, did you say?"

"I didn't. What is your name, so I know whom to blame in my report if I see or hear this type of behavior continue?"

"My name is Santor, Ivan. Ivan the Terrible," he grinned until he saw the apparent officer's burning glare.

"Jeretzian, Ara. That is my name. And I expect this is the last I will see or hear of such beatings or threats, or perhaps it is you who will become better acquainted with the temperature of the Danube." He finally reached into his pocket for a cigarette and produced a lighter from the pocket of his pants.

"Yes, Jeretzian, Ara. May I have one of your smokes?"

Jeretzian turned suddenly around to return to his waiting car. There was much to be done.

PART II

8

Jeretzian, Ara

Jeretzian closed his eyes as he pushed his slicked, black hair back with his right hand. With his left, he started to withdraw another cigarette from the breast pocket of his makeshift uniform, then suddenly remembered he already had one dangling from his lips. He patted the intended new one back into its package as he repositioned himself in the back seat of his car, and finally opened his eyes.

"Where to now, Ara?" his driver and longtime friend, Laszlo Nagy, gently asked. "Shall we proceed into 6th District, to the house you mentioned?"

Jeretzian exhaled out the car window as his gaze returned to the spectacle and sounds of the marchers on Margit Bridge. The island below it, lying just north of the bridge, was usually teeming with life; strollers, families picnicking, laughter.... Today, it was stunningly empty in comparison to the bustle of the bridge itself. "The hell with it, Nagy," he mumbled uneasily. "I'm going to need more than this pathetic uniform alone if I am to help my old friends. Drive over to the armory, on Bem Jozsef square. There's no way these punks will listen to me on the strength of my voice and good looks alone," he sighed without expression. "We're going to need some things before I figure out what, if anything, I can do for them."

Acquiring the new Arrow Cross uniform, or at least parts thereof, proved to be easier than he had imagined. *It's good never to burn bridges,* he thought, remembering his mother's advice repeated a hundred times throughout his adolescence. He quickly dismissed the irony of driving on Margit Bridge, and fixated his thoughts instead on the hope that he might have friends at the Armory to acquire weapons, just as he had to get the uniform odds and ends.

"What the hell am I doing, Nagy?" He wanted no answer and told Nagy so simply by raising his left hand and waving him off in the rearview mirror into which his friend glanced. Jeretzian looked both disgusted and defeated, at least for now.

After flicking his cigarette butt outside onto the cobbles, Jeretzian hastily rolled up the window. As the car swayed sharply to the right upon Nagy's turn, Jeretzian let himself go, allowing his head to lean against the window. He closed his eyes. His worst fears, from the moment he learned Szalasi was now in charge of Hungary as Hitler's puppet, were confirmed by this deathly procession and the inhumanity written on the faces of the Arrow Cross men herding and shepherding these Jewish people to their inevitable slaughter. *So, this is the end for them,* he thought. *If I don't do something to help … somehow.*

Minutes later, Nagy parked the car alongside 3 Bem Jozsef ter, a monstrous, pale, old building not far from the new Arrow Cross headquarters on Andrassy Street. It had served the military and police as a barrack for as long as Jeretzian could remember, but now had the fascist Arrow Cross flag draped over the entrance. Jeretzian had been here before, of course, but seemingly in another life.

"Is that a ghost walking in the door, or is this Jeretzian, Ara, former Arrow Cross Youth Director?" The bearded man in his dark blue Arrow Cross colors stood up from his chair behind the desk immediately and walked briskly around. He saw Jeretzian's outstretched hand but shoved it briskly aside and embraced him firmly instead.

Thank God, Jeretzian thought, almost aloud. He couldn't believe his good fortune. It was an old Youth Division assistant who worked under, and eventually with him, Balasz, Aron. "How the Hell are you, Balasz!

Yes, yes, it's me. I'm still here, old friend. I need some weapons to go with my uniform, can you help?"

"What? That's what I always loved about you, Jeretzian. You always get right to the point. So, you're back with us, then? The Arrow Cross? I heard nothing of it."

"That's a long story, Balasz. Surely you don't want me to bore you with the details," Jeretzian smiled warmly. "How is your wife doing? Do you have children?"

"Ah, Ara, it's good to see you, old friend. She's fine, of course, she'll be sorry to have missed you. But then all the ladies wanted to be with you back in the old days, eh friend? And look at you, you haven't changed a bit," Balasz laughed heartily. "So, where's your requisition form? What do you need?"

"I don't have the form, but you remember Kiraly, yes? At headquarters? He authorized me to come after giving me parts of the uniform. I like my new dark green shirt. I'll be heading back there imminently to get the rest of it. What do I need, grenades, a rifle, a hand-held…?"

Balasz scratched his chin and nodded. "Sure, Ara. Among friends, what do I need a requisition for? Besides, I imagine that not a hell of a lot happening now follows protocol."

"Thank you, brother. It's so good to see you. When I get everything sorted out, I'll come back to buy you a drink. You still like the Russian vodka, no doubt?"

"Does a leopard change its stripes … I mean, spots?" he laughed again. "Sure, let me get you what you need. I figure if someone, especially someone of your stature, wants to join the fight, we'll need them for what is still to come, eh?"

"It's frightening out there, Balasz, and, between us I don't appreciate Hitler, Eichmann and the rest telling Hungary what to do … but it is a great opportunity at the same time. For Hungary! Persevere!" Jeretzian suddenly shouted while clicking his heels together, reciting one of the many Arrow Cross slogans that were now in style.

"Jeretzian, the opportunist! Persevere!"

Balasz had no idea….

A few minutes later, Balasz returned with all the necessary weapons, and helped stow the grenades in his leather harness. "Your boots and pants aren't standard – are those your Civil Defense pants? Neither is this belt, Jeretzian," he informed while handing the weapons' safeties to him. "But like I said, if someone of your stature is here to join this fight, who am I to impede your plans?" He stood up, patted Jeretzian's sides, and again embraced him. "I'll expect that vodka soon, Jeretzian, you hear? Stoli!"

"I hear. And thank you, Balasz. I owe you." His words and warm, reciprocated embrace were all genuine, but in his mind, his thoughts immediately turned to his friends, acquaintances and business colleagues. Most of them were Jews, and many of them and their families were living, or at least now living at 1 Zichy Jeno utca, across Vilmos Csaszar utca from St. Istvan's Basilica. The Basilica, imposing in its neoclassical beauty and scale, and the neo-Renaissance Hungarian Royal Opera House on Andrassy utca comprised the heart of the 6th District. Jeretzian was aware that houses were being marked with Jewish stars, doubtlessly a prelude to ghettos and further deportations. Clearly the killings had already begun, to which the procession on Margit Bridge attested.

"I said, 'I'll see you very soon, then, right Jeretzian?'" Balasz looked wondering, but forgivingly at Jeretzian, as Jeretzian had appeared to become lost in thought and refused to release him from their embrace.

"Ah, Balasz, I'm sorry my brother." Jeretzian finally stepped back, opened the door, and turned around briskly. "If all goes well, brother, I'll buy you all the Stolichnaya you can drink – if you let me have some too!"

Jeretzian practically sprinted back into his waiting car. "Nagy, our good fortune continues," he said, breathlessly. "Now, my friend, on to 1 Zichy Jeno."

9

Strange Brotherhood

It had only been a few hours. Just a few hours ago, Arrow Cross men had entered 1 Zichy Jeno and forcibly removed many of the elderly residents as if they were going on a retreat together. But, despite the incessant questions, calls and yells demanding any news of their return – where had they taken them – the truth was known, even if no one wanted to admit it. They were gone. This was the beginning, surely. The beginning of the end. It had only been a few hours when a tall, dark man dressed in an Arrow Cross uniform appeared at the entrance and knocked.

People in the lobby screamed when they heard the knock and saw through the glass door the uniform. Within seconds, there was no one left in the lobby. All had run as fast as they could back into their rooms to brace themselves for something even worse than what they had just experienced. The Arrow Cross was back. So soon.

All had run away, except for Theo, the super, who was presumably duty-bound to serve as the house's front line. He didn't want to look at the man at the entrance. Though Theo was not Jewish, these were his friends here. This was his home, for all practical purposes. He didn't want to look, but reluctantly did as he approached the door.

"Are you kidding me?" Theo exclaimed while opening the door. "Jeretzian, Ara? But what…?"

"Theo, ah excellent! It's you. I had almost forgotten that my Civil

Defense house commander doubled as this building's 'super,' is it? Please let me in, I'll explain." Jeretzian flung the butt of another cigarette into the pavement just before entering.

"The uniform, Jeretzian. What…?" Theo unlocked the door and locked it again after Jeretzian had entered. He turned. "Tell me you're not one of them, Jeretzian. They took many of our residents just hours ago. Please…," he finally breathed.

"No, it's not what it seems, Theo. I'm here to help."

"In that uniform? You must be kidding, Jeretzian. These people are terrified – I'm terrified. They know what is happening."

"I'm here to see Volgyesi, Ferenc, the hypnotist and neurologist. I came to know him well through my Civil Defense work in this District – I've even learned a bit of hypnotism from him." Jeretzian playfully waved his fingers at Theo as if he was trying to hypnotize him. He instantly became serious again. "Is he here?"

"He's been away, Jeretzian, at the sanitarium, his hospital. But I believe his family is still here. Perhaps he came back last night, I don't know. I haven't seen him. Do you know Dr. Zahler, Emil?"

"Yes, of course. We have also worked together but I know him less than Volgyesi, more by reputation. He is a big shot in this building, no? Someone in his family owns it?"

"No – I mean, yes. But he must be out of his mind, Jeretzian. The Arrow Cross, they took away his…," he froze a moment as he again eyed Jeretzian's uniform. "How can we trust you while you're in this uniform?"

"I told you, Theo. You'll have to trust me. What choice have you got? I'm here to help. Now, can I go and see the doctors?"

"Sure, Jeretzian. Start with Dr. Zahler. He is on the second floor. He would also know about Dr. Volgyesi, I'm sure. But I warn you…."

Jeretzian had already turned around and began to ascend the weathered stone staircase. He thought he saw eyes peering between cracks of doors slightly ajar, watching his every step. And Jeretzian certainly could not blame them. If the situation was reversed, certainly he too would be terrified by the presence of a man in roughly the same Arrow

Cross uniform as the men who had earlier taken away many of their relatives. In fact, Jeretzian paused briefly as he reached the second floor. What was he thinking? Why was he wearing this uniform, in this place, today of all days? "Ah," he answered himself. "Time is of the essence. There is no time to change costumes as if in a play."

He stopped when he reached a door with the placard, "Zahler, Dr. Emil." He heard muffled cries inside but proceeded to knock, nevertheless. The sound of the knock startled him, and, even worse, set in motion horrified shouts down the hallway. *This is absolutely awful*, he thought to himself, both apologetic and embarrassed to be the cause of this new battery of fear.

"Who is it," dared a woman's nervous voice behind Dr. Zahler's door.

"Good evening, Madam. This is Jeretzian, Ara. I have done work with your husband through the Civil Defense. I am the Air Raid Protection Warden in this District. I am a friend. May I please come inside?"

"Jeretzian, you say," responded a man's voice softly. Jeretzian heard footsteps approach the door, and then the door slowly opened. Dr. Zahler, a distinguished but today disheveled gentleman in his mid 60s, immediately stepped back. On most days he didn't look a day over 50. Today was not one of those days. The woman who must have been his wife whimpered and practically fell into her husband's arms. A young, beautiful girl was seated on a chair beside another middle age, attractive woman, likely Zahler's granddaughter and daughter. Looking at Jeretzian, they wore horrified expressions, then returned to consoling each other, their faces burrowed inside their respective embraces.

"My God, Jeretzian," exclaimed Dr. Zahler. "What are you doing in that uniform?"

"Dr. Zahler, it is good to see you safe. I am grief-stricken to have heard what transpired here earlier. Listen, I can – and will -- explain my appearance and am sorry if this has frightened your family. Madam," he bowed to Dr. Zahler's wife.

"And this is my daughter, Erzsi, and her daughter – my granddaughter, Eva."

"The pleasure is mine, and again, I am so sorry." He turned again to Dr. Zahler. Doctor, is Volgyesi here? I would like to speak with him -- and you as well about how I might be able to help you all here at Zichy Jeno 1."

Dr. Zahler stepped away from his wife, who now went over to sit near Erzsi and Eva. "And why would you want to do that, Jeretzian? I know you – I mean, you are a good man as far as I know, but you do know what the Nazis – not the Nazis, our own fellow Hungarians -- the Arrow Cross is doing to us Jews? And what they have already done to all the Jews in the provinces of Hungary? We are next -- you know that, right?" Dr. Zahler did not mean for his voice to rise as it did, since he was trying to prevent his family members from hearing what they likewise already knew but did not want to discuss.

"Of course, I know, Dr. Zahler. With respect, this is why I'd like to speak with you both. And as for why I wish to help, I consider you all far more than acquaintances through the Civil Defense. You are my friends."

Dr. Zahler wiped his brow and leaned forward, closer to Jeretzian. He still had not asked Jeretzian to sit down. It was as if he was auditioning him for a part in a play. "Well, I suppose we'll see. He is over at the sanitarium. Let's go there together so we can talk more freely. To do nothing is no choice at all, so I suppose you're as good as it gets … 'friend.'"

Jeretzian smiled and patted Dr. Zahler on the back. He bade farewell to the women in the room as Dr. Zahler went over to explain things to them.

On their way out of the house, Jeretzian stopped when Theo moved in front of the door, desperate for information. "Theo," Jeretzian patted him on the right shoulder, "listen. Under no circumstances should you let any Arrow Cross people in the building."

"Like you, you mean," Theo mocked.

"Just listen to him, Theo," Dr. Zahler pleaded, more annoyed than anything.

"Just do as I say. And if anyone comes, you call for me and we will return immediately. We are going to the sanitarium to see Dr. Volgyesi. You understand?"

The drive to the sanitarium was a blur. Dr. Zahler steeled himself so he wouldn't cry while recounting the actions of "Ivan the Terrible," the courtyard, the removal of his mother and too many others and, most of all, the shouting and crying against the injustice of it all … why? Jeretzian refused to reveal his own encounter with "Ivan the Terrible" and the march. *No*, he thought to himself, *this wasn't the time. There could never be a time to recount any of this, to anyone, for any reason.* And yet, he knew this was truly just the beginning. There was no question in his mind. He had seen this Ivan; he had seen the look in his eyes; he had seen the look when he heard him, plain as day: "May I throw this man into the Danube?"

"Dr. Volgyesi, look who is here with me," Dr. Zahler announced as they entered Volgyesi's makeshift office unannounced.

Volgyesi looked up, perturbed to be interrupted from reading a stack of papers in his hand. His left hand had been propped against his left temple, but now let his hand fall away. "Jeretzian?" he asked, looking up through the lenses of his reading glasses.

"One and the same. Volgyesi, how the hell are you?"

"You really must ask? And why am I not surprised you are in this uniform – or should I be surprised?"

Jeretzian sat down first. It had been a long day already, and he knew there was much more to discuss. Dr. Zahler followed, and then explained the tragic events of the day at 1 Zichy Jeno, and then Jeretzian's curious arrival. "He claims he wishes to help," Dr. Zahler sighed.

Dr. Volgyesi stared intently at both men, but most of all Jeretzian, throughout the recounting of the day's events.

"Okay, Jeretzian," Volgyesi played along. "Tell me why I shouldn't do everything in my power to try and get my family and I out of that place immediately. But wait, most importantly, what are you doing here and why is it that you want to help in the first place? I've been working with you for how long now in your capacity at the Civil Defense – Zahler, do you know what his interest is here? Jeretzian, are you Arrow Cross or not? You're no Jew."

Jeretzian reached into his pocket for another cigarette, already dizzy from the predictable onslaught of questions. *Yes*, he thought, *this will be a long night indeed.*

"No," Jeretzian answered as he lit his cigarette. "I'm not Jewish, I am Armenian. For some reason, I don't know why, the Hungarian nationalists have turned a blind eye to my own heritage, so I've been rather fortunate. If you know your all too recent history, Doctor, you know that – how should I say it – I feel your pain. My family and all Armenians went through some of these same unspeakable horrors at the hands of the Turks just 20-some years ago. My parents left everything behind to escape to Budapest. I was only three then, and too young to remember. But I have heard the stories. My father died when I was only six, but my mother – even what she doesn't tell, I have learned. To see her face -- to look into her eyes, Doctor, is to know."

Volgyesi's gaze remained fixed on Jeretzian, who finally seized the moment to take a puff from his cigarette. Dr. Zahler, the eldest of the three men in the room, well over twice Jeretzian's age of 26 and more than two decades older than Volgyesi, stood up briefly and cracked open the window to let the increasing cool of dusk inside, and more importantly, the smoke out.

"And what about the Arrow Cross, then?" Volgyesi half-smiled. "How does an Armenian get an Arrow Cross uniform?"

"Now that's a longer story, but I'll get to the point," Jeretzian leaned forward. "Before you met me at the Civil Defense Commission, and before I started my successful chemicals business, I actually was in the Arrow Cross. For just over a year, in '38 and '39."

Dr. Zahler abruptly turned to look at Volgyesi, but Volgyesi, wire rim glasses at the bridge of a bulbous nose at the crest of his impressive, graying beard, continued to hold his gaze at the man in the Arrow Cross uniform.

"I was young. The slogans and hype of the national socialist movement appealed to me. Despite being the son of a seamstress, I attended prestigious schools thanks to my mother's connections. I resented the vast disparity in wealth and class and appreciated the ideas of brotherhood and working hard for the sake of society: 'To each according to their talents; abolish privilege.' In short, I joined the youth movement, distinguished myself and was promoted in no time to become the director of the youth section."

Annoyed by the trail of smoke rising and then drifting aimlessly in the room, Jeretzian abruptly picked up the cigarette butt and snuffed it out inside the ashtray at the edge of Volgyesi's desk. Dr. Zahler let out a large cough. "And then?" Zahler asked while wiping his lips with his handkerchief.

"Our hope, in the youth section, was to be more human, more Hungarian. This was ironic, of course, since I was not born a Hungarian and I have an Armenian name. Nevertheless," he continued, "They saw, in my youth, great leadership potential and they let me run things, if not in title, certainly by my deeds. We were achieving great things and were gaining popularity across the country. However, I was naïve. If you were to ask me what exactly our goals were, I couldn't have told you. I only knew *we* wanted to take power – abolish all that was wrong in Hungarian society and make it better. I was so busy – I hadn't even time to have read Szalasi's writings. In hindsight, of course I should have made the time, but I didn't know.... The upper echelon of the party surely promoted the ideal, "more Hungarian," but whereas I had come to admire Jewish success in economic life and wished to study and share it across the nation, Szalasi and the others were ... deeply anti-Semitic. There was no middle ground, you see. We were at odds; irreconcilable differences. Soon after, a circular was distributed notifying every member that I was no longer in charge of the youth division, and in fact, they disbanded the youth movement. So, I moved on ... and you met me afterwards."

As the sound of the rain ricocheting off the ceramic tile roofs around the men intensified, Jeretzian explained the rest. He told them how he was disgusted by politics and so he turned his attention to his business, Civil Defense and the connections he had made. But he was even more disgusted by what was happening to the Jews in the countryside, though he felt he could do nothing. And now that the Arrow Cross was somehow prematurely, but perhaps predictably elevated into this position of power by Hitler, he knew that all Hell would break loose in Budapest for the Jews. "And it is," he assured the doctors sitting before him. Unlike the situation in the countryside, Jeretzian explained, he did not wish to learn of the atrocities on the radio and in the papers while he sat at home, turning a blind eye…. He felt he could help, somehow. "You are my friends," he calmly told them. "Whether you know it or not. And right now, I believe I'm the best – and maybe the only friend you've got. So," he said, rubbing his hands together. "How can I help?"

"You must be awfully desperate for friendship to seek us Jews out at times like these," Zahler smirked.

Volgyesi picked up a pen from his desk and rubbed it between his fingers. He removed his round, wire glasses and propped them up beside his desk lamp. "How *could* you be so naïve the whole organization was predicated on its hatred of Jews, like the Nazis," his voice sharply cracked, surprising himself. "You'll have to forgive me, I am, as you can imagine, nervous beyond belief and now with Zahler's news — with today's news; the marches out. Well, this uniform. These weapons you wear. How did you get them?"

"I still have friends there. Not many, but I was popular among those with whom I worked. Through such friends, I was lucky and what you see that I am wearing is a combination of odds and ends I had, and what they have just given me. The uniform is fine. You see my armband -- it will suffice, especially now that I have these weapons."

"Good. Very good," Volgyesi nodded. He twirled his pen again, then set it down. "I will suspend my questions about your past, for now, and try and focus on saving my family; saving the Jews at Zichy Jeno 1. And you – your uniform, your weapons, your Arrow Cross involvement will be paramount. Emil, I wonder, how many physicians do you think are now living at the house. At Zichy Jeno 1?"

"There must be at least 25 now," Dr. Zahler wagered. "From over 300 or so Jews, there must be 25, 30 physicians there. Most of us have lived there for some time, others have moved in more recently as it is marked a "Yellow Star house," and so some doctors we all knew were invited in…."

"Jeretzian, you are still the Civil Defense Commander of this 6th District, yes?" Volgyesi interrupted. "That might count for something, if you are both Air Raid Protection Warden and with that Arrow Cross uniform…. We'll need more than that, but it's something."

"I would need to somehow get in more closely with the Arrow Cross, then. For me to help protect you beyond air raid protection…." Jeretzian started to scratch his chin, the flicker of a shared idea reflecting from one another's eyes.

Volgyesi again interrupted. "You will need to be accepted as Arrow Cross -- not just a man in a uniform -- to be of service to us; to our building's residents. If you are Arrow Cross *and* our Civil Defense Commander, then maybe you buy us some time to develop a better idea. I'm not sure what, but so many doctors in one house. Jewish doctors…."

"It's worth a shot," Dr. Zahler agreed. "If we are protected by your ostensible Arrow Cross elite membership … divert attention from the house, could it work?"

"So, can you do it, Jeretzian? Can you get deeper inside the Arrow Cross, or not? It is only our families; only over 300 Jews who'd be depending on us – on you. You say you wanted to help, so will you?"

Jeretzian reached for another cigarette. He stood up suddenly, and finally smiled. A crack of October thunder resounded like a violent scattering of bowling pins. The rain answered in turn, seemingly increasing its tumultuous descent from whatever lies above. "Gentlemen, I have work to do, but of course. Yes, I will help you."

10

The Next Day

Robert could not sleep. Judging by the movements and rustling of covers throughout his aunt's apartment, he wondered if anyone was really sleeping. It was too dark to tell, of course. But if anyone else awake felt remotely like he did, they were too afraid to wander out their door for any reason. Instead, they likely closed their eyes and tried counting sheep, or counting backwards, or tried to conjure a blank screen, puffy clouds ... anything to just fall asleep.

Robert tried to erase from his mind the images of the girl with the laughing eyes, Eva. His efforts were futile. The look of fear in those eyes, no longer laughing, when her great grandmother bade her farewell, likely for the last time.... The smug arrogance of the lead Arrow Cross man there, Ivan – the threats. They'd be coming back! The sound of crying; seeing such dignified people in the Budapest community break down for all to see....

Eventually, Robert willed his thoughts to the one rock in his life that never wavered: If only his father were here. How was he doing right now? What was he doing, and where was he? After not having received any news from him in a few months, a postcard arrived just a few days ago that seemed to be encouraging. For one, he was still alive! Second, it did not bear the postmark of the labor camp, Bor, but rather a different city somewhere in Yugoslavia whose name Robert couldn't even pronounce.

Robert and his family concluded this must be positive. Finally, it did not bear any censor marks on the card. Where the few previous missives were so heavily crossed through that there was nothing left meaningful beyond evidence of his continued existence, this one was unedited. He told Robert, his mother and family that, though he could not provide details, he was well and loved and missed everyone dearly. Curiously, he then digressed to caution not to "become swept up in the current of so many Jews changing their religion to save their skin. Stay true to who you are."

Sure enough, they had heard widespread reports of attempted conversions – even many suicides already in the wake of the regime change on the 15th. To so many Jews in Budapest, this event, in addition to the many men already in brutal forced labor camps and assignments, military conscripts in the East and news of what already occurred in the provinces, what was now occurring was the final precursor to ghettos and deportations. It was difficult to see otherwise from the vantage point of an apartment house adorned with the yellow Star of David, like so many others in the city. This was particularly true in the Jewish District itself, in the nearby 7th District.

Somehow, the topic of conversions never once arose. Maybe this was on account of Aranka's already "Christian" status, and a few others' false papers, but it just hadn't been a topic until Robert's father raised it, from so far away. It was curious to the family mostly because they all knew that his father was hardly religious – none of his side of the family was particularly devout in its Judaism, particularly in comparison to his mother and her family … now gone.

"Maybe he finally found God," one of his uncles laughed, "in the 11th hour." Laughs were immediately met with scolding and disapproval. Like this topic of suicide in the face of what was occurring, there were some things that would not be discussed in the apartment, at least not openly.

As the dark of night gradually released its stranglehold on Budapest, a soft light introduced shadows into the apartment. Robert rubbed his eyes and saw a figure seated alone at the kitchen table. It was his mother.

Robert discarded his useless cover and crawled around one or two uncles to approach his mother, who was obviously awake, but clearly not present.

"*Anu*," he whispered, raising himself onto a seat at the small, round table. "*Anu*, are you among the living?"

His mother turned slowly, from God only knows where. A moment later, she smiled. "Robi, what is it? You should get back to sleep."

"You know what I just remembered, *Anu*? There is something I just remembered about *Apu* that I wonder if you ever knew."

His mother, now clearly present, looked at Robert warmly, a trace of a smile at the corners of her full lips. His mother sure was "the cutest thing," as his father always said.

"What is it, Robi? What could you possibly know about your father that I don't?" she smiled wider.

"You know when we would go to synagogue," he didn't pause for a response. "During all of the songs, incantations and the like -- did you ever watch father?"

"What do you mean?" her surprising smile now defining her facial features. "Did I ever watch your father sing? Why...," she broke and stifled a whimper.

Robert moved closer to her and put his hand on her cheek. "*Anu*," he whispered. "He didn't know any of the words. He just faked them and moved his lips."

"Why?" Her voice cracked sharply.

"I know, right? I asked him once, *Anu*, and do you know what he said? He said, 'Don't tell your mother.' He winked at me and said he didn't want to let you down; to embarrass you."

"Oh, Robi," she took his hand and put it in hers. Robert used his other hand to use a cloth to wipe her tears even as she smiled. Lately, it seemed she always had one nearby for the tears that were always flowing.

By now, Aranka had awakened and gone straight to the sink behind them to start a pot of coffee. She saw that Robert and his mother were speaking quietly and did not interrupt.

"*Anu*, there is something else I must tell you. It's been eating at me for a long time now, but I must tell you."

His mother looked up, appreciatively, inquisitively.

"It was maybe over a year ago now, back at Rottenbiller. Klein, the proprietor of the antique store –"

"Robi," she interjected abruptly.

"--It was so obvious how much he was in love with you. I used to show up on purpose almost every day to see him walking with you; talking with you when you were coming home from the pharmacy. And you seemed to enjoy his company!" His voice unexpectedly rose before he shrugged off Aranka's deft glare and continued. "One day, both of you clearly saw that I was walking behind you, looking at you both. What made me so upset," now Robert broke.

"Robi, don't you doubt—"

"Once you saw me, you started to walk arm in arm, and I heard you laugh. You both turned to look at me and you, you laughed."

"Robi Holczer, don't you ever doubt my love for your father. Mr. Klein was, is, was only a friend. I have no idea where he even is right now."

Aranka blurted, "Well, everyone is up now. May as well turn on the lights and open the curtain."

"Aranka, please. Robi," she held both of his hands firmly with both of her hands. "Look at me."

He did, bleary-eyed himself now.

"Klein always knew about your father and my love for him. He was only a friend to laugh and talk with sometimes. But I am sorry, you are right. That was callous of us – of me. I shouldn't have tried to get your goat. Do you forgive me?"

Robert turned away.

"Do you forgive me, Holczer, Robert?"

"Yes," he finally whispered. Against his will, he smiled. He permitted his mother to hug him, warmly.

***

Jeretzian couldn't sleep. Not a wink. Between the images of the day on Margit Bridge, the looks of the faces of his Jewish friends at 1 Zichy Jeno and the conversations with so many Arrow Cross people that could have turned on a dime either way, he couldn't clear his mind enough to count sheep. Above all, he knew there was so much more to do.

He resolved that the first thing he needed to do – after he smoked the day's first cigarette – would be to try to "come in the back door" of the Arrow Cross by enmeshing himself within the 6th District Arrow Cross command. He felt he could do this because he lived in the 6th District, just about a mile away from 1 Zichy Jeno and, after all, he was the Civil Defense commander there. He felt he needed to do this in order to try and garner more protection for the Jewish residents of that Yellow Star house. Nevertheless, he was again apprehensive because he was obviously not an official Party member – not for almost five years.

When Jeretzian arrived in "uniform" to the 6th District Headquarters at 19 *Terez Korut* straight from Dr. Volgyesi's office last night, he got one foot in that back door. Although the current district leader, Lohonyai, Jeno was not there, Jeretzian was again fortuitously on familiar terms with the man sitting at the boss's table, Tiborcz, Simon. The two had come to know each other during their time serving in the old Arrow Cross Youth Division. Jeretzian had lost contact with him when he left the party.

Tiborcz freely divulged to his old colleague how unprepared the Arrow Cross was to take over the leadership of Hungary, let alone this district. "It's all happened so fast," he cried. Gesturing wildly to the lack of furniture around him, glass of Stolichnaya vodka in his hand, he explained how anyone with any intelligence had already zealously power-grabbed higher rank positions of leadership, leaving the "dregs" behind in the district offices. Tiborcz seemed oblivious to how he had just implicated himself. "So, my friend, we sure could use someone of your intelligence and experience in this District. Come back in the morning to see Lohonyai – I'll put in a good word for you."

Upon his arrival there this morning, he had to look up at the address to make sure it was the same building. Whereas last night there was little to no activity outside and sparse furnishings inside, today there were so many people lined up inside and out. Many were carrying furniture, clocks, sculptures and carpets inside; others – ordinary citizens -- were there trying to acquire many of these items for themselves.

"Excuse me," Jeretzian tapped the shoulder of a woman who seemed to be instructing people where to place things inside, "what is all of this?"

"Who are you? This property has been requisitioned for our use. Are you here to help or just get in the way?"

"I am Jeretzian, Ara, Civil Defense Commander for this district. I am here to see Mr. Lohonyai. And, I'm sorry -- this property has been requisitioned from whom?"

The woman now paused a moment to wipe her brow with her fleshy arm. She was bigger than Jeretzian. By a lot. Two men carried in an antique cedar grandfather clock in between Jeretzian and the woman. The woman raised her eyebrows that seemed to run continuously across her forehead and smirked.

"This property has been requisitioned from," she began, smugly imitating Jeretzian's proper tone and voice, "well, it's all been *seized* from the Jews of Budapest, you idiot. We've taken it from them once they *moved* out of their houses, get it? And I don't expect they'll be coming back for it any time," she laughed. "Ahhhhh, I kill myself sometimes. Lohonyai is back there, the one with his feet up … on his new furniture."

Jeretzian, appalled, instinctively turned to find Lohonyai. *That woman*, Jeretzian thought, *is no woman.*

Apparently, his visit with Tiborcz last evening must have made quite an impression, because Lohonyai immediately stood up to shake hands and greet him enthusiastically. It was difficult to hear him at first, as Jeretzian counted at least eight antique wall clocks ticking and chiming simultaneously. It seemed that as soon as the chimes were done, the men carrying in the grandfather clock practically knocked over Jeretzian, asking Lohonyai where they should put "this one."

In short, Lohonyai seemed favorably impressed by the names Jeretzian dropped and the fact he wished to assist him in his "difficult and responsible work." Jeretzian said, puffing out his chest sufficiently, he considered it a crime to ignore the districts since the Party, as well as the whole country depended on their effective leadership and administration. By the time Jeretzian left, he was appointed "deputy leader of the 6th District," and was told that his first act as deputy should be to attend an Arrow Cross assembly at *Szabadsag ter,* a large square and park in the 5th District, on Lohonyai's behalf. "You should get going now," he urged. "I'm all tied up with all of this damn property!"

When Jeretzian arrived at the square, the meeting had just begun. There were scores of Arrow Cross militiamen and local policemen there, and all of them started to march toward the police headquarters on *Mozsar utca* in the 6th District, near the Party headquarters on *Andrassy utca.* Finally, once all had arrived, including the various district leaders to which group Jeretzian now belonged, an Arrow Cross high-ranking officer read aloud a decree from Minister of Interior Gabor Vajna. The decree provided, to Jeretzian's dismay, all remaining Jewish males between the ages of 16 and 60 were to be apprehended and ordered to military labor service. Jeretzian knew that thousands of Budapest Jewish males between these ages had already been conscripted, most of them already killed on the front or at labor camps. However, there were clearly still many left, including most of the men at 1 Zichy Jeno. He listened carefully to the rest of the instructions, which set forth the houses and districts from which they would begin collecting men as early as today. To his great relief, they would not be going into the 6th District today. "Safe," Jeretzian muttered to himself, hoping not to be recognized by anyone around him. "For today."

Jeretzian proceeded out of the crowd, which was almost bloodthirsty now to have "legal" authorization to drag away Jews. He felt more tired than he could begin to measure. He looked for a streetcar or bus to take him in the direction of his home, hoping to briefly nap before deciding what to do next in the face of this decree. Surely, they would come to 1 Zichy Jeno in the next few days. Would his titles and persuasive powers alone save the people there? He found a bus to take him to his apartment, close to the police headquarters, and couldn't stop his mind from considering everything.

11

A Series of Escalating Events

What was intended to be a short, early evening nap gave way to another troubled sleep. Jeretzian closed his eyes in his modest apartment, reasonably confident that no danger would befall the residents of 1 Zichy Jeno, at least for a couple of days. He was mistaken.

From the shallow depths of another sleep marred by too many sounds, faces and stressful moments endlessly replayed in his mind, came a pounding on his door. When he was finally satisfied that the pounding did not emanate from inside his head, but instead from his door, he pulled his robe across the same uniform he was wearing the day before and trudged toward the door in his stocking feet. As soon as the person with the clenched fist on the other side of his door heard movement inside, followed by the sound of the lock being undone, there came a familiar voice. It was Theo, the super at 1 Zichy Jeno. Apparently just having discovered the doorbell, he pressed it for good measure.

"Theo, my God. What is it?"

Theo was out of breath, wild-eyed. Jeretzian glanced at his watch and saw that it was just past three in the morning. Except for the dim, yellow light in the building's hallway, he could see that it was still pitch-black outside. Theo grabbed his left hand and pulled, more firmly than he had intended.

"Come on. You must come at once, Jeretzian. Dr. Zahler told me to

93

get you – the Arrow Cross is there, in the building. They want to take the men away. Can you come now?"

"Of course," Jeretzian instinctively answered. There was not even time to straighten up, so he just tossed his robe in the general direction of the kitchen table and awkwardly stepped into his shoes beside the door. "How did you get here, Theo?"

"I ran, sir." He looked like he was going to faint, either from the stress or the exhaustion of his pre-dawn sprint through the 6th District. The balding, middle-aged Theo was not in the best physical shape.

"Fine. My motorcycle is up against the wall of the interior courtyard portal. Come with me, you can hop on back."

Upon their arrival, it was as if the scene described – was it yesterday or the day before – by Dr. Zahler was happening all over again. Jeretzian heard crying and shouting, and there were far too many people down in the lobby, bags haphazardly packed. Crying, shouting. He couldn't hear himself think. Using his taller than average height of 6 feet, he tried standing on his tiptoes to see through the crowd and the insufficient, pale light of the lobby where the Arrow Cross people were.

And there they were. Or at least some of them. Coming down the stairs with several Jewish men, there were two Arrow Cross militiamen as well as a local police officer. They spotted Jeretzian, standing there alone in an Arrow Cross uniform, and appeared to be alarmed.

"Who is in charge here?" Jeretzian demanded. He saw Dr. Zahler, together with two other physicians he knew, Dr. Armin Flesch and Gynecologist Dr. Jeno Stricker, standing behind the Arrow Cross men on the stairs coming down to the lobby. Sure, it was the middle of the night, or morning, but they all looked awful. In the pale, tired eyes of the elderly Dr. Zahler, Jeretzian saw terror, or surrender.

The policeman, smirking, pointed to an apparently intoxicated, young man – a boy, really -- in an Arrow Cross uniform. His stare was vacant, either owing to his inebriation or his lack of intelligence. Perhaps both. Jeretzian seized the moment.

Pulling his gray tie closer to the top button of his now wrinkled, bright green shirt, he introduced himself as the Arrow Cross 6ᵗʰ District Deputy leader. "On whose orders are you patrolling and acting here? I demand an answer at once!"

The lobby and stairs, just moments before a scene of bedlam and cacophony, was now silent. All eyes were on Jeretzian, and now to the Arrow Cross man on the stairs, as if watching a tennis volley.

"Well, we're here from the 5ᵗʰ District. We were picking up Jews across on the other side, but there aren't any left. I remembered that this was a Jewish house as well, so I thought we'd also cover this in one stride."

Judging by the timidity of this young man's voice, Jeretzian knew he had him where he wanted. At least for this day, this moment.

"I was at the same meeting at *Szabadsag ter* as you must have been. By no means were you to enter the 6ᵗʰ District. This is my territory. Now get out of this house and district right now before I report you to your district leader."

As if he was a magician waving a wand, the Arrow Cross men and policeman came down through the crowd, even apologizing to Jeretzian, before leaving. The residents close enough to have observed these proceedings, including a 15-year-old boy named Holczer, Robert, watched with awe.

Amidst the rising swell of appreciation and collective hugs and sighs, Jeretzian reached into his dark uniform coat for a cigarette. An unidentified man struck a match to light it, thanking Jeretzian profusely. Robert turned to run back upstairs to tell his family what he had just witnessed. Jeretzian exhaled, sending a wave of smoke upward to dance with the high ceiling light in the lobby.

"Zahler. Flesch. Is Volgyesi here yet? They murmured under their breath, shaking their heads. "I didn't think so. We need to talk."

"We can go upstairs to my apartment," Dr. Zahler offered. "No one in this whole place is sleeping; don't know when or if we ever will!"

Over a cup of coffee, served by Dr. Zahler's beautiful granddaughter, Eva, Jeretzian briefed the doctors on what had transpired the day before and what else he had learned. Although he was able to suppress this current attempt to drag away most of the building's men today on grounds that the Arrow Cross had not yet been directed to enter the 6th District, it was just a matter of time. He told them how Jewish property – likely much of these people's property was seized and was either being used to decorate Arrow Cross rooms or was being sold to non-Jews. He explained that even as the Soviets were coming closer to Budapest every day, Eichmann and Endre, at Szalasi's behest or acquiescence, were drawing up plans to move all the remaining Jews into ghettos, organizing for…. He told them the Arrow Cross was a gang of idiotic thugs, but dangerous ones to be feared. He had overheard while at the city square last evening that some Arrow Cross were even marching some Jews to the banks of the Danube, where they would then shoot them into the river below. More recently, Jeretzian recounted with his eyes almost covered by his hands, they would sometimes tie the Jews together by the Danube in order to conserve bullets: Shoot just a few and their fall would drag the rest down with them.

The doctors listened with revolting dread. Dr. Zahler thought early on in this monologue to tell his wife, daughter and granddaughter to go to sleep, but knew it was futile. Instead they all paced nervously around the kitchen in random, aimless directions until Eva finally asked to be excused so she could visit her friend, Marika. Erzsi, Eva's mother, finally went into the room she shared with Eva and closed the door. Dr. Zahler's wife remained in the kitchen, staring outside the window into the still, black-as-night courtyard, faintly illuminated only by the light inside their neighbors' respective kitchens.

In time, Jeretzian's distressing monologue gave way to shared, proposed solutions. After Dr. Zahler mentioned how so many here had Swiss or Swedish protection papers, for what these were worth, Jeretzian quickly pierced this bubble by saying that so did the Jews presently being marched to the Danube. "The Arrow Cross doesn't care," he fumed.

Dr. Flesch then offered how he had heard that the Swiss embassy had taken an entire building under its protection. "Could we get something like this?" Flesch asked. "That would be something even greater than any individual protection. In theory, we would be protected by international law, as such."

Jeretzian agreed that this was something he could, and would, pursue. Nevertheless, he expressed worry about the draft notices for the men, and undoubtedly soon enough, for women. "I'm no legal expert. I'm not sure if even international law can shield you all from their draft orders and … whatever follows from them."

***

The Swiss Embassy was located at *Szabadsag ter*. Upon Jeretzian's arrival there after a light breakfast with his old friend and colleague, Laszlo Nagy, he was stunned to see a line of well over 200 people. All of them were presumably Jews, standing in line at the embassy to apply for Swiss safe conduct, *Schutz* passes. Jeretzian knew by now that these passes were barely worth more than the paper on which they were being printed, but who was he to say so? Countless people gawked and pointed at him, undoubtedly fearful of his Arrow Cross uniform.

After initial skepticism by the front office staff on account of his ostensible Arrow Cross affiliation, he was ushered in to see the Swiss Embassy Counsel, acting today on behalf of the ambassador "for all matters to which I am qualified."

Jeretzian began. "Besides being a leader of the Arrow Cross Party," he lied, "I'm also commander of the Civil Defense rescue stations in the 6th District. Most of my underlings are Jewish doctors and nursing staff living in the house under 1 Zichy Jeno utca, a Yellow Star house. Due to my other commitments, I can't always personally be there to protect them, and considering this, I'd like to protect them from potential harassment by asking for the house to be placed under Swiss protection."

Smiling as he considered Jeretzian's words, the elderly counsel paused before answering. "Now that is an unusual request. I am not aware of placing an entire house under Swiss –"

"Please, sir. I'm sorry to interrupt. Surely you -- Jewish yourself, is that not correct -- can see my predicament and the good that such an order could bring to so many – over 300, so many of whom doctors and nurses. If you can just issue such a document, I will personally accept any consequences. I just need legal title to exempt the house from intrusions."

Whether because of the uniqueness of Jeretzian's request or his powers of persuasion, the counsel ultimately agreed, affording 1 Zichy Jeno utca Swiss protection. Escorting Jeretzian to the door, order in hand, the counsel shook his hand. "I am happy to learn that there are those even among the Arrow Cross who choose to act so humanely."

***

Robert reminded himself of a lesson his father had taught him: "Son, don't allow yourself to get too excited; too high when things are going well. And don't get too down; too low when things don't go as hoped in life."

Pacing in the courtyard and alternately climbing up and down the four flights of stairs for exercise and peace of mind, he was trying to remember the context of this lesson. And then it came back to him. Of course! It was the day his father shared the news he was being sent to Bor. Earlier that same day, Robert had been so excited; he had felt he was king of the world. He and his best friend, Matyas, had just won their first bicycle relay race at Varosliget Park. They had once come as close as sixth place out of over 100 entrants for their age group in the monthly park races, but this was their first and, as it turned out, only victory. Always shorter than his peers, Robert was, by no means, the world's greatest athlete. Instead, he was pesky; tenacious. This made this victory with his much more athletic friend so sweet.

The celebration was, however, much too short-lived. Just hours later, his father received his orders. Robert's reactions of protest, silence and then tears followed his father's rich lesson. How typically wise; how selfless his father was. Whereas his father should have been the one so far down in the dumps on receiving his order to Bor, a veritable death sentence, he somehow endeavored to assuage Robert and, in turn, his mother. It was as if he was teaching them a lesson that they would need to heed during more daunting times he could not have foreseen.

Those daunting times, becoming seemingly more precarious by the day -- if not the hour -- were now well at hand. If the day of the bicycle race victory and his father's order to Bor was one of dramatic contrasts, the last few days made his – and everyone else's at 1 Zichy Jeno – head spin. Every time he dared to hope things might be safer for the building's residents, there seemed to be new, more disheartening setbacks.

First, there was the stunning celebration in the house after the tall, dark-featured man with the perfect moustache and hair – wearing an Arrow Cross uniform, no less – stood down the Arrow Cross men who were there to take away so many men in the middle of the other night. Although Robert was just under the age minimum the men were intending to take, the whole building celebrated as if it were a soccer team that had miraculously eked out a last second victory in the final seconds of a championship match. Who was this man, Jeretzian? Everyone wanted to know.

The very next day, Robert and most others – if not already convinced – began to think of Jeretzian as a hero; their savior. When word spread that he had somehow won the entire building Swiss protection, most – Robert included – dared to believe that their fears were no more. "Any Arrow Cross who steps in this house," Robert heard one Jewish man triumphantly proclaim, "Violates international law. There's no way they can do it!"

It turned out there was a way they could do it. Robert's Aunt Aranka, as if echoing her brother's – Robert's father's advice, cautioned her family not to get carried away. "Danger is everywhere," she warned, causing everyone in their apartment to frown and scoff. "And who is there to hold the Nazis or the Arrow Cross – one and the same for all I care – accountable if or when they want to do to the Jews as they please?"

Later that day or the next, word spread like a wildfire that all women between the ages of 16 and 50 were required to report for labor service in the next 48 hours. Although Aranka felt safe because of her "Christian" identity, this order would include Robert's mother, among so many others. Did the house's Swiss protection order immunize them from this latest roundup? What of the men – did the original order of men aged 16-60 still stand? Did it apply to the 6th District yet?

Robert watched the news of this order quickly undo the courage and calm so many had previously shown. People were discussing how the wife and beautiful daughters of the famous hypnotist and physician, Dr. Volgyesi, were hysterical and crying, their wails carrying into the courtyard and staircase. "Where is my husband?" the wife cried. And few had seen him, in fact. Some said he was staying away at the office in his hospital out of fear, but then why was his family still here?

But before even Robert's mother could fully internalize the prospect of being taken away, it was Jeretzian to the rescue again.

Robert watched the scene unfold in the lobby, where the despair had lifted again. There was beautiful Eva, the girl with the once laughing eyes, smiling again as she stood beside her grandfather, Dr. Zahler. Apparently, Eva and her mother had both been subjects of this same order. The doctor, who had been despondent over the earlier news, was now hugging Jeretzian: "My God, Jeretzian," he exclaimed, tears in his eyes. "You must be the miracle my rabbi at Dohany Street Synagogue predicted to me; that in my greatest trouble a young stranger would appear and make everything right. Thank you. My God, thank you!" Robert was deeply moved by this incredible display of gratitude.

Aranka later learned that Jeretzian had somehow obtained blank Arrow Cross protection orders. Supposedly, she overheard doctors in the "inner circle" share that few at the Arrow Cross nowadays could read or write. So Jeretzian convinced someone to give him blank service orders that he would fill in for them. Once he obtained the required Arrow Cross stamps on the papers, he issued orders that the designated people in the house were performing Civil Defense duties so crucial that he could not do without them. Jeretzian advised the women in question that they might still need to report for the draft for fear of inviting closer scrutiny, but with these orders in hand they would all be safe. So, as Aranka explained, this has apparently bought everyone more time.

"What will happen, Aranka," asked Robert's Uncle Joszef, "If some higher up at the Arrow Cross finds out what this Jeretzian is doing? I mean, is he even an Arrow Cross?"

Aranka took a long sip from her cup of coffee. "I don't know," she said, at last. "Everyone has their theories about who he is or why he would help us, but all I do know is that he's as good as it gets for us, right now. As to what will happen to him if he is caught trying to save Jews? Probably the same fate as us if they take us—"

"Death," Robert interrupted glumly.

12

Higher and Higher

Jeretzian stared into his reflection of the bathroom mirror on the first floor of the Ministry of Interior's offices and spat at it. He considered his distorted reflection for a moment, then cursed aloud. He cupped his hands beneath the running cold water and, after first wetting his face, threw water at his spit dripping slowly down the glass. "How am I supposed to do this?" he whispered to himself.

It was only a week ago when Jeretzian and the residents of 1 Zichy Jeno had been jubilant. He had somehow obtained Swiss protection for the entire house, then managed to secure blank, stamped Arrow Cross protection orders which he had forged in order to protect Dr. Zahler's daughter and granddaughter, Dr. Volgyesi's wife and daughters and so many other young women. The Swiss protection order, for the time being, seemed to be keeping the Arrow Cross at bay, away from the men in the house.

The mood of the building was guardedly optimistic. Dr. Volgyesi moved back into his apartment, using his reputation and relative fame and influence in the community to invite several other esteemed Jewish physicians, nurses and their families. Dr Zahler did the same. Everyone seemed to believe this was a kind of safe haven in comparison to the unpredictable dangers that seemed all around them. It was chaos outside.

And now chaos was again engulfing this "protected" house. A new

Arrow Cross decree from Interior Minister Vajna ordered that all Swiss protection passes would be void; useless unless the pass bearers moved to the new, so called "international ghetto" in the 13th District, beginning November 12th. This was an area between Szent Istvan Park and Grand Boulevard. Only the most naïve or delusional deigned to even hope that a chance for life could exist beyond the indefinite tenure of ghetto life, such as it was. Conditions were becoming intolerable immediately, with gross overcrowding and genuine fears of inadequate food supply, utilities, and sanitation. In some apartments meant to accommodate three or four, there were as many as 12 people — most often strangers — inside most. And winter was still to come.

In the meantime, as many as 25,000 Jews were being marched on foot from Budapest to the western border for forced labor. In addition, there were death marches – brutal, torturous marches that included the widespread looting, beating and murder -- of over 50,000 Jews to the Mauthausen concentration camp in Austria, part of the Reich, Nazi-controlled territory. Civilian traffic in Budapest was prohibited as of November 10th.

Amidst the hysteria everywhere, the Arrow Cross returned to 1 Zichy Jeno to take all residents with international "safe conduct" passes to the international ghetto. The rest, the Arrow Cross militiamen said, would need to relocate to the ordinary ghetto "soon enough." Jeretzian's frantic efforts, both to keep this news from all the residents so as to maintain a degree of calm, and to save the residents, were only partially successful.

Jeretzian, producing various protective orders and stamped papers, argued that the whole house was under Swiss protection because the residents were indispensable Civil Defense or medical personnel. The Arrow Cross scoffed, equally unimpressed by Jeretzian's credentials. They indicated that all matters pertaining to Jews were now within the exclusive province of Minister of Interior Vajna. They allowed, however, that if Jeretzian could obtain permission from the police chief to permit "only those truly necessary" to Civil Defense or otherwise, then maybe "some Jews here could stay a little longer. But be serious, it's all just a matter of time – they are all fated in the same way," the senior-most Arrow Cross man told him snidely. "What difference does it make?"

After so much debate and discussions among the senior physicians, including Dr. Volgyesi and Dr. Zahler, as well as resident Civil Defense engineer Gyorgy Koller, it was eventually agreed that 20 names would be offered, "in good faith." Dr. Zahler needed to recuse himself from the discussion; the memories of having already lost his mother in a similar fashion far too near and painful. "I cannot be a part of this; playing God." Still, the others reasoned, 20 people would be "sacrificed" in order to save more than 250.

This was a disastrous situation. However, doing the best they could to keep order, a handful of senior doctors knocked on doors and informed certain people they needed to pack a bag and relocate to the international ghetto. There were Arrow Cross men in the lobby to escort them there. "No, don't worry," a doctor would try to reassure. "This is not what you think. You will have either Swedish or Swiss international protection there. You will technically be safer there, under better conditions," they lied. "You are one of the fortunate ones."

Dr. Zahler looked like he had seen a ghost. He refused to come out of his apartment throughout the process. He felt ashamed. Dr. Volgyesi voiced his grave concern that all any of them were doing was just trying to delay the inevitable. They all discussed whether they should disclose that if anyone had any other potential living arrangements, places where they could hide or could voluntarily go rather than into the international ghetto, they should do so.

Following this discussion, Dr. Volgyesi himself moved back out, this time taking his family with him to his medical offices "until things settle down," he hoped. A few others also left, some choosing to reunite with family in the ghetto. Dr. Zahler, however, chose to remain, putting his hands on Jeretzian's shoulders. "So far, you have provided us more protection from the protective passes. We will stay here, with you, hoping we figure something out. If not, it's all the same whether we die here or elsewhere."

***

Jeretzian finally took a cloth from the washroom dispenser and hastily wiped the mirror of his spit. It was still a mess. He gave up and tried to focus again on the task at hand. He straightened his tie, pulled down his dark gray jacket and pulled a piece of paper from his breast pocket. He unfolded it and smiled. He hoped -- he believed that, if he could get this paper signed by someone here in the Ministry, this could save the Jews at 1 Zichy Jeno. Despite Dr. Volgyesi's comings and goings, there had been an influx of more and more medical personnel into the house since the building had come under Swiss protection. It was ironic that so many of these people were coming on account of Volgyesi, yet he was the noncommittal one. Regardless, Jeretzian had a bold idea: His plan was to transform the building into a working medical facility. If this order was granted, they would convert the first two floors into doctors' offices. They would then move some of the current occupants to the upper floors to live with others. No doubt they would all be living in less than ideal, more crowded, conditions, but, if all went as hoped, they could live. Volgyesi and Zahler had agreed. Non-physician family members would instantly become nurses, helpers or couriers.

Desperate idea in mind, Jeretzian had earlier visited another old acquaintance he had heard worked at the Ministry of Total Mobilization on his way here, to the washroom of Minister Vajna's offices. At the Total Mobilization Ministry, he practically blurted to Andrej, his acquaintance: "I want to set up a free medical center and emergency clinic manned by Jewish doctors under Swiss protection. I'd like to get a permit for that."

Andrej stared at Jeretzian, anticipating he would burst out laughing. When he did not, he sat back in his reclining chair: "I don't see you in what, two … three years? Since we did business together? No foreplay? No 'Andrej, my dear old friend, how the hell are you?'"

Jeretzian remained stone-faced.

Andrej could see this was not a cordial visit. He gulped, and then explained, "You will get thrown out if you go to my boss, Minister Kovarcz, with Jewish matters. Really, if it has to do with Jews now, then it's only Minister of Interior Vajna who could give you permission." He sighed, then chuckled. "As if…. But wait, maybe I can help you somehow."

"I appreciate that, Andrej, and I am sorry for my lack of bedside manners," Jeretzian realized. "Look, if you can give me your letterhead, let me draft what I want the order to say, and then I'll take it to Vajna myself. Fair?"

Andrej shrugged. "It's no problem to me. Might be a problem for you, but that's your business, Jeretzian." Andrej produced a few sheets of blank letterhead, and Jeretzian gratefully took them.

***

Now, here he was in the washroom of Minister Vajna's offices. Minister Gabor Vajna was a virulent Jew-hater who seemed to enjoy -- and carried out with single-minded purpose -- the torture and murder of the Jews. Jeretzian read aloud to his marred mirror image the order – on Ministry of Total Mobilization letterhead – that he hoped would save Jewish lives. He wondered if he spelled everything correctly, but remembered the Arrow Cross leadership, in disarray, was not distinguishing itself for its intellect. The "order" read:

"Ministry of Total Mobilization

Direct Order!

I order Brother Ara Gyorgy Jeretzian, Block Group Leader, Sub-Center 61 of the Civil Defense League, to requisition Jewish occupants of the Swiss-protected house under 1 Zichy Jeno utca for military labor service to set up and operate a free-to-use medical center and ambulatory care clinic in this house. The medical center must provide medical care free of charge to those injured and ill in the district.

Persevere! Long live Szalasi!"

Satisfied, despite it being almost laughable to him now, Jeretzian hoped to take advantage of the disorganization he had seen in all Arrow Cross offices. He prayed no one would connect the dots and realize he was not even a legitimate Arrow Cross party member. Above all, he wished with all his might that Vajna would not be there. Vajna's presence might lead to questions and the possible recognition of Jeretzian's ruses to protect the Zichy Jeno house. Jeretzian inhaled, then exhaled deeply and finally opened the washroom door. There were three agitated men standing outside in line for the washroom. They glared at Jeretzian. "Persevere," Jeretzian winked, then saluted them.

The situation in the Ministry was even more chaotic than Jeretzian could possibly have imagined. There was no Vajna, nor any of his direct reports, and people just seemed to be standing around. What fortune! After exchanging pleasantries with three lovely secretaries, each one blushing, then directing him to the next office higher up in rank, he finally met with a young man clearly inexperienced and not indoctrinated to Arrow Cross ideology. He reminded Jeretzian of himself when he had first joined the party several years ago.

The man was duly impressed, both by Jeretzian's order on behalf of the Ministry of Total Mobilization, "a very high ministry, indeed," and by the idea that Jews would be "put to such invaluable use" under the guise of a labor service order. "Excellent idea," he said to himself. Without closely examining the document, he instructed his secretary to have it stamped, signed and issued.

In this way, the words Jeretzian had previously drafted became an official order, signed and through the Ministry of Interior but on Ministry of Total Mobilization letterhead. He prayed that no one would notice that this order was on a different ministry's letterhead; or that it directly contradicted Vajna's previously and personally issued order that no international protected houses or Jews could exist outside the international ghetto. To top it off, Jeretzian's fabricated decree was ordering Jewish doctors to treat Christians, contrary to a much earlier decree forbidding this practice. Despite the inconsistencies that could be detected by anyone reading the order carefully, Jeretzian felt proud of his accomplishment and took the order, practically running out of the building, and rode his motorcycle as fast as he could to the house, "protected" once more.

13

Hope

For the first time in weeks, there was laughter, singing and, dare Robert say it, happiness within the walls of 1 Zichy Jeno. Theo had uncovered the phonograph, and was playing a scratchy, but splendid collection of Liszt's "Hungarian Rhapsodies" and other such melodramatic compositions loudly throughout the lobby. He was like a mad scientist, wiping his shiny brow all the while. The entire area was alive, in stark contrast to the prevalent mood of uselessness, fear and disillusionment.

For the first time since October 15ᵗʰ and the Arrow Cross takeover, the people in this building finally had a purpose. One cannot underestimate the importance of being busy and feeling useful, in comparison to lethargy and endlessly waiting in limbo; bored and terrified all the while. Within hours of Jeretzian's return to the building, news had spread that the house would now be protected by one high ministry or another because the first and second floors were being turned into a working clinic and hospital.

Although neither Robert nor his Aunt Aranka could discern how or why this would protect them beyond all the other protections that the residents and house already had, the building's esteemed doctors seemed sure this would make all the difference. They hugged, they shouted, they called everyone down to the lobby and courtyard and gleefully announced the plan. Everyone would have a role, spare no one. Women would be trained as nurses and assistants, and men who were not physicians would perform various construction work and odd jobs in and around the house. Younger people, like Robert, would work as couriers, delivering and obtaining whatever was needed, as well as assisting the physicians as necessary. The physicians explained, a tired but proud Jeretzian by their side, that there would still be danger with the Arrow Cross, especially outside of the house. However, from this day forward the house and its residents would be "necessary" to the Arrow Cross – a fact which no one in the building could even believe – and, therefore, "protected."

This irony was made even bolder when Jeretzian took out of his bag a metallic Arrow Cross placard. He instructed two boys, young yet older than Robert, to get the appropriate tools from Theo, go out and remove the yellow star sign beside the address, 1 Zichy Jeno. They should then replace it with the Arrow Cross and International Red Cross signs, the latter symbolizing that the building was now a hospital. The mood was positively celebratory, even as people immersed themselves in work.

Robert recognized one of the two boys now talking to Theo about the tools. He was a year or two older than him, and quite a bit taller. His name was Kohn, Norbert. He had only arrived at the building recently, apparently having come from the only forced labor military detail, Company 107/302, that attempted to follow Horthy's final order to disarm the Nazis. Kohn impressed Robert immediately by his industry and proud swagger. Robert never saw him resting; he was always trying to carry things for people, asking various doctors about the nature of their work and how he could help them. It now appeared as if he might get that opportunity.

In the next few days, the work "party" continued. The doctors expressed the need to obtain more of their instruments and supplies from their homes or offices, many of which were either locked down, Yellow Star houses, or else already taken over by non-Jews. Jeretzian wrote orders, on behalf of the "Minister of Interior of Hungary," to requisition necessary medicine, instruments, and other supplies to the building. Even more incredibly, he used these "service notices" to requisition several more doctors and their families from the international ghetto. There were now more than 40 doctors in the house, and nearly 400 people in all. This fact made conditions in the building much more crowded, especially considering that most of the first two floors were being converted into doctors' offices and surgeries.

Regardless, Robert heard all the newcomers from the ghetto proclaim how much better things were here than there. Apparently, the Arrow Cross was outright refusing the legitimacy of individual protective passes, swearing that there were too many forgeries and fake documents. As a result, there were frequent raids, almost daily, during which the Arrow Cross would round up random Jews, march them to the nearby Danube and shoot them into the river. "It is overcrowded there, far beyond what you can imagine," one woman cried, weeping into the arms of her husband, Dr. Orban, while addressing Robert, his aunt and at least 30 others near the base of the stairwell and steel cage elevator leading up from the lobby. "But the fear is the worst part. Like hunted animals! So much for international protection!"

Robert turned to Aranka and, looking at each other deeply, they didn't have to exchange words. Now they well understood that conversion of the building into an "Arrow Cross hospital" would likely be their lifeline, for better or worse. Aranka headed straight upstairs after this news, but Robert remained. He felt alive when he worked, and so he, like the older boy, Kohn, refused to rest. In these days of industry in the house, despite the increasingly bad news beyond its walls, Robert worked with many other young people to assist engineers and doctors creating and painting countless signs: "Internal Medicine, Obstetrics, Surgery, Dentistry, etc." Others, including the beautiful Eva, whom Robert could never help but pause to admire, were preparing scrubs and armbands, moving furniture in and out, and scouring rooms, sanitizing especially the rooms to be used as a surgery. Even Dr. Volgyesi, who had just returned with his family because the sanitarium was no longer habitable, was offering up his first floor apartment for "the greater good." He moved upstairs with another doctor's family. Because there were already 10 people inside Aranka's apartment, she was not asked to take in anyone else, at least for the time being.

***

Now more than ever, Jeretzian felt hopeful that his plan to help save so many Jewish friends, physicians and their families might actually work. As preparations for the clinic continued, he began to turn his attention to advertising the clinic's existence, for a clinic with no patients is hardly a clinic. He anticipated that, as the Soviets drew nearer, the likelihood of catastrophic injuries due to city fighting between the Soviets on one side, and the Nazis and Arrow Cross militia on the other, would inherently increase the number of prospective patients. But until that time, how could he make the clinic – and above all, its Jewish residents – "indispensable" so as to avoid their sharing the same fate as the other Budapest Jews?

Minister of the Interior Vajna, striving relentlessly to attain leader Ferenc Szalasi's goal of the total separation and elimination of Hungary's remaining Jews, finally ordered at the end of November the creation of a larger, ordinary ghetto for all Jews without international protective passes. Jews could bring only a handful of belongings into an area in the 7th District, including the Dohany Street Synagogue. Christians living there were ordered to move out immediately, with the promise that they would be given new residences, typically previously occupied by Jews. The area, about only one quarter of a square mile, would ultimately hold between 70,000-100,000 Jews, and was being enclosed with a wooden fence and stone wall. News quickly spread that conditions were unbearable, featuring many of the same problems faced in the international ghetto, but to a much larger extent given the substantially higher number of people being forced into such a small area. And by now, winter conditions were at hand!

Jeretzian knew that the best chance for survival was to broadcast that the clinic would treat Arrow Cross personnel free of charge. He wagered that, once even their oppressors would see and receive the free services of these Jewish doctors and nurses, word would spread, and the house could quietly slide into the fabric of Pest's Arrow Cross rule. He ordered several younger people inside the house to create various fliers bearing Arrow Cross logos and propaganda, advertising the services of the clinic. These were then placed in and around the house, beyond even the parameters of the 6th District.

Jeretzian also knew, however, that he continued to walk on a tightrope. Everything they were doing could end in tragedy, for him and everyone in the house, if any Arrow Cross high-ranking officer divined that Jeretzian was not even a Party member. Not to mention the fact that the very orders by which the clinic existed were conjured up on patchwork Arrow Cross letterhead, and in violation of virtually every other order concerning the Jews. And then one afternoon, in the midst of continued clinic preparations, two men in Arrow Cross uniforms appeared at the door of the house. "We have an order of arrest for Jeretzian, Ara," one of them said to Theo with a smile. "We were informed he would be here. Is he here?"

Theo, as well as a few others within earshot, froze with fear. Trying not to let news of the arrival of these two men spread further, he kept them at the door. He sent a young man who had been gathering posters for distribution to the second floor to get Jeretzian. Theo knew he was there because he was finalizing preparations with Dr. Zahler.

On hearing the news, Jeretzian immediately put out his cigarette in the ashtray on Dr. Zahler's cabinet. He inhaled deeply, trying to steel himself for what might lie ahead. Dr. Zahler, clutching his wife's hand, gasped. Out came no words. Jeretzian turned to them. "Don't worry about anything. We'll be alright." He patted his Arrow Cross gray coat pocket to ensure he had with him the vital order of the Ministry of Interior. He asked Dr. Zahler and the messenger to please send for his friend, Laszlo Nagy, and have him meet him at the Party headquarters at 60 Andrassy utca.

Jeretzian resolved that he should be as compliant as possible, conveying the idea he's done nothing wrong and is simply carrying out the orders of the Ministry of Interior. He greeted the men warmly, offering to ride his motorcycle to headquarters behind them. "Come, let me answer their questions, brothers!" His jovial attitude seemed to surprise the Arrow Cross men, and they agreed.

At headquarters, hours passed waiting for the local regional Party leader, August, to arrive. Jeretzian struggled to guess what had happened to lead to his arrest. Had someone figured out that both he and his orders were fraudulent? Despite his inner turmoil and fear, he resolved to remain outwardly calm and good-humored to help maintain the appearance of innocence. Maybe no one had discovered his subterfuge, he wondered, or had identified only one small discrepancy in his story. Jeretzian's jokes, flirtations and small talk fell on deaf ears, for no one had the authority to override August's order that Jeretzian be arrested. At least he was permitted to wait in the lobby, despite the fact he was forced to turn in his pistol and armband upon his arrival. After a short while, Laszlo Nagy joined him and they were able to discuss the possibilities if things should not go well for Jeretzian. The priority was to convey any bad news to the house immediately so that the residents might get a head start to evacuate before they would be taken to the ghetto or, even worse, to the Danube.

Hours passed, and still no August. Jeretzian wondered what the people at the house were thinking, assumed they would be terrified and so sent Nagy there to indicate everything was fine. Meanwhile, his banter at the station paid off with crucial information. He learned from one associate who had stopped to chat with him what he feared most: August had him arrested because he intended to prosecute him for the crime of harboring Jews in defiance of Minister Vajna's order that all Jews be relocated to either of the two ghettos. Jeretzian knew that, for this crime, he, and everyone in the house, could be executed. As the time for most officials to go home arrived, Jeretzian had succeeded in winning over the confidence of the office staff to such an extent he was permitted to return home and come back first thing tomorrow morning. "I know you know where to find me, and I have nothing to hide, so I will return right away," Jeretzian confirmed with vigor.

Jeretzian knew August by reputation and feared the worst. He had had enough time throughout this long day to think of one person who might be able to help him, Karoly Wirth, the Parliamentary Representative for the Organization of Labor in the country. Jeretzian hoped that if he showed his old school friend, Wirth, the Ministry of Interior order establishing the house as a medical facility indispensable to the country, he would agree this was both legitimate and a proper use of using Jews for labor. He again hopped onto his motorcycle and drove the short distance to the grandiose Parliament building near the Danube.

Not only was Jeretzian right about Wirth's ability to help, but even better, it turned out fortuitously that Wirth despised August. Perhaps driven in part by animosity and an unexpected chance to bring August down a notch, Wirth drafted a service notice on Jeretzian's behalf, ordering August to withdraw the order of arrest. Wirth also personally vouched for Jeretzian's character and legitimate service in the name of Hungary, using Jewish physicians and assistants under labor directives to serve the Arrow Cross and war effort.

The following morning, when Jeretzian returned to the Party headquarters and produced Wirth's order and letter to August, all hell broke loose. "Who is this Wirth to tell me anything?" he seethed, practically frothing at the mouth. "He answers to me, not the other way around!" Further, he screamed for the head of the man who let Jeretzian leave yesterday afternoon. "On whose authority did the service leader let this man go?" he asked, more using his hand as a weapon than pointing at Jeretzian.

In short order, August put Jeretzian and the hapless service leader in a cell so he could "get to the bottom of this." Before being confined, however, he managed to convey to his friend, Nagy, to fetch Wirth here right away. In no time, Wirth arrived. Jeretzian could hear everything from his cell.

"Did you not think to ask Mr. Jeretzian about the order he bears from the Ministry of Interior?" Wirth yelled at August before August could open his mouth. "If you did then it is you that would realize you could be in trouble, not Jeretzian. You, Mr. August, are standing in the way of his direct order from above to assist Hungary and the Party in the war effort. Have you ever heard of a war without the need for medical personnel?"

Reluctantly, August ordered the cell opened and asked to see "this order." Upon careful examination of its contents, he could scarcely believe it. It was true, Jeretzian and the Jews at 1 Zichy Jeno were free to proceed.

August looked up, unapologetically. "Something isn't right about this, and I will have the last laugh in the matter," he bristled again. "I will discover the truth – tell me why Minister Vajna wants all Jews in the ghetto, and yet he doesn't? Never mind. Don't go far, Jeretzian." He refused to look at Wirth, who turned to wink at Jeretzian and offered him a cigarette. Jeretzian gladly took it, bowed before August, and walked out the door with Wirth.

"Thank you," Jeretzian told Wirth. "You'll see. You'll see how invaluable my Jewish physician friends will be."

14

"The Fascist Clinic"

There was only one person in the room not laughing. Everyone else was laughing so hard it hurt, even if the humor was dark as a moonless night in a mountain forest.

Dr. Volgyesi would not allow himself to see the humor. He finally walked into the washroom that still technically belonged to him but was now an extension of the new "Arrow Cross" clinic's command office. Behind the desk in the center of the room, where once there was a life-sized portrait of Volgyesi standing proudly, almost defiantly, at the painter within a gorgeous, gold-plated frame there was now an immense portrait of Arrow Cross leader Ferenc Szalasi. And the laughing did not abate even as the other doctors and families in the room saw Volgyesi exit.

"Hey," Dr. Orban elbowed Dr. Stricker, "Be careful. He might hypnotize us all and make us bark like dogs."

Dr. Zahler, the eldest of the crowd, interjected. "Easy, friends. Let's not get carried away. This is, after all, Volgyesi's apartment. If it weren't for him, our hero, Jeretzian likely wouldn't even know of this building's existence, and therefore wouldn't be here to help. Isn't that right, Ara? You worked quite closely with Dr. Volgyesi through your Civil Defense work, yes?"

Jeretzian looked appreciatively at Dr. Zahler, whom he was coming to admire more every day. This man, so highly regarded both in the Budapest

Jewish community and in the medical field, was so selfless, so loving and protective of the three remaining women in his life: his wife, daughter and granddaughter. Jeretzian saw how deeply wounded Dr. Zahler remained from having lost his mother to that first Arrow Cross roundup before Jeretzian had arrived. He saw it again when the building agreed it needed to sacrifice 20 residents to the international ghetto, purportedly to save the lives of everyone else. He saw it in Dr. Zahler's eyes. Even when he smiled or laughed, there was now sadness, a soft glimmer in his eyes that would not dim or dry.

Though Jeretzian had not known Dr. Zahler nearly as well before this all began, he knew that sad expression of grief that refused to yield. He knew it in the eyes of his own mother, Sophie, who had lost nearly her entire family just over two decades before when the Ottomans slaughtered over 1.5 million Armenians in Turkey.

Jeretzian placed his right hand, cigarette in his left, on Dr. Zahler's shoulder. "Friends, let's be humble. We must respect and help one another, as Dr. Volgyesi has done by permitting us to use his apartment for the clinic office."

The washroom door opened and Dr. Volgyesi reappeared. His wife, younger than him by at least 10 years, stepped through the crowd to take his hand.

"We have done very well by now to publicize our existence," Jeretzian continued. We have a police officer standing guard in front of the house around the clock, and the signs in and around the house clearly show we are an Arrow Cross medical clinic. Arrow Cross commanders have come here for treatment and have been duly impressed. My friend, Laszlo Nagy, has helped me connect our clinic through the Arrow Cross to help treat refugees from Transylvania."

There were three or four claps among the group, crowded in the apartment-turned-clinic office.

"But the worst is yet to come, isn't that right, Jeretzian?" Volgyesi asked, half embittered. "The Soviets are all around us."

"Yes," Jeretzian paused. "Very nearly. And then, my friends, not only will there be more chaos, but there will likely be terrible bloodshed all around. Our clinic – if we play our cards right – will become more a hospital than an outpatient office."

"Here, here," Dr. Orban cheered. "Then we become more 'indispensable;' more necessary to the Hungarian effort and, therefore, safer. Isn't that right, Jeretzian?"

"I hope so. But that's the tricky part." Jeretzian gained momentum. "We are all hopeful the Nazis are expelled from Hungary – and the Arrow Cross with them. But who knows how the Soviets will view things: The Jews here; the Jews in the ghetto; an Armenian Hungarian posing as Arrow Cross and wearing the uniform? For now, let us consider opening our doors to all who are wounded; treat everyone. And maybe," he extinguished his cigarette in an ashtray below the new Szalasi portrait, "all will appreciate us and be grateful."

Before the gathering in Dr. Volgyesi's former apartment retired for the evening, the conversation shifted gears. News and rumors were shared. The large ghetto walls were now enclosed, encasing over 70,000 Jews in such a small area in the 7th District. The international ghetto, despite the presence of Swedish emissary Raoul Wallenberg, Swiss representative Carl Lutz and many other diplomats held nearly 40,000 Jews in protected houses meant to accommodate under 4,000. The Arrow Cross thugs continued to beat, loot and murder Jews for whatever reason they invented. They continued to shoot many dozen Jews per day at the Danube. Further, until just recently now that the Soviet encirclement of Budapest was nearly completed, Jews continued to be marched out toward the Reich, unless they died of exhaustion or starvation or were murdered along the route.

"What will happen during a siege, Jeretzian?" asked Laszlo Nagy as they exited the house and took in the cold night.

Jeretzian patted the back of the police guard standing outside, smoking a cigarette. "Persevere," they said to each other simultaneously.

"Well, we are about to find out, my old friend." Jeretzian sighed before turning to walk in separate directions to their respective houses. "Many of the Arrow Cross higher officials have already fled to safety; outside of

Budapest somewhere. I didn't want to tell the others inside this, but the Ministry of Interior – the same entity that unknowingly ordered this clinic's existence and protection – has practically dissolved, or at least relocated. I'm not quite sure, but I do know Vajna remains. The worst one. Who knows where the German authorities, Eichmann and all, have gone. I know there are Nazi offices in Buda – in the castle, as well as at the Hotel Astoria … other places too, but I don't know anymore…."

"If the Red Army begins shelling the city…," Nagy began.

"*When* the Red Army begins shelling the city…."

PART III

SIEGE OF BUDAPEST

15

Going Underground

First came the sound of a single explosion. So powerful, so near that it rattled the porcelain plates on Robert's Aunt Aranka's cabinet. Everyone in the apartment took in a collective deep breath and froze. They all looked at each other, as if wondering if anyone could offer up an explanation other than the obvious. They didn't.

Instead, the first explosion invoked almost total silence as far as Robert could hear. And then came another explosion. Then another, louder, nearer. The air raid sirens suddenly began; so loud, so obliterating of thought. There was the drone of the stubby, low-wing Soviet *Polikarpov* I-16 "rata" planes overhead, then booms and sporadic bursts of shells and artillery fire seemingly enveloping Budapest. Like the Soviets themselves. And now there was no silence at all. In its place there were hysterical screams, cries and shouts that began as a call and response with the barrage, but now became part of the collective soundtrack.

Robert remembered hearing and feeling the bone-shattering effects of American bombs in Budapest the preceding March or April, but that experience seemed so much less terrifying. For one thing, Robert was still living at his Rottenbiller home, and thus, they had been further away from the city center where relatively few bombs dropped. In addition, he did not then feel trapped as he did now, like a prisoner awaiting an unknown fate, along with all the Jews in this house and throughout Budapest. He was now living as if by permission only, and he despised this feeling more than he feared death itself. He was a passenger on a ship whose destination was not revealed to him, assuming there was any future at all. That his mother and his family inside the apartment shared this predicament made him only feel worse. He wanted to scream for his mother, for himself, but he had grown too old, too fast and so he already knew that such antics could change nothing.

There was yet another layer of uncertainty that sucked the air from the cold winter day: Here were the Jews desperately hoping the Soviets would win and liberate them from the German and the Arrow Cross fascists, but would they all die in the process? And even if they survived, what would Soviet rule mean for Hungary? Even Robert, quite taken with some Communist ideals, had heard enough from the elders in the building about Soviet victors' despicable treatment of their conquered citizens, as well as how Stalin and the Soviets had treated so many of their own Jewish citizens. Regardless, the building consensus seemed to be that Red Army liberation, should the residents live to see the day, was infinitely preferable to the hell of Nazi and Arrow Cross tyranny -- particularly for the Jews.

Robert had been working on some Algebra problems at the kitchen table. Ever since Jews were prohibited to attend school after Robert's 8th grade year, his mother had managed to find different tutors to keep Robert reading, writing and learning mathematics. Robert did not initially enjoy these sessions, but he had come to appreciate them as distractions – first, from the boredom and monotony, and more recently, to prevent him from obsessing over the almost perpetual fear. Plus, having a shared tutor in this building allowed him to see, and be near pretty girls like Eva, the girl with laughing eyes, Dr. Zahler's granddaughter, and one of Dr. Volgyesi's daughters whose name he was still desperately trying to obtain. Although he still had not achieved the victory of shared conversation beyond greetings with any of them, let alone being noticed by any of these beautiful, until recently wealthy young women, just being in their presence gave him a brief sense of feeling young, free and alive. And there was always the hope that each ensuing day would be the day he spoke with them. Any of them.

Robert was aware that the clinic on the first two floors was readying itself for the likelihood of increased traffic. In a strange way, this was what the doctors were all hoping for, because the consensus was that the more patients there were, the more the doctors would be needed and, therefore, the more *safe* would be the Jewish residents at 1 Zichy Jeno. Jeretzian, as Civil Defense commander, had been running the residents through regular evacuation drills into the small, very cold and musty basement. They needed to prepare for the worst, he kept saying. "You need to get down there quickly. Take nothing with you, just get to safety, as orderly as possible."

The siege, the total encirclement of Budapest by Red Army troops, began in earnest on what was Christmas Eve. Despite the Arrow Cross orders that all Christians living in Yellow Star houses leave, a few residing in 1 Zichy Jeno defied these orders and still insisted on living there. Robert was amused to see the few remaining Christians find ways to celebrate Christmas despite the dangerous times. One family, now sharing their apartment with two Jewish families on the fourth floor, wrapped a large, indoor plant with aluminum anti-radar strips as decorations to serve as a Christmas tree. Robert heard them singing carols together on Christmas Eve. They sounded happy, somehow.

Earlier on Christmas Eve day, it was reported that Nazi director and overseer of the Jewish "question" in Hungary, Eichmann, had escaped from Budapest. By now, no Jews could be deported from Budapest to any destination. Instead, with almost all Budapest Jews in one of the two ghettos, the Arrow Cross members remaining -- seemingly younger, more belligerent, and more lawless -- turned their attention increasingly to tormenting and murdering Jews. Perhaps they too, assuming they could formulate intelligent thought, realized their predicament, and so they did the one thing they knew how to do well: Be murderous bullies.

Robert was trying to find the value of an elusive variable when the first explosion shook everything, even his bones.

At the same time, inside Dr. Volgyesi's former apartment that now served as the clinic intake office, Jeretzian had been in the middle of a conversation with a handful of physicians. "To this point," he explained, "We are okay. But this may not last unless we somehow get more patients. The Arrow Cross orders are clear in that there should be no Jews whatsoever living outside of the ghettos. And I understand that they are now trying to move the Jews from the international ghetto into the ordinary one, making everything even more miserable. Food is already scarce, people are starving, and most utilities out there are not working on account of the siege...."

"I understand," interjected Dr. Volgyesi. "The provisions and protection we have so far is not infinite unless we can blend in; be more useful. What is the state of our own food and utilities?"

"For now, we are fine. As a medical facility, we continue to be guaranteed a certain amount of supplies, food … but this may not last when the bombs fall. And who knows what electricity, water there will be."

Suddenly, the first blast interrupted the conversation like a hammer smashing down onto Dr. Volgyesi's desk. The men in the room looked at each other, shaken, as Dr. Zahler braced himself against Jeretzian's shoulder for support. They all rushed to the windows, crowding together amidst ensuing blasts, artillery fire, and then the sound of Soviet rata planes spraying shells everywhere. Across the street, they could see people lying injured outside the bakery at O utca and Vilmos Császár utca.

Jeretzian ran downstairs to sound the alarm. Almost immediately thereafter, as rehearsed many times, down came the remaining non-working residents toward the small basement shelter. Meanwhile, the doctors, together with those functioning as nurses and assistants went to their respective places, many into the lobby area to help assign the incoming injured to the appropriate rooms and physicians. Even those with limited to no surgical experience were instantly being pressed into emergency duty. Many younger assistants, including Norbert Kohn, served as casualty transport personnel and went outside into the dangerous fray to carry or usher in the injured. It was already a bloody mess everywhere.

The screams of agony, pain and loss competed at terrifying levels with the deafening sounds of battle, however one-sided things appeared. There were no Arrow Cross or Germans to be seen outside 1 Zichy Jeno, only civilians, too many of them wounded.

Jeretzian, seeing the number of injured vastly exceed his support personnel, took in a deep breath and joined the exodus into the cold to help. Outside an Italian gelato stall beside the bakery, he saw a man lying motionless in the stiff, frozen air. When he reached down to pick him up, the man seemed to weigh almost nothing. Jeretzian looked down again and discovered, beneath the man's long winter coat his entire lower torso was gone. His lower half had remained on the road when Jeretzian lifted his body. He saw the man close his eyes for the last time, having taken in one last gasp, before nothing....

The ack-ack of the rata planes firing from on high shattered windows. Glass fell, sometimes in whole shards, like rain or ice from buildings all around. People dove to take cover beside buildings but, in truth, it was difficult to tell who was lying down for cover versus those who were wounded or dead. Sometimes the glass fell directly onto those taking cover. Jeretzian, still shaken by the sight and near weightlessness of the man cut in half by shrapnel tried desperately to gather his wits. He saw shattered windows in several apartments at 1 Zichy Jeno but was pleased to see so many people carry wounded, or crawl into the clinic. He finally saw young, wounded Arrow Cross personnel enter. *Help was help after all*, Jeretzian thought, *regardless of the race or religion of those administering it*. The policeman stationed there never fled, but instead assisted in getting the wounded inside.

The rata planes now appeared to shift their attention across the Danube to the Buda side. Seizing this moment of comparative calm, Jeretzian was able to get off his knees. He saw blood on his coat sleeves, realizing it belonged to the half man. He looked down the street of his own apartment, Vilmos Császár utca, and, for the first time, saw at least a half dozen dead or dying horses lying in the middle of the street just south of St. Istvan's Basilica. There were soldiers lying around the horses, but Jeretzian could not tell from this distance whether they were Nazis or Arrow Cross. He knew that there were cavalry units attached to the defense of the city, but for the life of him, he could not now discern how a cavalry detail could assist in this kind of war; in a siege in which liberator bullets and bombs were flying all around them any and everywhere.

As Jeretzian returned to the other side of the street, he came to a young man carrying a beautiful young woman in his arms. Despite the unforgiving cold, now even more imposing with the competing smells of artillery, blood, building dust, smoke and death all around, the man was sweating, tears streaming down both cheeks.

"Please, sir, can you help?" he cried frantically. "This is a hospital?"

"It is now. Of course, where is she hurt?" Jeretzian immediately felt stupid, for he now saw that the girl was bleeding badly below the waist. "I'm sorry, come inside right away."

As the three of them entered the clinic that was now an emergency hospital, Jeretzian could not even see through the lobby to find the designated intake personnel. There were so many wounded or dead people and relatives all around. "Theo," he finally called out, grateful to have found a face he recognized, "where are the nurses? We have an emergency here. This man…."

"They are all emergencies, Jeretzian," Theo muttered without expression.

"Help my wife, please," the young man screamed above all other noises in the lobby. "She was struck by shrapnel; a shell fragment, I don't know. I have been all over the place looking for help. There are no doctors. No doctors anywhere! I will give you everything if you only save her, my love! My love!" It was a cry; a call from the depths of the man's soul.

Jeretzian gently took the woman from the man's arms and, realizing what happened the last time he held someone, he cradled her gently, as if she was a child. "Come with me. We will go to the surgery upstairs."

Jeretzian and the young man finally found Dr. Stricker's staff and attending personnel, who were clearly overwhelmed. There were more bodies than beds and cots. It seemed like all the physicians in the building were here, even the dentists and psychiatrists. Dr Zahler, a pediatrician, and his daughter and granddaughter, newly minted nurses were busily helping as they could. The rooms designated for surgery now occupied all the rooms on this floor, at least. As the doctors immediately began to evaluate her, the young man, now numbly, told the nurse and Jeretzian that his wife's name is Zsofia.

"We were married only three months ago." The young man, a Hungarian soldier, arrived home from the front on leave just a day before the Soviet encirclement closed. His wife surprised him with news that she was pregnant. Over the man's shoulder, Jeretzian saw the medical personnel transfer Zsofia to an operating table and attach cardiac monitoring gear, administering boosters. Jeretzian knew this did not look good.

"We were so happy," he continued, with growing emotion. "We were still in bed, and she wanted to surprise me with a cup of tea. But the water is out in our house already on account of the…. She told me she knew the water was still on next door. I said it was too dangerous. She insisted. She laughed as I called out. She wanted to treat me. I was too stinking lazy to get out and go with her. Oh God, curse me! She cannot die! She cannot die!"

Jeretzian took out a cigarette and offered one to him. He declined, so he took it for himself and lit it. It wasn't much of a waiting room, and most others were standing but all were reverent toward one another's worry, fear and loss. No one seemed to even look up when the young man cried out.

"She had only gotten maybe 10 meters out of our house's gate when I heard the first blast. It must have been the very first blast that got her. It must have been…."

"Take it easy, brother," Jeretzian told him. "You have the best doctors in Hungary right here. If they can't save her, then…."

"No!" he screamed suddenly. "If they can't save her, you must promise me something right now." The young man looked wildly into Jeretzian's eyes. "If Zsofia does not live through this then you must kill me also. You must!"

Hours passed. Although the bombs and bullets outside seemed to have stopped, it was hell on earth inside. There was so much suffering, so much sorrow and pain. The young man was finally enticed to step away to let the surgeons work. He began pacing like a wild animal in an enclosure, walking up and down the stairs over and over again. Every time he returned to the waiting area, he demanded: "Zsofia? Zsofia! Someone here, please tell me she will live. I will give you everything I have!" This continued for nearly six hours.

Jeretzian had managed to disengage from the young man for a couple of very brief spells. He learned a great deal. For one, there was already significant damage done to the house. Windows were broken, and one apartment on the fourth floor seemed to have taken a direct shrapnel hit that caused substantial interior damage. The water and electricity still functioned, but clearly things were much too dangerous in the building itself. Gratefully, all non-medical personnel were in the basement and so no resident was hurt. However, there was another, more pressing problem. The basement area below the house was insufficiently large to accommodate even the non-medical residents. If the building was too dangerous for the residents to be in their units, it was also far too dangerous to constitute a hospital. One nearby blast was so close that it sent two doctors crashing up against the wall of the first floor. Where were they to go?

Before Jeretzian could further process this issue, he saw the young man pass him by again on the stairs. He followed him back upstairs. As the man continued his rounds up and down the stairs, Jeretzian meandered his way through the crowd and approached the window that allowed him to see into the waiting room. He was tall enough to see over the heads of a few onlookers closer to the window. For nearly 15 minutes, he watched the physicians bravely, tirelessly perform with the greatest calm, the greatest expertise. They inserted one needle after another, employed the cardiac booster twice more in this time span, yet nothing seemed to enable Zsofia's heart to beat on its own. She had lost so much blood. Jeretzian watched Dr. Stricker finally motion to a nurse to pull the sheet over her head. She had been feeling Zsofia's pulse and began to cry. Dr. Stricker, too, seemed to be on the verge of tears or passing out. Instead, he gave a sad glance to Jeretzian. "I did everything I could," Dr. Stricker mouthed through the glass. "If only she had gotten here sooner...." Dr. Stricker glumly turned to heed the call of another nurse beside another patient.

Jeretzian stood motionless near the glass. The nurse who was assisting Dr. Stricker with Zsofia came out and approached Jeretzian. "Where is the young man, her husband," she asked gravely. "Wasn't he with you?"

"He should be right back here in a moment. I don't know what to...."

"I can tell him, if you'd like," the nurse said, tenderly. "Do you know? Dr. Stricker and the others said...."

"What is it, Madam?"

"They said they would have been able to save her had she arrived sooner. She had lost too much blood.... And do you – does he know that she was … pregnant?"

Jeretzian placed both of his hands on the nurse's shoulders and smiled through his own teary eyes. He had no idea how long this young woman had even been a functional "nurse," but at this moment, he felt one with her in spirit. Just then, the young man came up, saw the look in Jeretzian's eyes and frantically pushed his way to the window. There was Zsofia, the young love of his life, beneath a red-stained sheet.

"Can't be! This cannot be!" he howled with the full desperation of a wounded beast. He then forced his way into the makeshift surgical room, where he removed the sheet from Zsofia's face and kissed it. Over and over again, each kiss increasingly drenched in his own bed of tears. He caressed her slowly. Neither Jeretzian nor the nurse – no one -- dared to interrupt. They both stood and watched the young man once again pick up his beautiful wife's motionless body. Jeretzian followed, safely securing his passage down the stairs and out the door.

"Young man!" Jeretzian called out, desperately from the door. "Sir, what is your name? Please, it isn't safe!" His calls fell on deaf ears. If they were heard at all, through the pain and heartbreak, they were ignored. Jeretzian could only watch as the young man, his darling Zsofia wrapped in a blood-stained sheet in his arms, disappeared around the corner of O utca. The indifferent sun, barely visible through the dense, gray clouds, was setting. In the distance, Jeretzian heard the almost perpetual barrage of shells and bombs. The sounds were coming closer.

***

The respite between the earth-shaking artillery fire, shells and bullets was not nearly long enough to call a meeting of all those required to devise a plan for the safety of the building's residents and the hospital itself. Jeretzian, visibly shaken as was everyone by the day's events so far, was relieved to see a familiar face. There was Dr. Zahler, holding the hand of his granddaughter, in the middle of a conversation with two other doctors. Not surprisingly, they were discussing the same issue that now preoccupied Jeretzian.

"Ah, Jeretzian," Dr. Zahler exclaimed. "How are you holding up, my friend?"

Jeretzian sullenly shrugged his shoulders. There were so many people all around them, and so much noise. Families and residents huddled together from the lobby to the stairwell, too apprehensive to stay in their upstairs apartments. "This is terrible; beyond what I could have imagined. Were you gentlemen discussing the basement situation?"

"Yes," blurted the voice of a doctor whom Jeretzian did not know by name. He spoke loudly in order to be heard. "I am Dr. Szasz, a surgeon. My family is on the fourth floor. A shell blasted through the window and destroyed everything."

"Yes, I saw that. I am sorry and happy only that no one was upstairs at the time," Jeretzian empathized. "What do you have in mind?"

"Go on," urged Dr. Zahler, motioning for his granddaughter to go to her mother. Jeretzian bade her farewell, obviously taken in by the young woman's beauty. Her striking green eyes seemed to smile despite everything, like a rainbow amidst a devastating storm.

"Well," Dr. Szasz broke in, uncomfortably aware that Jeretzian's attention had been diverted. "We need ample space both for our residents as well as for our … our hospital. A lot of space. Right next door to us here, as you well know, is the porcelain store of Haas & Czjzek. My wife once worked here and tells me that she used to run downstairs to their storage to place and gather inventory. Their storage … their basement is at least five times the size of our own, and, as this whole block is connected through access doors underground, why don't we spread out into their area? They have cleared out now on account of the siege; they are no longer there."

Jeretzian looked at Dr. Zahler, Dr. Klein and finally, Dr. Szasz. "Of course. We could move their inventory, if necessary, to one place and move everyone and everything down there in the name of Civil Defense." Jeretzian exhaled, reaching into his pocket for a cigarette. "I don't know why I didn't think of this before." He composed himself once he drew in from his cigarette, then put his left hand on the shoulder of Dr. Szasz. "Let me go down to police headquarters and draw up the necessary paperwork to requisition this basement for our work and safety. We will all go underground," he smiled briefly. "It will be a lot of work, but time is of the essence."

In short time, amidst intensifying shelling and the almost constant influx of severely wounded patients, Jeretzian secured the necessary permission to move all hospital operations and residents underground. It took nearly a full day to move the porcelain store's delicate inventory into one smaller space, then clean and arrange the rest of the now much more sizeable basement. It was cold, and, understandably, dark downstairs. No matter how many times one entered below, and no matter how many people were circulating there, there was a pervasive smell of cool, damp mustiness. But this would be an awfully small price to pay for evading the shelling above ground.

Every resident not already assisting in hospital operations had a hand in the establishment of the move to the basement. They transported all mattresses and cots and placed them close together in open areas toward the back and alongside the walls. There were not nearly enough mattresses for everyone, considering that so many needed to be used for the patients, and, by now, there must have been over 400 residents in a building meant to hold maybe half that number. All lanterns and candles were brought downstairs, and Theo and his vice-super, Bodor, succeeded in drilling holes to wire electricity into the medical areas. They hoped the electricity would last. Water pipes ran downstairs, so they simply exposed the pipes and showed people where and how to open the faucets. There was no viable option for washroom facilities, so several young men took shovels and picks and dug large holes into the basement floor to serve as a kind of latrine. Once again, this was hardly desirable, but desire was now an almost delusional commodity considering the circumstances.

And so it was, within just three agonizing days of relentless shelling overhead and countless surgeries, deaths and myriad miracles, all personnel and operations were relocated underground, below 1 Zichy Jeno and the connecting storage basement of the porcelain store next door. Underground, they rang in the advent of a new year, 1945. The new year came devoid of celebration. Those few that were both aware of it and acknowledged it gave reluctant thanks to a god fewer believed in that they were still alive, and hopeful that their liberation, let alone survival, would come soon. When it was evident that they needed even more space underground, they expanded into the firewood storage basement of another house next door, 21 Vilmos Császár utca. There, they set up 30 more beds as an additional operating room area. They feared what they knew: They would soon need every bed they had for what was to come.

16

Frozen

There were not enough blankets to combat the cold outside that chilled the basement residents to the bone. There was no music to inspire or distract them, or even to muffle the sounds of the patients' agony and suffering. The relentless loud pounding of shelling outside drained the hope and smiles from every face. For all the medical miracles achieved in the makeshift hospital, there were at least as many disappointments and losses. The only thing any of them could do was to keep busy; to be useful; to serve the interests of their great endeavor to try and survive.

Robert explained to his family, huddled and crowded on four mattresses not nearly far enough away from the "potty pits," what he was being asked to do. "Three men assisting Jeretzian -- a Mr. Laszlo Frank and two brothers, Paul and another Laszlo something or other -- want me to assist in the removal of dead bodies and," Robert paused, "the limbs that have been removed; amputated."

Silence.

"And," Robert continued, "I would also alternate with some others my age to deliver messages, pick up supplies … things like that."

More silence. Robert's grandmother put her fleshy, tender arms around his mother, whose eyes were lifeless.

Finally, Aranka broke in. "And where – how far away are you supposed to put these bodies … and limbs? Which square? And the messages and supplies, how far away are they requiring you to go while the shells are falling?" Both Aranka and Robert's mother were now functioning as newly trained nurses, or at least assisting in the hospital operations in one way or another. No one in the building was oblivious to the gruesome wounds, amputations and the dead around them. Clearly, they could not keep the bodies and limbs among those living, working; trying in vain to sleep.

Robert, sitting on the edge of a mattress with his legs folded beneath him, closed his eyes and took in a deep, cold breath. He shivered uncontrollably for an instant. "The limbs are to be stacked neatly in that small section of the courtyard, next to the outdoor basement entryway."

"Oh my God," cried his mother. That was almost directly below where Aranka's apartment was situated, though Aranka's window faced outward, not inside to the courtyard.

"It is so frozen; so cold outside, at least for the foreseeable future, that they won't decay. The dead bodies, it's the same thing. Only those will be taken out some ways to another square, I'm told. The ground outside is too frozen solid to bury the dead. Some may have to stay in our courtyard until we can safely get them out further. But I understand it's terrible all over," Robert continued. "So bad that there are dead bodies, frozen, starved or shot to death, lying among dead horses in the middle of streets. And in the ghetto…," he stopped, seeing the effect of revealing the facts he had learned from Mr. Frank, Paul and Laszlo, whom people were dubbing "The Three Musketeers."

Even Robert could scarcely believe he was articulating such words. He was 15, or maybe 30 now. He had no idea if his father was alive. He didn't know if he and his family in the basement of 1 Zichy Jeno would survive either the bombings, the Nazis, the Arrow Cross or the Soviets. And he saw dead or dying people every day. They were all around him. He was living in a basement to avoid being killed by shells or artillery. His mother was still a ghost of her former self. Her entire side of the family had been killed because they, like Robert and his mother, were guilty of being Jewish. Friends were gone, relatives … and so many were simply missing. Should they be presumed dead? Nothing of this made sense to Robert, but he had long since grown accustomed to this recognition. And how he missed his father!

Aranka, stoic as usual, turned to Robert's mother. "He must do what is needed, Cornelia. He is a man now. He must help. We all must help."

Robert followed his grandmother's lead and drew closer to his mother. "*Anu*, I love you. I will be okay. Let me do my part."

Within the first hour of his new assignment, Robert, wearing white gloves that became soaked red after the first three deliveries alone, carried and neatly stacked 18 limbs; arms, legs, feet and hands. He was told to put like body parts together. For some reason he could not discern, he was to keep identifying name tags attached to each limb. Next up were the dead bodies. He was already growing numb, as much to the nature of this grisly work as to the cold.

***

In between the incoming patients and the messengers and supply gatherers coming and going there entered a high-ranking police officer looking for Jeretzian. The man, introduced by the guard posted outside the building, was named Jeno Szinyei Merse, Commissioner for the Ghettoization of Jews.

"Is there somewhere we can go to speak quietly, Mr. Jeretzian?" Merse asked, surveying the front area of the basement hospital.

"Well, not exactly down here, Sir. As you can see…. But I do not hear shells or the ratas at the moment. Perhaps we can go upstairs to the former office?"

In the office, still intact despite broken windows that let in the frigid January air and missing furniture, much of which was now in the basement, Merse wasted no time. "Let me get to the point straight off, Mr. Jeretzian. You have Jews here. How many?"

Jeretzian tried not to blink or show concern. "Nearly 400 medical personnel, sir. Let me show you the order from the Ministry…."

"I've heard of this order. Let me see it."

Jeretzian produced the Ministry of Interior order, the Swiss order of protection and various service notices associated with the Civil Defense. He had kept them all folded inside his Arrow Cross coat pocket ever since he received them. "Everything is right here. As you can see from them, and as you saw downstairs – these Jewish physicians and their assistants have been, and are absolutely necessary...."

"I see," Merse acknowledged, cursorily surveying the documents through slight reading glasses perched near the tip of his nose. "I will have to check on the authenticity of these documents, particularly with Minister of Interior Vajna. The main thing, as surely you must already know, is that there should be no Jews living outside the ghetto. Your order must be a mistake." He looked more seriously at Jeretzian, who was refusing the urge to lean back against the wall, in the absence of any chairs in the room.

"I assure you it is not," Jeretzian deadpanned. "This hospital's work – these people are indispensable."

"Four hundred Jews, you say. How many, do you think, are truly engaged in 'this hospital's work?'" Merse was studying Jeretzian's face for his response.

Jeretzian did not know how to immediately answer. If he overreached, it could present further problems. If he estimated too low, would he be sacrificing lives without their knowledge? He had already done this once, a few weeks ago, and had barely come to terms with the choices he and some of the physicians had made in this regard. "At least 200," he finally offered.

"Impossible. Out of the question. There can't be such a high number of Jews outside the ghetto."

"Mr. Merse, the order," Jeretzian practically whined. "You saw what you saw. The work they are doing. The order is authentic." Jeretzian was now at a loss. For the first time, he did not see a clear way through this problem. He knew that if this man reached Vajna, all would be lost for everyone, including himself for his part in the deception, forgeries, and above all, protecting Jews against absolute orders and decrees.

"Mr. Jeretzian, between you and me, are you aware of what is happening out there?"

"What do you mean?"

"I mean, just yesterday the Swede, Wallenberg, closed his part of the international ghetto on account of the shelling and daily Arrow Cross raids. He relocated most of the Jews there to the large ghetto, where he believes they will have a better chance for survival. Jews, more than anyone, are starving to death, freezing to death. There are no supplies, utilities don't work. People are rushing out between artillery fire, trying to carve up the frozen cadavers of horses for meat, for God's sakes! Yes," he practically shouted on seeing Jeretzian's horrified expression. "They get there, then Arrow Cross clowns grab them, beat them for the food and, well, because they are Jews, after all. The Danube is … well, you wouldn't believe it. They have shot and killed so many Jews in the river there are naked and half-naked bodies frozen on the embankment, and others are just floating down the river."

Jeretzian finally leaned back. He felt gutted. "Do you smoke?" he asked, offering a cigarette. Merse took one, then pulled out his lighter to light his own cigarette and that of Jeretzian.

"May I ask you, Mr. Merse," said Jeretzian between puffs. "You know all this. You ask me if I know all this. You see my orders and the work we – they are doing downstairs. Why bother?"

"Regulations," Merse smiled almost apologetically. "We all know they can never deport all of the Jews on account of the siege, and it's just a matter of time, it sure appears, before the Soviets come to liberate we Hungarians and, I suppose, your Jews. The Nazis keep talking about some wonder weapon, or some miracle weapon that will still appear and win the war, but…. The Jews, though," Merse paused again. "Szalasi, Vajna, Hitler, Eichmann, who knows? They still want to kill all the Jews, win or lose the war."

Jeretzian just shook his head, unable to comprehend the logic in any of this. "Does any of this bother you, Mr. Merse?"

"What do you mean, the—"

"What I mean is, you are Hungarian. Szalasi, Vajna, the Arrow Cross…. I haven't seen Hitler or Eichmann, have you?" Jeretzian didn't wait for a response. "It is now 1945. We have heard what the Germans were doing to the Jews in Poland and in the East for how many years now? And all along we kept saying we Hungarians are better than this. In Budapest the Jews are our friends – certainly mine. And yet, here we are, Mr. Merse. We Hungarians are doing this by ourselves … in the provinces and now in Budapest. The war is lost for Germany and still here we are; round up the Jews and kill them all. Aren't we ashamed? Shouldn't we be ashamed?"

"I will make my calls to check on your order, Jeretzian. You take care in the meantime, and don't go anywhere."

"And wherever would I go?"

***

"Beans. More beans. A hell of a lot of beans," Eva, Dr. Zahler's granddaughter, complained to him. She was somehow still smiling, if only in her eyes.

"You have no idea how good you've got it, you spoiled beauty," smiled Dr. Zahler standing beside her in line for their daily ration of beans and potato flour bread. With a little luck, there would also be some diluted coffee. Something was better than nothing.

Just then, Laszlo Frank, one of Jeretzian's associates in the day to day operations of the building came down with the teenage Norbert Kohn. Kohn had quickly established himself as one of the, if not *the* chief courier. He proved to be fearless, fast and, most importantly, successful. "Fearless," he scoffed when Frank previously complimented him in this way. "I'm not fearless, I am terrified, and that is why I run so fast through the artillery barrages!"

Frank called out to the man behind the serving bowls and dishes, Laszlo "Laci" Spitzer. Spitzer, unshaven and in his mid-30s, acted as the head "chef" in the building now that everyone was out of their apartments and dwelling underground. He was a miracle worker with beans, among the other very few provisions they had. Spitzer, who had never previously been known as "Laci" until he arrived here where there were far too many men named "Laszlo," successfully fled his forced labor detail on October 15th, when the Arrow Cross took over. He was grumpy, demanding and quick-tempered, a perfect recipe for a cook limited to preparing and serving only beans and bread. No resident dared complain, at least not to his face.

"What do you want, Frank," Spitzer shot out. "Time to change your diaper again?"

"You and Kohn here – you know, the one who *didn't* run from his forced labor and actually attempted to disarm Nazis—"

"That's quite enough, Frank," Spitzer seethed. He ladled another serving of beans on to Dr. Zahler's plate, who quickly put his head down and walked straight back to the cramped eating area where his wife, daughter and granddaughter already sat. He moved much more slowly in his old age, but he was wise enough to know when it wasn't "a good time" to loiter.

"Alright," Frank conceded. "It's time for you to go along with Kohn here to bring what flour we have and take it to Schlederer Bakery. You can take the flour in these sacks here; just sling them over your shoulders. At present, we don't have the wagon, so you'll have to get it there to bring back the bread they'll give you in return. I'll take over here in your absence. I wouldn't expect you to be too long. It's not so far, right? Half an hour there?"

Spitzer set down the ladle and wiped his hands on his apron. The cooking and serving areas were far too dark and dirty for his liking, but then, he didn't like much of anything. "Don't screw it up, Frank. You have my weapon?"

Frank reached into his pocket and produced a pistol. Spitzer took it, inspected it, and inserted it behind his belt on his back side. "Kohn here have one too? A weapon?"

"Of course," Kohn replied.

Spitzer sneered.

Schlederer Bakery was on Kiraly Street. For as long as this building was "protected" by order of the Ministry of Interior, Spitzer was able to produce the necessary paperwork to get a decent allocation of bread from there in exchange for their flour. In this way, they were also able to secure the flour. As such, the residents of 1 Zichy Jeno were able to get their hands on some kind of food, which was far more than anyone in either ghetto was afforded. The bakery was, at this point, the nearest Arrow Cross baker. Lately, the city's flour supply had diminished to the point the bakery was mixing what it was given with god knows what. Potato? Rice? Who knew?

To get there, they would have to cross the Liszt Ferenc Square. Under normal circumstances, the Square would be a busy area, filled with restaurants, shops and revelers. These were not normal circumstances, owing more to the siege and attending shells, artillery and bullets than to the fact almost all Budapest Jews were compressed under desperate circumstances inside the ghetto. The Square also happened to be one of the main areas where Kohn and others from the building had been bringing dead bodies from the hospital. They were stacked in plain view, for all to see, frozen as they were on frozen pavement. It was already a ghastly sight.

It was now dark outside, and bitterly cold. A soft snow was beginning to fall, but it was too cold for it to accumulate with any significance. There were distant gunshots but, for the moment, nothing substantial. Kohn had already grown accustomed to the sight of bodies lying frozen on the streets. There were more bodies every passing day. It was the smell that bothered him more. It was unbearable. Blood, death and incremental decay despite being frozen, gunpowder, defecation everywhere….

The two men had nearly crossed the square when a voice called out from behind them. "Spitzer? Laszlo Spitzer?"

Spitzer did not want to, but he quickly turned around. He placed his hand beneath his coat and to his back side.

"Why, it *is* you," beamed a short man wearing an Arrow Cross beret, but nothing else obviously identifying himself as Arrow Cross. "You, my old friend, are a Jew, if I'm not mistaken." The man became more excited. "Why are you wearing the Arrow Cross emblem --and you are without your yellow star," he declared. "I am arresting you, and this man beside you! Time to take you to—"

Before the man could complete his sentence, Spitzer pulled out his pistol and, in seemingly one continuous move, shot him in the face. The man's head practically exploded before their eyes.

"My God," Kohn exclaimed, breathless. His heart pounded violently to be freed from his chest. His ears rang loudly. The smoke from the pistol seemed to freeze where they stood, refusing to dissipate.

Spitzer looked quickly around. There was hardly a soul to be seen. Two or three men were on the opposite side of the square, but perhaps on account of these times, they ran away, rather than toward the gunshot. Spitzer set his sack of flour down.

"What was this man doing out, all alone," Kohn asked, trying to fill the void of the immediate silence.

"Doesn't matter. Quick, help me drag him over beside that shop. Do you have a pen, by chance?"

Kohn always carried with him a pen on these "missions," because he had to sign for what he received or gave. As Spitzer approached the window of a restaurant now closed, he stripped off an Arrow Cross propaganda poster, tape still intact. On the paper, he used Kohn's pen and wrote the following lie: "This is the fate of Jews who hide their identity." He taped the amended poster to the body of the man and propped up what was left of him against the façade.

Kohn learned that the dead man was a former classmate of Spitzer's. Stringing more words together than Kohn had ever previously heard from him in total, Spitzer explained that they needed to put a sign like this on "this dead Christian. Otherwise, if the Arrow Cross ever figures out his identity, they might come hunting for us: for Jews not in the ghetto. He obviously was not killed by artillery or a shell, and the Red Army is not yet on these streets, so they would suspect Jews like us are on the loose. It could only get worse for us."

Kohn was not sure how anyone could possibly figure out this man's identity. His head was practically blown apart. Plus, even if he was wearing nothing else distinctly Arrow Cross, wouldn't the lie become exposed once someone pulled down the man's trousers and discovered he was not circumcised? This was how the Nazis and Arrow Cross discovered which males were Jews, since Jewish men were typically circumcised, but not gentiles. Even so, Kohn said nothing.

The two men continued silently on their increasingly frigid journey to Schlederer's Bakery. Kohn, who tried to pride himself in believing how much tougher and hardened he had become to living, dying and all that lay in between, was stunned. Worse, he wondered what he would have done if the situation were reversed, or if he had been alone. Could he have killed someone so instantaneously like that? Would he have been … *fearless* to do what was needed without even thinking about it?

***

Their journey was far from over. Before Spitzer and Kohn had even reached the bakery, they heard rata planes overhead and witnessed and heard relentless rounds of shelling. The Red Army seemed to focus its sights on a wide area at or near the enormous Parliament building. This majestic, white brick, gothic-style building stands beside the Danube on the Pest side, in between the Margit and Szechenyi Bridges. The men had already experienced more than they had bargained for tonight. Nevertheless, they agreed to take in the spectacle of whatever the damage was there. They both knew that the Margit Bridge had already been partially blown up in a tragic accident in early November, well before the siege had begun. The Parliament building, normally illuminated spectacularly at night, appeared from their relatively short distance away to be alight now only in small pockets of flame.

Like moths drawn to the light, Kohn and Spitzer detoured toward the building. Their pace was slightly slowed. In part, this was because they walked with more trepidation and less purpose than on their way to the bakery. In addition, this time they were towing the wagon loaned to them at the bakery to transport the bread and flour back "home." Suddenly, Kohn saw a shadow move beside the locked gate to a building's courtyard, and Spitzer heard a soft voice, like a whimper, in the same direction. They both froze and turned to see a man, in his 30s, and pretty, young woman, maybe 20, huddled together on the pavement for warmth. They were shivering, almost violently. They were both wearing only underwear.

"You there," Kohn called cautiously.

The half-naked, freezing couple recoiled in terror. Seemingly fixated on the green, white and red Arrow Cross emblems that Laszlo Frank had affixed to Kohn's and Spitzer's coats for these "errands," the pair drew even closer together. They were the most terrified-looking people either man had ever seen.

"Hey," Spitzer intervened, stepping closer. "We are not Arrow Cross. We are Jews. Who are you? What are you—"

"Oh my God! Alfonzo," Kohn uttered in disbelief. "Alfonzo, the famous comedian and actor in all of Hungary, is that you?"

The freezing man, whose huge eyes looked as frightened and sad as an abused pet, dared to turn his attention to Kohn. It was difficult to tell if he nodded, he was shivering so hard.

"Yes," the girl managed to say. "This is Alfonzo."

Kohn immediately took off his coat and gently draped it over the shoulders of the girl. Her skin was red from the cold. Spitzer, following Kohn's lead, did the same, placing his over Alfonzo. Noticing that Alfonzo was so cold he could not even raise his arms to properly position the coat, Spitzer helped him.

"Alfonzo! I can't believe it," Kohn continued. "If my parents were here to know that I was meeting you…. We just saw you perform last … when was it? It must have been last February, before the Nazis came in. Oh my God, has it been nearly a year?"

"Enough blabbering, Kohn," Spitzer returned to character. "Can't you see we need to get them back with us?"

"Where," asked the girl suddenly, still frightened. "We can't go back to the international ghetto. We can't. No, please…."

"No, no. We are members of a Jewish hospital in the 6th District," Spitzer explained. Despite the girl's undress and obvious beauty, Kohn couldn't take his eyes off Alfonzo, a hero to him and so many elite citizens of Budapest fortunate enough to have witnessed his already legendary performances. Spitzer continued. "We have both Swiss and, yes, Arrow Cross protection … kind of. It's complicated but take my word for it. That is why we have these coats. We are Jews and, as far as I know, it is far safer to come with us than to go to the big ghetto."

The girl looked at Alfonzo, who must have nodded in the affirmative. "Yes, thank you. We will come with you." Securing Kohn's coat more securely around her, she stood up. "I am Hanna, one of … well, Alfonzo's lone assistant now. And this, you know, is 'Alfonzo,' Jozsef Markstein." Alfonzo still did not look into their eyes.

It was now late at night. Kohn and Spitzer had been away far beyond Frank's expectations, and they were out past curfew. This was as much a crime as being Jewish. Given the circumstances, and the facts that Alfonzo and Hanna were barefoot and now Kohn and Spitzer were without their coats, they were all freezing cold. Spitzer told Kohn there was no way they should cross the Square again, so they took side streets and hoped for the best. The wagon made noise, so they sped as fast as they possibly could, playing a veritable game of hide and seek between shadows and light. Luck was in their favor, and they saw no one near enough on the streets until they finally arrived at the entry door to 1 Zichy Jeno.

"Kohn! Mr. Spitzer," called out Robert, who had just returned himself from picking up medical supplies for the first time. He squinted. "Who is this … oh my god! Alfonzo? The famous Alfonzo?"

The police guard opened the door, then stepped in front of Robert to help usher in the visibly distressed Spitzer, Kohn and their guests. Robert's jaw hung open as he clung to the package of medical supplies. Seeing

Robert's awe, the slightly older Kohn, shivering like the rest of them, managed a smile to Robert. "I know," he whispered excitedly. "Can you believe it's him? And this is his ... one of his ... his associate, Hanna."

"Nice to meet you," she almost cried, cold as she was.

"I am Holczer. Robert Holczer. Let me help you inside." He was simultaneously star struck and in love.

***

In the basement, after some time and under the supervision of the medical staff, Alfonzo and Hanna regained color and a degree of life. Their feet had likely incurred a mild case of frostbite, however, so they would need to remain bedridden and under care for a while. Nurses needed to clear the area of residents, so excited and curious to see the great Alfonzo in their presence. Robert and Kohn were permitted to stay; Kohn to be examined with Spitzer for exposure to the cold, and Robert, because he overstated his role in delivering the new patients. Kohn did not object, and Spitzer, once cleared, returned to his "kitchen" before contemplating sleep. It had been a hell of a day. And night.

In the soft dark of the basement, to no one in particular, Alfonzo finally began to speak. He spoke gently, as if reading a story to a child. If the rest of his body had thawed, it appeared that his eyes had not. They seemed frozen with the same look of terror he wore when Kohn and Spitzer discovered him. When he began, Hanna leaned over from her bed beside him and placed her right hand on his shoulder.

"We were in the 'international ghetto.' A Swiss-protected house. Me, Hanna and ... and my other assistant, Nora. She is -- she was -- just 17, younger than Hanna here," Alfonzo began before cutting himself short. His eyes still did not seem to rest on anyone or anything in particular. "We had heard, of course, that the Arrow Cross wanted to move everyone to the ordinary ghetto. It was so bad, so crowded. We were so hungry already that it made no difference to us. How could it be any worse over there," he almost smiled, as if seeing something comic.

"Yes, we had also heard about atrocities by the river. That they would take Jews there and shoot them. But, I don't know, we thought we were 'protected.' We didn't really believe it, you know? Well, what do you know? What did we know," he almost finally cried. "A priest – what did they say his name was? Yes, 'Father Kun.' A priest," Alfonzo shouted suddenly. Calming himself, he continued. "So, they told us to get in a line. 'You are going to the big ghetto,' they said. But I know this city. We were not going to the 7ᵗʰ District; to the ghetto. Instead, there we were. By the bank of the Danube. 'Take off your clothes,' they yelled, guns waving in the air...."

Hanna now hobbled over a couple of short steps and sat beside him on his bed. Alfonzo remained in his bed, but his whole upper torso was suddenly leaning forward. He quickly surveyed the dark of the room as if finally aware of his surroundings. *He was no longer by the river.* He leaned back.

Robert began shivering himself. It was cold in the basement, but he was not shivering from the cold.

"So, the clothes came off. The shoes came off. They made two lines. Took Nora from Hanna and me and forced her down with … maybe there were 20 people made to kneel. Our group, Hanna and me, were next. We stood behind, maybe at the back of the cobblestones. Not far. One or two men kept their guns on us so we wouldn't run. But why would I run," his voice suddenly cracked. "On the other side of the Danube there was Buda; the castle," he digressed. "We could hear gunshots over there, but there it was. Beautiful…. Nora, our Nora was right there, kneeling. She had no clothes…." Alfonzo was now crying. A nurse, crying, gave Hanna a tissue, because she too was crying. Hanna gave hers straight to Alfonzo, but he refused it. There were so many tears. Robert knew them far too well. His mother…. He looked down at the ground.

"Then this 'Father Kun' steps out. He had a gun himself, with an Arrow Cross armband, wearing a long cassock," Alfonzo reported without irony. "He yells out, 'this is for the Holy Father; this is what you Jews get! I call down --' What did he say, Hanna? Oh yes, I remember: 'I call down fire and damnation on everything that is Jewish!' The Arrow Cross men with Kun raise their guns and point them. I'm looking straight at Nora. Nora turns around to look at us – Hanna and me. She mouths softly, 'goodbye, sweet life.' She was smiling. Her shoes were right behind...." Through tears that now evolved into near convulsions, Alfonso concluded: "Right then, Kun commands: 'In the name of Christ, fire!'"

Hanna, seeing there was no way Alfonso could continue, broke the silence surrounding the collective tears. "They all fell," she sobbed. "Into the river. They had to kick some over so they fell down. They kicked shoes also into the river. Some remained – the shoes, not the..... They ordered us to take their places. We did. People wailed -- a couple tried to fight but they were shot instantly. Alfonzo and I, we were ... paralyzed by despair. Nora...." Hanna seemed to return from some dark universe. "That's when the Soviet planes came and started shooting everywhere. Everyone ran. The Arrow Cross ran for cover. And we ran away. That's when the two men found us; brought us here."

No one listening could move. No one could breathe. All at once, it seemed everyone around Robert was crying. He, too, was crying. Nora's final words, "Goodbye, sweet life...." He was crying, for everything.

17

Ode (Silence for the dead)

18

Through the Open Door

"Under normal circumstances, I would say it doesn't make sense," Jeretzian explained in a tone of resignation. "Would it help us get food if I pounded my fist on the table?" He pounded his fist on the table of the makeshift office of the makeshift hospital.

The shelling, almost constant the past three days, had taken an enormous emotional and physical toll on everyone, Jeretzian included. The food supply was running so low that they were no longer above sending their couriers to scavenge outside in the dark. The closest Arrow Cross bakery, Schlederer, had become far too dangerous to safely get to and back, and the International Red Cross' and Office of Public Welfare's food supplies were just as dangerous to reach. There were enough beans to last another week, maybe two if they further minimized the rations. However, with over 100 patients currently in their care, and more coming in every day, they needed help. More shells had hit the upper floors of 1 Zichy Jeno and neighboring buildings. Laszlo Nagy, Jeretzian's longtime friend and business colleague, had just informed Jeretzian that Jeretzian's apartment on Nagymezo utca had been destroyed. Now, together with Laszlo Frank, the three men were trying to plot the course ahead. Though each day presented so many unexpected situations, crises, and, only on occasion, glimmers of hope, Jeretzian realized early on that the best course was to focus on the day at hand, one at a time.

"I seriously doubt it," offered Frank, without humor. "I don't know. How much longer can the siege last? We hear gunshots nearby now, not just shells or artillery. The Red Army must be close, maybe even in our district."

"Yet still the Arrow Cross is intent on killing the Jews … getting them all into the ghetto so they can die, one way or another." Jeretzian kneeled at the desk in frustration, pushing his two hands through his slicked dark hair.

"Have you heard anything from that Merse?" interjected Nagy. "The one who came here a few days ago…?"

"Nothing. But it might not be Merse we hear from," Jeretzian looked up at the two Laszlos. "A knock or – hell, they don't need to knock. The Arrow Cross could come at any moment and declare our protection void," he paused. "Again, what sense does that make, the hell if I know! They could kill us all, and one hour later the siege is over; the Soviets come to liberate Budapest. Hurray Arrow Cross! Hurray Hungary, are you happy now?"

Frank and Nagy looked at each other. Neither of them dared to initiate the question they knew must also weigh heavily on Jeretzian's mind. Assuming they all survive to see the Soviet liberation, how would the Soviets treat Jeretzian, let alone the rest of the house? Jeretzian was wearing the Arrow Cross uniform. He may not technically be Arrow Cross, but there are numerous papers to the contrary. Numerous witnesses. No, they would save that question for another day.

"Well," Frank dared, "we are still doing okay in terms of medical supplies. Apart from the anesthesia, of course. We have been out of, or too low on that for a while now. How those doctors … those patients…. Anyway, our couriers have been successful in getting to and from our suppliers for some medicine. The food, we'll just keep having to take chances … hope for the best. One idea I had was, there is a baker on O utca – closer by. If that one is still baking, couldn't we reach that bakery by going underground; through the air defense emergency exits from one basement to another?"

"Hmm, that might be possible," Nagy considered. "Let me take care of that and see. Since I, a non-Jew like Jeretzian, can still travel more freely outside than any Jew, I will see if that bakery will take our flour and bake it. If so, I'll take what we have there."

"It's the morale I worry about, too," Jeretzian stated coldly, having moved on from the topic of food and supplies. "The sounds, the pounding, the fear, the losses…." He stopped himself, turned, and walked over to the window.

Through the blinds of the window still miraculously unbroken, Jeretzian saw a young woman in a long overcoat suddenly collapse in front of the police guard in front of the house. Jeretzian turned again and hurried past the two Laszlos to run outside. They followed, oblivious to what he had seen.

"What is it," he demanded to the guard. Then to the woman, "Are you hurt?" he cried.

Weakly, and in apparent distress, the young woman pointed to her belly. "Baby," she managed. "I'm pregnant. Help?"

Without words, the guard held open the door as the three men carefully helped the woman up. They carried her carefully into the basement. Jeretzian called past the entry nurse on duty, coincidentally Dr. Stricker's wife. "Dr. Stricker, Dr. Stricker, we need you! We have a baby to deliver!"

All heads within earshot of Jeretzian's shouts turned. This was the first ray of light any of them had seen in too long, the prospective birth of a child!

Alfonzo, the famous, beloved comedian whose condition was slowly improving in the days since his arrival, was trying to put his comedic talents to use. He was working as an orderly in the hospital, cracking jokes and trying to make light of the traumas with which he too was sickeningly familiar. What the hospital lacked in anesthesia, they made up for with the prodigiously talented, human anesthetic, Alfonzo. He came beside Jeretzian and this woman while Dr. Stricker performed his own magic.

The woman, Marina, who was not a Jew, was the wife of an Arrow

Cross officer. She did not know where he was, or even if he was alive. She had not seen him since the first day of the siege. She looked everywhere, but no one could tell her anything. She was staying with her mother for the past few weeks, but, starving as they were, her already frail mother had died. Her water broke earlier today, and she went out, desperate to find someone to help. Someone pointed toward 1 Zichy Jeno, "the Jewish Arrow Cross hospital," and so she made it here, barely.

"Marina, Marina, how lovely 'tis to see ya," began Alfonzo, dancing beside her bed in between the contractions that were becoming more frequent. "All the boys in Budapest, what they wouldn't give to kiss ya. Marina, Marina, don't ya worry, your sweet baby shall defend ya!"

Jeretzian and the others laughed. Soon after, a beautiful boy was born. Marina, desperate to honor her Christian upbringing, looked and asked if anyone was Christian. Dr. Stricker and the crowd around them looked at each other, unaware why she was asking. "My husband is gone," she explained, caressing her baby boy's chubby cheek. "He needs a godfather."

Everyone looked to Jeretzian at once.

"Uh, me. I'm Armenian – Christian. I would be honored, if you'll allow me…."

"Yes, you then," she exclaimed, her warm smile wholly masking the pain her face had worn over the past hour and a half. "Will you be my boy's godfather?"

"I would be honored," Jeretzian beamed. "What will you call him?"

"What is your name?" she asked.

"Jeretzian, Ara Gyorgy."

"Gyorgy is his name, then. Gyorgy Kristos – my father's name – Horvath."

***

"Hey, you … Holczer, isn't it?" called Hanna, Alfonzo's young assistant. "What on earth are you doing with that? Is that a … oh God, an arm?"

154

Robert turned around suddenly. He wasn't used to conversation while transporting limbs from the basement to the area in the courtyard dedicated for amputated parts. Once he saw who it was, he stopped and smiled. "Oh, you mean this arm," he waved it to Hanna, smiling childishly.

Hanna gasped.

"I'm sorry. You never really get used to it, what I'm doing. But," Robert looked up at the taller, pretty girl with almost auburn hair, "If I don't make jokes about it, I'll lose my mind."

Hanna took two steps toward him, toward the smaller, darker basement stairwell that led out to part of the interior courtyard area. "Show me what you're doing then, will you?" Though Hanna was maybe five years older than Robert, she sounded and looked like a little girl at this moment. She was wearing an oversized gray sweater and baggy pants, as well as a pair of decent, brown shoes donated by one of the families in the house. Like Alfonzo, she was doing much better each day, trying to assert herself to feel useful and reciprocate the kindness shown to her. She followed Robert up the dark stairs toward the light.

Once outside, the brightness blinded the two of them. Not because of the sun, but because of the snow. There must have been five inches on the ground, and the snow was still falling. It was cold, but not substantially colder than the basement.

"So, how's that working out for you — trying not to lose your mind?" Hanna asked, intent to make footprints in the snow apart from where Robert walked ahead. The snow easily surpassed the height of her shoes, but it was good to be up from the basement. The small courtyard in which they stood was more of a landing or facilities area than a proper courtyard. It opened up to the wider, proper courtyard. Even so, it gave Hanna her first glimpse of the interior apartments, the ones that faced the courtyard. There were four floors from the first, with common balconies facing inward. She could not see any of the reported damage to the building from this view.

"How's that working out for me?" Robert repeated. "Terrible, actually.

I *am* losing my mind. The bombs, the darkness, the beans…. But, who am I to complain? I'm sorry … considering what you experienced, I suppose I must be grateful."

"Thank you, Robert. But you are entitled to complain. Everyone here has surely lost so much already, I'm quite sure you are no different. I don't know how much longer this will last, but it can't be long, right?"

"Don't ask me," Robert laughed. "My uncles and aunts are sick of me asking, 'when will this end, when will it be over, will my father ever come back?' I don't know, Hanna. I have lost all perspective on time. I don't know if I am more sad than angry that it – time, my father, my father's father and my mother's family, your friend Nora, everyone – has been stolen from me; from all of us. I mean, time never stops, right? But I resent everything happening *to* me; *to* us … and I don't have any say in the matter. I hate it!" Robert turned back to look at Hanna, who was stunned again as she watched Robert using his hands to push away a layer of snow. Beneath the snow there were rows of what must have been close to 100 body limbs. She couldn't believe her eyes.

"What will happen," Hanna asked, eyes wide open. "Why do they want to keep these … these body parts here?"

"I think they just needed a place to put them so they are out of view of everyone downstairs," Robert explained, looking up. "Dr. Stricker and the others are saving a lot of lives in this way even though they barely have the necessary instruments to do so." He placed the arm he brought up onto the top of a stack of other arms and then stood upright.

Hanna finally took her eyes off the pile and diverted her attention to the snow, beautiful despite the surroundings and circumstances. First, she cupped her hands to try and catch the snow, but then gave up on the endeavor and outstretched her tongue. She was smiling, and Robert was enamored with her. She had such a calm, easygoing sense about her. He didn't feel shy, as he normally did.

"How I wish we could walk outside. Safely, and as far as we could go until we became tired. Better yet, I miss my bike," Robert remembered. "What do you miss most, Hanna? I mean," he quickly clarified, "other than people, friends or family that may be gone." His mood suddenly turned sullen again.

"Oh, Robert," she said, perceiving his mood turn. "I miss my bedroom. My books, my childhood dolls…." She too became sad. "I also miss university – that's what I was doing, going to university and working with Alfonso to help make ends meet. How about you, how old are you, anyway?"

"Come on," he changed the subject. "We're wasting time," he smiled. "We'd better get back inside. There are some more … parts I need to bring out here. You can help me if you'd…." Coming out of the light and back onto the stairs leading down, Robert's attention was drawn immediately to a small, round object on the third stone step down. Covered by the building itself, there was no more than a slight dusting of snow on these stairs. He bent down and lifted the object up.

"What is it?" Hanna asked, behind him.

Robert turned and showed it to her. It was a marble. It was blue in some places, white in others and transparent in the absence of these colors. It looked like … a different world.

"How did that get here?" she wondered. "Is it yours?"

Dreamily, he slowly twirled the marble around in his fingers, holding it back toward Hanna; back toward the light. A distant memory reverberated in his head. *This one won't escape me down the gutter*, he smirked. "I have no idea at all, sweet Hanna. None at all…." He stuffed the marble inside his pocket.

***

When they opened the door to enter the basement, there was a large commotion at the opposite end. There, by the main entry door to the underground hospital were several men in Arrow Cross uniforms.

"Come on," Robert urged Hanna forward, through the sea of compressed mattresses, blankets, and scattered people trying to nap or just close their eyes for a while. Underground, day was irrelevant to night for purposes of the dark. People took turns working in shifts of about six hours at a time, though most never had any idea what time of day or night it was. There were just the sounds of shelling, trying to fight fear, desperation, and boredom by keeping busy and wondering whom or what would come through the hospital's open doors hour by hour. Robert reached for and twirled the marble inside his pocket. The two of them meandered toward the scene unfolding.

To Robert's surprise and their great relief, it was calm. Rather than the end --another roundup to the ghetto, or worse, a march to the Danube, there was an Arrow Cross commander and three associates conversing respectfully with Jeretzian and two doctors, one of them Dr. Zahler. Beside them on the ground there were stretchers on which five wounded Arrow Cross men lay. Two of them were unconscious, all of them bloody. Suddenly, Robert did a double take and more closely approached one of the Arrow Cross men; one of the men who was unconscious.

"You must be kidding me … oh my God," Robert exclaimed softly. He looked like he had seen a ghost. He twirled the planet marble rapidly now between two fingers in his right pocket.

"What is it, Robert?" asked Hanna.

Just then, seeing Robert and Hanna approach one of the unconscious men, Dr. Zahler, curious, looked more carefully. He covered his mouth with his right hand. His eyes, wide as globes, betrayed his silence. By now, Jeretzian looked over the shoulder of the Arrow Cross commander and back. He suddenly looked again. Lying on the ground unconscious and bloody was the man he saw that first day on Margit Bridge.

What did he say his name was? 'Ivan the Terrible' -- the man who wanted to throw the old Jewish man he had been beating into the Danube, Jeretzian remembered to himself.

Dr. Zahler suddenly looked at Robert, who looked up at Dr. Zahler. Robert was correct. "Hanna," Robert turned back to her, "this man came into our building within the first few days after the 15th of October and took away Dr. Zahler's mother and 15 or 20 other elderly people. They have never come back. This is—"

"Ivan the Terrible," Dr. Zahler finished, almost whispering. He slowly seated himself on the edge of a cot to try and steady himself.

"Is there a problem, Jeretzian?" asked the commanding officer.

"What? No, I'm sorry, of course not. You there," Jeretzian suddenly called to Robert. "Can you make yourself useful and help get these men into open surgery beds?"

"Yes, but what if…?"

"I will help," Dr. Zahler interceded. "And Hanna, can you go with these nurses and clear the way, help them set up the intake and assessments?" Hanna touched Robert's shoulder, then dutifully followed their lead.

"So, as I was saying, Mr. Jeretzian, the Red Army front is nearby, in this district," continued the commander. "The fighting is very close. My unit, over 40 Arrow Cross militants, is fighting to hold off the Soviets at the Szittya Mozi theatre. The Soviets are at Terez Korut, and we are awaiting reinforcements."

"What of the Nazis' 'miracle weapon' I keep hearing of?" Jeretzian scratched his chin.

The commander was no older than Jeretzian, in his mid-20s, but shorter by a few inches and with a substantial gut. He coughed. "Well," he pulled out a kerchief and wiped his lips, "we're still waiting for that, too." He changed the subject. "So, as you can see, we are incurring casualties. I assure you, so are the Soviets! Anyway, if you could help treat our wounded, we would sure appreciate it. There are too few hospitals now that are not destroyed, and yours is the closest."

Jeretzian considered whether to try to stretch this stroke of good fortune. He went for it. "Of course, Commander. This is the reason we are here. Only … with so many more patients and our non-stop operations, we are running short on food," he dared imply.

"And so … you'd like me to get you more food," the Commander smiled, "In exchange for treating our wounded…. And you say you're not Jewish? Ah, never mind. Certainly, I will see to it that you get what you need."

Jeretzian shook the commander's hand. "Persevere," he smiled. "Persevere."

The next day, a dozen baskets of food were delivered to the front door by Arrow Cross couriers. The police guard could barely believe it when he opened the door and called for Jeretzian and Laszlo Frank. The brothers, Paul and Laszlo, were the first to arrive and opened the boxes before bringing them back to Laci Spitzer. Inside, there was coffee, bacon, ham, cheese, fresh bread and, of course, more beans. It was an answer to their prayers, or at least their hopes.

Apart from taking a short nap and running a few brief errands for the doctors and Mr. Frank, Robert had not left the bedside of Ivan the Terrible. Oh, the irony! How he had left that gray, drizzling October day, swearing to the Jews in the courtyard and loud enough so that those in hiding in their apartments could hear: He'd be back "for the rest of you;" the Arrow Cross would be back to "finish you off." And now here he was: lying here, dying here. The doctors had already saved the other four Arrow Cross men who had come in with Ivan. Three had already been released and returned to combat, expressing sincere thanks and appreciation to the Jews who had saved them. The other man who had come in unconscious was now out of the woods but would need to stay under supervision and for recovery for another couple of days in order to fully recover. Ivan's injury, on the other hand, was fatal. Dr. Orban told Robert that this man's bullet was lodged so firmly into his brain there was nothing they could do for him; it was just a matter of hours.

And so, Robert waited. He didn't know why, exactly. His mother, assisting doctors in different rooms, would check on him from time to time, but Robert insisted he wanted to wait out this man's life. Hanna came by sometimes, bringing him some coffee, water and bread. She didn't bother to ask Robert why he wanted to sit there -- she just knew – even if Robert himself couldn't quite explain it. Dr. Zahler, too, must have known, because he walked by regularly in between his rounds to just stare at the comatose man lying beneath him.

The first time he came by, Dr. Zahler put his hand on Robert's shoulder and said defiantly: "He's gotten what he deserves, young man."

Robert nodded. Alive, powerful … a predator and murderer of Jews and then … nothing. Just an anti-Semite lying on a bed in a hospital manned by Jews…. "Oh, the irony," Robert smiled.

When Ivan the Terrible finally took his last breath, Robert stood up. He folded his chair, brought it over to one of the nurses in the front of the room, and asked, "Where would you like me to set this chair? I am done with it."

On his way back toward his family's section of mattresses, he saw Hanna beside Alfonzo in a patient's room. She looked at him, inquisitively. He winked, clutching his marble between his fingers in his pocket.

19

14 January 1945
Does it Matter?

"Wake up, Robi. Robi, wake up!"

"Apu? Father? Is it really you?" Robert felt his tired, hazel eyes slowly open to see the image of his father smiling tenderly as his father kneeled beside his bed. Robert returned the smile, crossing his face from ear to ear.

"Is today the day, Apu," Robert implored, almost breathlessly. He scooted backwards so he could sit up against the cold stone wall and look into his father's increasingly wizened face, which was still beaming. "Are you really here to finally take us from this godforsaken place somewhere … safe?"

"Not yet, my son. But soon, I promise. But now you must wake up. Szeretlek, Robi. I love you, but you must wake up!"

"Holczer, wake up! I'm not going to ask again. Wake … Up!"

"What? What's going on, wha…?" Robert vigorously rubbed his eyes to try and see through the darkness. When his eyes became sufficiently accustomed to the dark, he saw, to his utter dismay, not one, but two faces, neither of which belonged to his father, and neither of which hosted loving smiles.

"Paul … Laszlo, what…?"

Paul, the younger of the two brothers, was the first to smile, then wink at his older brother. "Hey, Laszlo … of which beautiful girl do you suppose Holczer was just dreaming? Volgyesi's daughter – what's her name? Zahler's granddaughter, Eva? Or was it that comedian Alfonzo's assistant he's always with? Hanna, right?"

"Maybe all three," Laszlo cracked, then suddenly deadpanned. "Listen, kid, sorry to disappoint your fantasy…."

"I wasn't…!" Robert protested halfheartedly.

"Doesn't matter, now get the hell up. And shush … you'll wake everyone else up. At least have the decency to let them sleep while they can." Laszlo seemed to whisper and yell simultaneously.

Paul interrupted. "Jeretzian needs someone to go pick up two light boxes of supplies, and your number's up – it's your turn to go again. No need to wake anyone, just get your sack."

"Where – what time is it? Now?"

"Yes, now," Laszlo blurted. The brothers seemed to continue each others' thoughts as though they were one. And why not, they had survived over 30 days at the Russian front with a Jewish forced labor battalion conscripted by the Nazis, Hungary's ally -- or wasn't it master? The brothers' earlier escape was beyond lucky. Nevertheless, here they were, side by side in the basement of 1 Zichy Jenő Utca, destined to share whatever fate lay ahead for everyone there.

Dangerous or not, certainly Robert would attempt the pickup. He would do anything necessary in order to help keep his mother and 10 other relatives alive in this miserable, but at least for the moment, life-saving place.

"Okay, let me get my things. Where is it – I mean, where do you want me to go to get these supplies? Is it really only 4:00 in the morning?"

"Does it matter, Holczer?" Laszlo impatiently asked. "It's the same place you went the other day, over behind the Opera House. You know the place, right?"

"Yes, it's a few blocks away." Robert paused, listening intently. "Has the shooting stopped at least?" Robert looked over at his sleeping mother in admiration. How he wished he could still be asleep, or, better yet, that it was his father with whom he was now conversing, not Paul and Laszlo. But his father, dream notwithstanding, was gone. He had been in Bor or wherever for, what was it, nearly two years? He hoped the dream was a good omen, a sign they would all be together again "soon…."

"Just go now. Stay in the dark, and along the walls. If you're careful, you'll be fine. It should be routine by now."

"Routine? Seriously? None of this will ever be routine." He was now most definitely awake. "How can you say that, 'routine'? Nothing is ever routine, especially after what just happened with Kohn and Spitzer … finding Alfonzo and Hanna like that? Routine?"

Paul smiled as he patted Robert's arm, then continued. "Holczer, I like you. I'm going to tell you something our father taught us when we were up to no good and scared we might get caught – which was always, right brother?"

"Oh, seriously, Paul?" Laszlo whined as he was surveying all the sleeping bodies around him. "We don't have time for this; it will be dawn too soon."

"Our father gave us advice for a reason, brother. We must share – we honor our father in this way." Paul, whose hand never left Robert's shoulder, finally looked back to Robert. Robert politely waited. "If you act like a dog sniffing around for the best place to piss," he grinned, "You will look like you belong where you are. Does anyone ask why a dog chooses where he pisses? Of course not. No one will ever notice you; you will be part of the background. And if no one notices you, you don't get caught, see?"

"Ah," Robert offered a half smile, "Thanks … again. I'll definitely keep that in mind."

Robert put on his overcoat and cap and deeply inhaled, trying not to wake anyone. He knew there was danger everywhere. Hell, there was danger just existing in Budapest at this time, and if you were a Jew like him, you could multiply that danger ten times. Regardless, he decided to wait to put on his boots so as not to wake anyone until he reached the steps to head outside. Over two hundred steps later, through the darkness and past the bodies of a few hundred sleeping Jews, and then, by the doorway, moaning, whimpering and crying patients in various states of distress, Robert pulled up his collar. He laced his shoes nervously, and slowly opened the door to enter the frozen hell of war-torn Budapest.

It is almost too quiet, Robert thought to himself. *Almost too easy. So far.*

Robert followed the same route he did just two or three nights ago by making two quick right turns out of the building. On that occasion, he was asked to run out with two other couriers and be the first to bring back a horse killed by artillery fire. Food -- especially meat -- was in tremendously high demand, and the competition on the streets for fallen horses was extreme. The horses were there courtesy of Nazi and Hungarian cavalry units. Sadly, there were now far too many frozen horse cadavers in the middle of streets. They did not begin to rival the number of dead humans -- Christians and Jews alike -- but truly, death was everywhere.

Robert's turns led him onto Hajos Utca, to avoid the larger streets on which there would likely be more of those scum of the earth Arrow Cross patrols. If they found him, Robert knew, he would have nothing, no one to save him. His only hope was to avoid detection altogether, and so far, so good.

"A dog looking for the best place to piss," he whispered to himself, smiling again despite the cold. He entered the open gate and found the correct name beside the door buzzers: "Meszos, Viktor." He pressed the buzzer exactly five times, as Laszlo had instructed him. After some seconds, the buzzer in the corridor sounded and Robert was permitted to walk up to the third floor. He did so, taking the marble stairs encased by iron rails there, then knocked.

The voice of a man called out from inside. "Yes?"

"*Ich bin blau,*" Robert said sheepishly, the embarrassing German "secret code" he was instructed to tell Meszos, the man behind the door. The expression technically means, "I am blue," but it is an idiom for "I am drunk." Robert, 15, had never been drunk before. This fact had only added to the laughter of Paul, Laszlo and their third partner, Laszlo Frank when they taught him what to say. Robert thought this whole dialogue was ridiculous, but still he played along, believing it necessary.

The door quickly opened, but only partially. Out came a waft of cigarette smoke. Coughing suddenly, Robert never saw the face of the man whose arm held out two small boxes. "So, are you, young man? *Blau*," he cackled. Robert took them, turning back to try and fit them into the sack slung over his shoulder. The cold seemed to grip him all at once.

"What are they, do you know?" Robert ignored the man's laughter at his expense.

"Does it matter?" asked the voice. "Now get out of here before we're both shot at the Danube, you fool. God bless you and be safe." The door closed, and Robert turned to consider his return route. "Stay sober," Meszos chortled more loudly.

Robert decided to go back the way he came. He felt obligated to put his curiosity to rest and peek inside the two small packages. Looking inside, he discovered that the boxes contained only some gauze, tape and a few vials of pills. *More boring items*, Robert thought. But, as he turned around the corner without looking ahead of him, his heart exploded from his chest in terror.

"Stop, Jew!"

Robert froze in his place. Two Arrow Cross patrol officers, neither of whom could have possibly been more than a year or two older than him, rifles in hands, took rapid steps toward him. Clumsy in their obviously ill-fitting boots, the one with the peach-fuzz moustache was grinning like a cat that had caught its mouse. "You're a filthy Jew, yes? Roland, we've got one, eh?

Robert remained frozen, hoping that his fear wasn't as apparent to them as it really was. He began to shake his head 'no,' when Roland, the younger one, rifle trained at Robert's head, blurted with a mouthful of derision, "Drop your pants!"

These words, these murderous, heated words spewed amidst a cloud of veritable smoke into the Arctic air were a sure sign of ensuing death; *his* death.

Robert knew this because, was it just a week ago, when he learned of his cousin Peter's death under these identical circumstances? Their Aunt Aranka had relayed to the family the devastating news that Peter, at 13 two years younger than Robert, was caught by the Arrow Cross while scavenging for food to bring back to his parents' hiding place at the north end of the city. He was ordered to take off his pants. When Robert asked his aunt why ever someone would utter such an order as this, Aranka explained without hesitation: "It's because Jewish boys, unlike any other European, are circumcised at birth. So, if they see a boy … man, whomever, circumcised, they will know they are a Jew…. When Peter dropped his pants and they saw he was indeed a Jew," she continued, "One swine, scum Arrow Cross man grabbed hold of your cousin while the other pressed his two thumbs into … Peter's eyes, until…." She broke off.

Robert's jaw dropped to the floor while his mother burst into heavy sobs. There had been far too many tears in their lives for as long as he could remember. He hadn't seen Peter in at least a couple of years, but this was appalling.

"I said drop your pants!"

Hesitating, Robert slowly reached for his belt as if in slow motion. He thought of his father and now realized he wasn't afraid to die. Just, he hoped, at least with his pants on. Suddenly, he heard galloping footsteps precede the sight of an older, better-dressed Arrow Cross man as he careened around the corner and shouted, "Hey! I'll take care of this stupid kid! There are maybe half a dozen Jews right on the other side of the Opera House. You go deal with them; I'll handle this one and then join you when I'm through with him. That's an order! Now, go!"

The men lowered their rifles and unquestioningly turned to run in the direction of the Opera House. "How many, did he say," one asked the other.

When he was sure they were out of view, the fair-skinned man turned angrily to Robert, whose hands remained fixed around his belt, perhaps frozen.

"What the hell are you doing out here? Are you stupid? Listen, I'm a Jew posing as an Arrow Cross. There are no Jews down the street, so those two will be back here in a minute. You're really very stupid, aren't you?" He didn't pause for an answer. Robert could almost feel his head nod, 'yes.' Was he dreaming? Already dead?

"All you need to do is stay hidden. Go back to where you came from. In another few weeks this will all be over, and we'll all be free, but if I ever see you out again, I'll personally kill you for the crime of being too stupid, do you hear?" Again, he didn't wait for an answer. He put his right hand on the gun in his belt, but never took his eyes off Robert. "Now here they come. I'm going to kick and hit you a couple of times for show, you understand? –They need to see I've handled this situation. I'll hit you, then you run home as fast as you can -- stop for nothing!"

Instinctively, Robert muttered, "Like a dog looking to piss…."

"What?"

There was a kick or two to the butt and the back of the legs. A hard swing of an arm across the back of Robert's head, but he felt nothing. Finally, he put both of his arms up to cover his head. He asked the man his name, almost doubled over as he was, but all he heard was, "Does it matter? Run, you idiot!"

Robert ran as fast as he could. He wished he had fastened his belt buckle so that it would stop clanging annoyingly. He wished he could see what happened when the other two men returned. He wished he could have learned the name of the fair-skinned "Arrow Cross" Jew who saved his life so that he could remember, so he could tell this story properly. But mostly, he wished for … his father.

When he opened the door to 1 Zichy Jeno and ran down the perpetually dark basement to where his family was now readying themselves for another day, his mother and Aunt Aranka demanded in unison, "Where the Hell have you been?" His Aunt's voice drowned out that of his mother, of course.

Out came tears Robert didn't recognize to be his own. So many tears, so many tears. Cursed tears. "Where is *Apu* … When will this be over … I didn't even get the man's name," Robert blubbered in between the tears of a child he no longer recognized.

20

Darkness Before Dawn

"Ich bin blau! Ich bin blau!" Robert exclaimed to brothers Paul and Laszlo. "Are you happy now … I'm not *blau* -- drunk – I'm 15, but I may as well be!" He was still hysterical, eyes now creased with dried tears. He had just returned from his closest encounter with his death, ordered to take down his pants by Arrow Cross thugs bent on murdering Jews, until the blond Arrow Cross man ordered them away. His body was aching from the kicks and hits the blond man administered to disguise the fact he was apparently saving him. Robert's mother sat up beside him at the edge of his mattress. Aranka was asked to assist as a nurse up in the surgery, so she needed to go there.

"I'm – we're so sorry but we are so relieved you are back, Holczer," Paul offered as earnestly as possible.

"Here are your damn supplies!" Robert threw the packages at the brothers.

Despite their attempts of propriety, the brothers turned to each other and couldn't help but laugh. Robert's mother almost scowled at them.

"Ich bin blau…," Paul managed. "Holczer … Robert's mother – I'm sorry, Madam, what is your name?"

"Cornelia," she offered, despite a furrowed brow.

"Pleasure to meet you, Madam. I assume you both know the Danube, yes?"

They both nodded, suspiciously. Robert's grandmother and the other family members leaned forward to listen. They were now, make no mistake, awake, even though the hour had not yet reached 5:00.

"Have you ever seen the Danube look *blau* ... blue? Ever?" Paul waited and saw them answer 'no' by slow shakes of their head.

Paul's brother Laszlo rolled his eyes. "Oh, brother!"

Paul continued. "Well, of course not. It's not *blau* – it's never *blau*. It's green. It's even brown sometimes, but I've never seen it *blau*. So then why, one might ask, did Mr. Johann Strauss call one of the most famous compositions of all time, *"Blue* Danube – *An der schonen blauen Donau,* By the Beautiful Blue Danube?"

Robert, still upset about his near death experience, looked, puzzled, to his mother and grandmother. They were both, however, becoming amused. Perhaps they knew the punch line to this joke, or riddle, or whatever it was. "Why, then, Paul?" he finally asked. His mother smiled; her mouth opening. It was wonderful to see her smile, even at his own expense.

"Because Strauss was a drunk, *blau!*" he shouted. If anyone around was still sleeping, they were now awake. "The Danube, friends, is not blue ... unless you are drunk! He was drunk and became sick into the Danube ... 'blue' Danube, you get it?"

Robert's mother was belly laughing together with her mother-in-law and other relatives by marriage. They were all she had left, of course. Hanna, having been awakened and briefed about Robert's adventure by brother Laszlo, came over. She saw everyone but Robert laughing. He was still fighting it, still not wanting to let the brothers or anyone else off the hook for his recent trauma. When he saw Hanna -- her smile, he too finally burst out laughing. It was the first time he had laughed – any of them had laughed -- like that in as long as he could remember. He wasn't even sure why he – they -- were laughing like this. But it seemed like the right thing, the necessary thing to do. Hanna smiled even wider, so tenderly.

Amidst all the laughter in the sleeping area, there suddenly arose yet another great commotion. Robert and the others strained their eyes to see what was occurring, and there they were: Arrow Cross militiamen armed with machine guns surrounding Jeretzian. These were not the same Arrow Cross people who had been steadily sending their wounded to this hospital for the past week and a half, and there was nothing cordial or even transactional about the nature of their conversation. "How could this be?" Robert thought aloud. "It just is," Paul replied without expression.

"The fighting must be no more than two or three blocks away, yet still they come for us?" Robert turned, first to his mother, then to Hanna. There were no words left to say.

"You all remain here," Paul told them. He and Laszlo then walked briskly forward through and around the mattresses and countless people in relative states of wakefulness and dread, again.

***

"I am Hidasi, Law Enforcement Commissioner of Budapest," declared a man who, by uniform insignias and tone clearly held the highest rank of any previous visitor to 1 Zichy Jeno. He was speaking directly to Jeretzian, whom Hidasi and his men had just awakened at gunpoint. Jeretzian now stood, not far from his impromptu command desk in the front of the basement. He was surrounded. "I am holding a report that indicates you are harboring 400 Jews here. We will now inspect the premises to verify the report. If this is true," Hidasi smirked, before becoming serious, "Everyone here is to be executed on the spot."

Jeretzian, cobwebs of sleep so abruptly eradicated, searched for what to say. He realized that this visit must be connected to the visit of Merse, maybe a week before. Because they had heard nothing, he dared to assume either Vajna had left Budapest, or maybe Merse had had a change of heart. He couldn't know for certain.

"Certainly, you are aware, Mr. Jeretzian, of the Ministry of Interior's recent decree that all previously granted privileges afforded Jews are null and void," Hidasi continued, almost exasperated waiting for any response from Jeretzian. "The decree is posted at practically every corner outside."

"With respect, sir," Jeretzian finally began, "We don't get outside so often now with the siege closing in; the front so nearby. But yes, of course I know of this decree. However," he paused, reaching into his pocket for a cigarette.

Hidasi suddenly swatted the cigarette from Jeretzian's hand. "You listen to me, Jeretzian," he scowled. "This is not a game; not a drill. We have your building surrounded. Outside, your police guard can confirm that there are 15 Nazi SS troopers and 15 Arrow Cross militiamen, all of them armed with machine guns. They have closed every exit and are prepared to follow my orders. Our search will begin—"

Jeretzian, still struggling to see a clearing through which he could successfully navigate the building's residents on this, their most daunting threat, interjected. "Nazis too? The SS is here? That is the first we've seen them this close."

Hidasi was beyond agitated.

"Listen, sir," Jeretzian began, more calmly as he saw Hidasi's temperament was like a lit fuse. "You say you are here to enforce the Ministry of Interior's decree, but I have the same Ministry's order in my pocket that says that our work here is necessary, indispensable to the war effort. And it is truer than you can know. Why, we have been treating any and everyone that comes through our doors, including Arrow Cross. Do you know the commander of—"

"Enough. I have heard enough," Hidasi declared.

"Please, sir. Be my guest. Please walk through our hospital here, and you decide – is our institute necessary, or are we doing no more than 'harboring Jews,' as you suggest."

Jeretzian stood more erect. For the first time, he realized through the crowd of surrounding Arrow Cross men how many doctors, nurses, and other support staff had been standing nearby to witness this spectacle. He straightened his collar. "Ladies and gentlemen," he called to them, "please, resume your duties; return to your areas and let these good men observe your work. Thank you." The staff, pale as ghosts, did as requested.

Satisfied for the moment, Hidasi likewise ordered his men to permit everyone to do their work. He began instructing them what to note, the counting procedures and so on. At once, there was a spectacular blast outside. The entire building shook, and Jeretzian and many others were jolted, several falling. Dust was everywhere. The blast was quickly followed by a volley of other nearby shells. The sound of bullets and artillery was almost deafening.

"Quickly!" Jeretzian shouted to Frank, Paul and Laszlo, wiping off his uniform as he stood back up. "Get out there; get out our casualty transport personnel and bring in the wounded."

Hidasi, visibly shaken, ordered his men to remain calm. He directed them to hold steady and do as ordered, temporarily putting another man in charge as he followed the hospital personnel upstairs, through the lobby, and out the front door to assess the status of his force outside and to observe what was occurring.

Immediately, the transport personnel brought in one stretcher after another of, in most instances, terribly injured people. Shells had struck so close that some civilians foolish enough to still be in their apartments in neighboring buildings were bombed right out of them. Other people were wounded Arrow Cross and SS soldiers. There were so many.

Hidasi stood beside Jeretzian as he positioned himself near the door to help get the wounded inside to the basement. In an instant, a body fell from almost directly above them, dully thudding against the ground in front of the building. Jeretzian looked up and saw nothing, then, horrified, back to the ground. It was the body of a woman who was a Jewish resident in the house. She must have thrown herself out of one of the upper shattered windows, Jeretzian was stunned to realize. She went up and decided … she could not take it anymore; the shelling, the uncertainty … the Arrow Cross back yet again....

But time inevitably pressed forward, and with it, the casualties and call to action. On one stretcher, a young civilian man was laying there, one leg contorted up beside his head, and the other dangling from the stretcher by no more than a narrow strip of skin. Hidasi convulsed.

Through the dust and smoke came still more wounded, running, crawling, limping on others' shoulders, being carried on stretchers.... From around the corner came Bodor, Theo's vice-super. He was bleeding badly.

Theo emerged, practically in between Jeretzian and Hidasi near the crowded entryway. "Bodor!" he shouted.

Bodor's head was bleeding. He did not look good, limping to the door. He pointed directly behind him, to a man carrying a young girl.

"Dr. Szollosy ... is that you?" Jeretzian asked, moving beside Theo, who was already bringing in Bodor.

"Dr. Szollosy? The former Regent Horthy's personal physician," blurted Hidasi, almost delirious with fear and amazement.

"Help ... help her, my daughter!" Dr. Szollosy cried. He lived nearby, two or three houses down Zichy Jeno. His building was not on the same foundation as 1 Zichy Jeno, and so their basements did not connect. He was bleeding almost all over. In contrast, Jeretzian observed, his daughter's eyes were closed, but he did not see any blood. Perhaps she had just fainted.

"Of course, Doctor, you are most welcome." Jeretzian took the doctor's daughter from his arms and led the way. Limp as she was, she seemed weightless. He still did not see any injury, confirming his suspicion that she must have fainted amidst the shelling. Hidasi, part dutifully and part in awe, took Dr. Szollosy by his right arm.

"Follow me," Jeretzian told Hidasi. He led him back down. Motionless girl in his arms, he called loudly for more people from the sleeping area to come forward and help. Seeing everyone around him already occupied, he set the girl down on an unoccupied cot on the floor. She was beautiful in her youth, not even a teenager. Light brown hair, fair skin. Hidasi led her father, the bloody Dr. Szollosy, forward into another part of the basement, following Theo and the bloody Bodor. Dr. Szollosy, still dazed and seriously wounded, turned back to look for his daughter. Jeretzian saw him and waved. "I have her here, Doctor," he called. "I will bring her to you when you are out of recovery."

Jeretzian turned back to the girl, whose eyes were still closed. He kneeled to feel for her pulse at her wrist. He felt nothing. *Impossible*, he thought, desperately. He reached for her neck, touched her vein. Again, nothing. She was dead. Jeretzian looked around him. Everything was spinning. It was so loud. So impossible. So meaningless. He called for a nearby doctor who was already in the middle of treating two, maybe 10 patients. When he saw Jeretzian's urgency, he came over.

"Doctor," he couldn't even articulate the words to come, "please, I feel no pulse. This is a little girl. I don't see an injury, but I feel nothing. Could –"

The doctor placed his stethoscope over the girl's heart. He listened for breath. He turned the girl over in her cot, looking for any entry wound, scanning bottom to top. First nothing, then nothing still. But there, in the back of her head beneath her gorgeous light hair. There … there was the slightest entry wound. The doctor looked up, holding the girl's gorgeous light hair up so Jeretzian could see. "It must have been the tiniest shell fragment," he said apologetically. "It must have gone straight to her brain … it doesn't take much."

Jeretzian became a ghost.

"I must go, sir. I must go," urged the doctor.

"Yes," he mouthed without sound. Louder, "Of course, I will tell the doctor … her father, Dr. Szollosy."

"Dr. Szollosy … are you serious?"

Jeretzian put his head into his hands until the noise of screams, shouts and yells reminded him where he was, what he needed to do. He blindly reached for a cigarette and lit it, eyes still closed. He heard Hidasi's voice: "Jeretzian, the doctor is in surgery. Where to now?" Finally, Jeretzian looked up to see … Alfonzo!

Alfonzo practically skipped forward and bent down beside another new patient, a wounded Arrow Cross militiaman screaming and in pain. He placed his hand on the man's forehead and started to whisper a joke.

The patient stopped screaming and turned, suddenly, almost grinning, to see who this whisperer was. Alfonzo curtsied and swirled around. He was, quite simply, amazing.

Hidasi, the color now fully drained from his cheeks, pointed. "Is that ... Alfonzo?" he asked no one. "The famous comedian?"

Jeretzian took hold of Hidasi's coat sleeve. "Come, see our work."

Jeretzian led Hidasi, room by room, patient by patient, doctor and nurse one after another for what seemed an eternity. They were forced to step over dying and whimpering wounded men lying on and beside stretchers on the ground. There were so many, and still, the shelling outside continued. It seemed that, at least outside, the end was nearer than ever. One way or another. Jeretzian resisted his urge to ask the burning question he wanted Hidasi to answer: Why was the Arrow Cross still so intent on killing the Jews when they and the Nazis were losing the war? Then again, he didn't know this Hidasi. Maybe he too deluded himself into believing that the Nazis would still unveil their so-called miracle weapon to deliver victory in the 11th hour. Jeretzian knew, almost as impossible as such a scenario was, that a Nazi victory would invariably mean the end of the Jews in all of Europe.

When Hidasi overheard someone ask for Dr. Volgyesi, he interrupted: "Volgyesi? Dr. Ferenc Volgyesi, the famous hypnotist and doctor is also here?" He shook his head. "I can't believe this." Jeretzian led Hidasi upstairs to the first floor to Volgyesi's apartment, which was sustaining more damage. There was Volgyesi with his wife and daughters, gathering some extra towels and cloth to bring downstairs to the hospital. Again starstruck, Hidasi initiated conversation with Dr. Volgyesi, who sent his wife and daughters back downstairs with the additional supplies. While they spoke, Jeretzian finally managed to light another cigarette, the smoking of which he enjoyed more than any recent cigarette. Several minutes later, Hidasi, now armed with a few souvenir books autographed by Dr. Volgyesi, looked back to Jeretzian. "Let's return downstairs, Jeretzian. Call everyone not in the middle of medical care forward, as close to the entry as possible."

Jeretzian, just having begun to feel that he – that the building residents had yet again succeeded in dodging the fate that was befalling too many of the rest of Budapest's Jews, was now unsure what to make of this request. *Was this it?* he wondered. *Is it possible this man has seen all we are doing and still, not enough?*

Jeretzian proceeded. He summoned everyone possible, all the residents of the building, to the front of the basement. The only ones absent to listen were the quite numerous doctors and nurses tending to the wounded.

There was Dr. Zahler, standing proud and upright as ever, lovingly beside his wife, daughter and granddaughter, Eva, the girl with laughing eyes. There was Norbert Kohn, exhausted from one trip after another outside, almost ceaselessly finding, gathering and bringing in the wounded, one after the other. There was Laci Spitzer, apron around his waist and serving spoon dripping beans from his hand, cursing and mumbling at no one, or everyone. Theo, the super who was not a Jew but wouldn't dare leave friends, no matter what. He had his friend, Bodor's blood on his sleeves and pants, but Bodor would survive, and that was all. There was Alfonzo, probing through the crowd for Hanna and then finding her. Their eyes met, and they joined hands. Hanna then turned and beckoned Robert. He closely followed, with his mother and the rest of the family apart from Aranka, who was still assisting a doctor. Robert had just come back inside from the partial courtyard, having had to stack several more amputated limbs. It had been one hell of a day. Again. There they all stood, waiting, wondering.

Hidasi, "Law Enforcement Commissioner of Budapest," stepped forward. Wanting to make sure he was heard by the large basement crowd of over 400 Jews and some non-Jews, he began. "I was sent here today – I'm sorry, this isn't going to work. Jeretzian, can you have someone get me a chair to stand on? I can't see a damn thing – how can everyone possibly see me?" Jeretzian motioned to Laszlo Frank, who reached over by Jeretzian's basement command desk to get, and then hand, Jeretzian the chair. Jeretzian placed it beside Hidasi, who nodded appreciatively while stepping onto it with Jeretzian's assistance. The crowd did not move, nor could a word be heard.

"Thank you for your patience. I was sent here today with orders to find the 400 Jews harbored here and slay them all, along with their leader, Jeretzian. I came here to do so," he paused, seeing nervous eyes steal glances from one another. "I came here to do so … but what I saw and experienced here far surpassed my wildest fantasies.

I would never have thought, and indeed, no one could have imagined such a perfectly operating institution could be set up in the heart of Budapest on such short notice. The work you are performing here is a feat so outstanding that I must laud it, even if I know that it's being done by Jews."

Robert turned to his mother, wide-eyed. It seemed everyone was looking at one another, asking, "Could this be happening? Is this possible?" Several doctors and nurses who were tending patients looked up and came closer to hear.

"From this day forward," Hidasi continued, "your amazing work will be disturbed by no one; I'll personally see to that."

It was as if 400-plus people breathed at once; a collective sigh of relief from so many humans who had almost forgotten what it could be to feel … safe. Safe, so that perhaps they could get back to the business of living their lives; trying to pick up the pieces and … just live.

"Just hold on for a few more days, ladies and gentlemen. One way or another, the end – the beginning is near. The Germans' magic weapon will arrive and set everything straight. And as for the reward for your extraordinary feats and heroism, rest assured, I'll make sure that everyone who is and has been taking part in the great work of this hospital will receive due recognition. I guarantee you that in the new Hungarist State you won't be considered 'Jews,' because if all Jews would be working this heroically and selflessly, then Hungary wouldn't have a Jewish question in the first."

Jeretzian turned to Dr. Zahler and Dr. Volgyesi. They had both been embracing family members like everyone else, but Hidasi's last words caught their attention, causing them to look for, and then at each other. They raised their eyebrows in unison with Jeretzian, then shrugged their shoulders. "What can you do?" they asked each other without asking.

Hidasi finally stepped down from his chair, amidst rounds of applause and exhilaration. The celebration, in the basement "hospital" of a house still enveloped by the Red Army's siege, then swelled even greater. To Jeretzian's wonder and awe, Hidasi began to shake the hands, one by one, of every doctor, nurse and support personnel he could find. After a long while of hand shaking and reciprocal appreciation, Hidasi finally arrived to Jeretzian. Jeretzian had been waiting in the front, by his command desk, assessing the situation of the continuously incoming wounded. He had never been more exhausted in his life. Of course, he could have said this about every day since the 15th of October 1944.

"Mr. Jeretzian," Hidasi exhaled, "This has been quite something, I must say. I assure you that I will convey the news of your role in organizing this hospital to our leader, Mr. Szalasi himself. If I have anything to do with it, I will recommend that you receive a high office in the coming new Hungarist State. You have truly displayed extraordinary abilities here."

"Thank you." Jeretzian adequately disguised his significant doubts both that the German-Hungarian alliance could possibly still win and, even if so, that he and the Jews had any future therein. He offered Hidasi a cigarette. This time, Hidasi smiled. He took one. Jeretzian lit the two cigarettes, and they took in their first puffs in unison. Hidasi smiled again, then amicably slapped Jeretzian's shoulder.

"Hold on, Jeretzian. It shouldn't be more than another couple of days – maybe less." Hidasi patted him again, then started to turn to leave.

"You're not worried," Jeretzian called out, "about what will happen when – if the Soviets win? It won't be a good thing for people affiliated with the Arrow Cross if…."

Hidasi did not stop smiling. He turned back to face Jeretzian: "I always plan ahead for alternate outcomes, Jeretzian. I assume you have done the same." At that, Hidasi reached to retrieve the bag which held his complimentary books autographed by Dr. Volgyesi, as well as an autographed page from a notebook, signed to Hidasi's daughter, by Alfonzo. His associates followed him up the stone steps and back into the cold. Into the fray.

***

Dr. Szollosy had lost a great deal of blood. The doctors worked on him, doing everything they could, for four days. Each time he would regain consciousness, he would ask for his daughter. "You take care, Doctor," the nurses and doctors -- all of whom in the know – kept repeating. "She is smiling on you now, praying for your recovery." For four days this went on until two doctors, believing he was sleeping or still under what little anesthesia they had to give him, were again discussing how they would handle telling him his daughter was dead when he, as they predicted, fully recovered. Dr. Szollosy heard. Later that same fourth day, Dr. Szollosy died.

His wife had come to the hospital on the third day. She was never sure what had happened, or where her husband and daughter had even gone, or if they were alive. She only knew that they were outside going for bread when the terrible shelling occurred. For three days she lived with this uncertainty, this terror. When she finally learned they were both alive but injured, and that they were at 1 Zichy Jeno, she went straight there. "Your husband was badly injured," a doctor finally informed her. "But he is recuperating. We expect him to fully recover. You can stay here, if you like. We'll come get you when he is stable and fully conscious."

She was relieved. "And my daughter … where is she?" She leaned to the left and right, to either side of the doctor, excitedly scanning the crowd of unfamiliar faces. "Where…?"

The doctor looked down. He, like the rest of the staff, had been deliberating what to do when they were obliged to inform Dr. Szollosy of his daughter's fate. He was not prepared for this.

"Where is my daughter?" she now shouted, almost in slow motion. Heads turned.

"I am so sorry, Madam … a shell struck her brain and…."

The woman, wife of Dr. Szollosy and the mother of a beautiful girl with light brown hair, stood up at once. She turned around to ascend the steps outside. Went out, into the cold. She never came back, not even to check on her husband's condition. Days later, it was Dr. Zahler who learned that she had taken her own life that same evening. An overdose, poison, something.

***

At dawn the following day, the Soviets entered the basement to liberate the residents of 1 Zichy Jeno. It was the 18th of January 1945. The Pest side of Budapest was liberated. Twenty-five days later, on February 13th, Buda, too, was liberated. In no time, Budapest went from Nazi-occupation and Arrow Cross terror to the rule of Soviet leader Josef Stalin. For Hungary's alliance with Hitler, Stalin proclaimed: "Hungary must be punished in an exemplary fashion." The Soviets finally expelled remaining German units and Arrow Cross collaborators from western Hungary in April 1945.

In March 1944, when the German occupation commenced, there were approximately 760,000 Jews living in Hungary. By the middle of February 1945, less than one year later, over 500,000 were murdered or died from maltreatment, including starvation.

The Jewish population in Budapest numbered approximately 200,000 before the occupation. Although Budapest was spared the outright deportations to Auschwitz unlike the Jews in the Hungarian provinces, its Jewish population was cut almost in half to just over 100,000. As many as 20,000 were shot and killed, thrown into the Danube. Throughout the liberated ghetto there were so many bodies lying dead in the streets from starvation or murder. In a garden beside the Dohany Street Synagogue, serving as an outer "wall" of a part of the ghetto, 2,281 victims were buried in 24 mass graves. The synagogue, like the Orthodox Kazinczy Street Synagogue also in the ghetto, was used by the Arrow Cross as, among other things, a horse stable throughout the siege.

PART IV

21

From the Basement to....

Every building in Budapest was required, by law, to bear emergency entry and exit ways between the basements of neighboring buildings, or at least in and out of its own basement. What this meant at 1 Zichy Jeno was that in between its basement, already vastly enlarged during the siege, and the one next door the layer of wall was much thinner at a certain point. And beside that thin layer of wall, on both sides, there was a pickaxe which could be used to break through in case of emergency.

The Red Army had been going both above and below ground, one building at a time, to force out enemy combatants. In many buildings they met resistance, either armed or at least emotional. Many Hungarians who were not Jews were still pulling for a German victory and were far more fearful than pleased to see their liberators enter their living spaces. This fear far transcended the mere feeling of realizing that the side you were rooting for had been defeated.

In the days in between the drama of Hidasi's visit, the terrible shelling and the 18th of January, the most frequent incoming patients to 1 Zichy Jeno were women physically abused and worse by the advancing Red Army. The hospital staff tried to keep this news quiet among the other basement residents, while at the same time trying to take extra precautions and plan ahead. Notwithstanding Hidasi's emotional, but naive assurances to the contrary, Jeretzian and everyone else clearly preferred a Soviet victory because an opposite outcome would absolutely mean the end of them. Far beyond Hidasi's words just a few days before, it was clear there was no place for Jews in a Nazi- and Arrow Cross-controlled Hungary. The writing was on the wall, let alone the placards on practically every street post and shop in Budapest.

Therefore, presuming the seemingly inevitable Soviet liberation, most residents at 1 Zichy Jeno were already disguising wives and daughters, putting on extra clothes, covering their hair and otherwise trying to somehow lessen their feminine appearance. Most who did not live in this building were already planning a swift return to their own homes, daring to hope their homes still stood. Regardless, there was a feeling of both fear and excitement in the air. They had been dodging bullets for so long now that, with some sort of an end finally in view, they were ready for just about anything.

It was not quite 5:00 in the morning on the 18th when Robert sat up abruptly in his bed. He wasn't sleeping. Not even close. There was too much tension and anxiety in the air as ground fighting could be heard as if it were occurring next door. It was. Now came a hard rapping against the basement wall, no more than five or six mattress lengths away from the mattress Robert shared with his Uncle Bobby. As usual, he was still sleeping, but seemingly everyone else around them also heard the same sound and looked in the direction of the wall.

And then the wall finally revealed a hole. Several hard strikes later, in came the head of a man wearing a military *ushanka*, a fur hat with ear flaps. The *ushanka* fell onto the dirt below the man's head, and he leaned nervously back, exposing a rifle beside him. Two or three other faces pressed up near his, looking through the hole at the Jews in the basement of 1 Zichy Jeno. A man near Robert asked: "Soviets?"

The man nodded affirmatively. He responded in passable Hungarian: "Are there Germans or Arrow Cross in your house?"

"No," maybe 15 voices responded in unison. Then, all at once, a cheer began, which became louder and louder, rolling like an ocean wave from the back of the basement to the front. The Soviet men looked at each other, smiled, and kicked open the hole so that they could get through. They did not get far before they were besieged by hugs, kisses and absolute gratitude. Robert managed to get a partial loaf of bread to share with his family from one of the men. The girl with laughing eyes, against her grandfather's wishes, broke through to kiss and hug them all –and there were at least 20 Soviet soldiers. Her exuberance was finally harnessed by Dr. Zahler, who successfully pulled her back, wary of what the Russians might do next. Her friend Marika just rolled her eyes.

One by one, the Soviet soldiers began demanding every and anybody, pointing to their wrists: *"Davai chassyi*, Give us your watches!" At first confused, many residents relented, as if in a drunken haze of happiness, impervious to self-interest. Once the soldiers received their share of watches, the next requests were for alcohol, of which there was exceedingly little in the building, and finally, ultraseptyl, an antibacterial medicine used to treat, among other things, venereal diseases.

***

Jeretzian's plan, both on behalf of the building's residents and for himself, was to continue to be indispensable. They, and he, now must become necessary to the Soviet occupation. Perhaps to a fault, he had never separated the interests of the many in the building from those of his own. He hoped this approach would protect them … and him. For the moment, he was less concerned about possible Soviet anti-Semitism than the fact that they were, after all, Hungarians – on the wrong side of the war with the Soviets. He immediately shelved his Arrow Cross uniform he had been wearing essentially around the clock up to this point and presented himself to the Soviet commanders as the hospital's "manager." The residents barely recognized him out of his uniform. The language proved to be an obstacle until one of the officers understood that Jeretzian was of Armenian origin and spoke Armenian. "We have Armenian," he managed to say in Hungarian. Minutes later, he produced a Soviet soldier of Armenian descent. When this man learned that Jeretzian too was Armenian, he embraced him excitedly.

Within a short while, Jeretzian succeeded in conveying that this was a hospital and the medical staff would treat the Soviet wounded free of charge. The Russian commanders were grateful, and indeed, they began to bring in their wounded for treatment almost immediately. Upon learning that the building's residents were hungry, the Armenian Russian, still overjoyed, brought in bags full of peanuts. They were better than nothing; in fact, the best peanuts the residents had ever tasted.

Since the shelling had finally stopped in Pest, people finally felt free and secure to explore their surroundings, look for loved ones and, in so many instances, leave the building for good to return to their own homes. This assumed, optimistically, the homes had remained intact. Remarkably, most of the apartments in 1 Zichy Jeno remained habitable. There was damage, no doubt, and so many broken windows, but those could be replaced. In the interim, at least any broken or missing windows could be boarded up.

Reports from the people who went to look for loved ones in the ghetto, however … that was an entirely different story. Dead bodies, dead horses everywhere. People starving to such an extent that they were still dying every day. There was typhus, there was an infestation of lice, excrement all over the streets…. The pressing concern was to somehow bury the dead, which still proved exceedingly difficult on account of the frozen earth. Equipment was brought in, people convened and covered their faces, trying to hide too many tears and not wanting to catch anything. It was hell out there; hell on earth.

As wonderful as it was for those fortunate enough to still have homes outside the building that survived the shelling, this caused a new problem that was undermining Jeretzian's plan for survival and protection for all. With so many of the support personnel and many doctors and their families exiting, there were nearly 200 patients still in need of care and treatment. There was no longer staff sufficient to care for everyone and continue to keep the hospital functional. In addition, Dr. Volgyesi, whose apartment was being used in earnest for treatment and care again, wanted his apartment cleared out immediately so that he and his family could resume living in it.

***

"*Anu*, I'm going. I must," Robert declared excitedly. "Why don't you stay here with the others? I have to see our apartment – if it is still in one piece."

"Yes, I too want to know. And your piano, the things we left behind," his mother reasoned, "but the streets are still too dangerous, from what everyone is saying." Apart from the frozen dead -- so many still lying in the streets -- the threat of disease, lice and, especially for women, the Red Army, there were also so many ruthless, desperate people on the streets capable of doing almost anything. Bands of Soviet soldiers and, alternately, civilians were looting stores, stealing almost anything in sight and prone to hurt or kill people in their way. Beyond that, across the Danube in Buda, the fighting was still severe as the Nazis were defending their positions in and around the castle.

And still, Arrow Cross units were resolved to round up and kill Jews there. In the last days alone, a group led by Father Andras Kun, the errant monk who had killed Nora, the friend of Alfonzo and Hanna, was on a rampage. Wearing the Arrow Cross emblem and a pistol strapped over his cassock, he led his gang to murder over 170 Jewish patients and others hiding in a Jewish hospital on Maros utca. On January 19th, his gang killed 90 people in a Jewish almshouse. He was accusing any Hungarian not fighting in the defense of the city of being a "coward" and a "bastard."

"I am not a boy anymore, *Anu*. Haven't you noticed? That was a long time ago," Robert nearly shouted, deepening his voice in the middle of his protest to emphasize his point. "Don't you want to know about *Apu*? We haven't heard a thing about him since the siege began. If he sent a message or note, it's more likely it would go there than ever reach us here. So, I will go, be careful. There won't be Arrow Cross on the streets anymore, and the Russians … they won't have any interest in me. Is my yellow star still inside your bag?" he remembered. The consensus among the building's residents, based on what the soldiers were saying, was that the Red Army had no issue with any Jews in Budapest but was rather much more suspicious of the Hungarians who might be Arrow Cross or Nazi sympathizers. Therefore, many of the residents who had left the building in search of surviving loved ones and their own homes actually put back on their yellow stars. How ironic it was that the stars were now being used as protection, rather than a mark of people about to die.

His grandmother turned to her daughter-in-law. "Why not let Robi go … see if his father – my son has sent any word. Robi has been out there, Cornelia," Robert's grandmother calmly tried to reassure her. "Aranka is in the middle of her shift with the doctors – and you work in an hour or so, yes? I know she – we intend to see what is left of my house in Kobanya, maybe as early as today also. You can come with us, if you'd like."

"*Anu*, I will be right back, I promise. It shouldn't take me more than an hour or two at most." Robert had hoped that Hanna might be able to join him on his quest, but she had just begun her shift working alongside Alfonzo in the hospital. There were fewer and fewer residents remaining – fewer by the hour -- to assist in the daily operations of the hospital, so those still there were being asked to work extra. Even Robert's uncles were busier than ever, assisting in retrieving supplies, rations and other items from the various relief organizations now in Pest.

Robert was so nervous and excited all at once that he could barely stand it. What would his family's home on Rottenbiller look like? He knew that it could never be the same, if only for the people who would no longer be there. Although there were not so many Jewish families who lived there in the first place, as far as Robert knew, they had all gone to the ghetto and who knows if they survived. Plus, he already knew about Matyas, obviously, and many other of his old schoolmates who were put on a train to Auschwitz that one fateful day last fall. But still, Robert hoped home would still be his home and that his father would soon return. He was also hopeful that he could find and reunite with some of his old friends from his scout group. Most were not from his neighborhood; he hoped they were as fortunate as he was.

"Just where do you think you're going, Holczer?" asked Laszlo Frank. Robert had one hand on the door handle. He had just waved goodbye to Hanna and Alfonzo. He had an empty sack over one shoulder. He wasn't sure why. Perhaps there would be some extra food he could bring back from his home – assuming it was still there.

Three or four Red Army soldiers stood near the door of the lobby, probably about to go out on another raid of nearby shops and buildings for food, clothes, alcohol … whatever else they could carry.

"What, you have more limbs for me to put away? I can do them later," Robert said, dismissively.

"You're coming back though, right?"

Robert nodded. "Of course, my mother – my family is all still here … for the moment."

"Good then. I see you have a sack. Let me give you one … two more. There is a Jewish relief organization … a few different ones, actually, over by the ghetto … er, by the Dohany Street Synagogue. On your way back from wherever you're going, can you swing by there with the sacks, show them this-" Frank produced a card identifying that the carrier of the card was a resident of 1 Zichy Jeno, a Jewish house. "—And, when you do so, they will give you some more flour and whatever other food packets they have. That will be a big help, Holczer."

"Of course. Please tell my mother that I will be a little longer than I had originally said."

***

The nearly two mile walk to 39 Rottenbiller *utca* was a breeze. It was still cold outside this morning, but there was no snow on the ground. Very few people were outside, and there was still very little car traffic. The street cars were still not working. Robert tried to ignore the horrific scenes on some of the streets he traversed, but purposefully avoided the ghetto area where he knew the state of things was even worse. Plus, he would have to go over there on his way back to pick up the flour, as requested.

The first sign that something was very different at his old home was when he approached the building and looked up at the windows of his apartment. The windows, even the overall condition of the entire building seemed quite good, apart from some bullet holes and marks on the façade. However, his windows had different curtains than the ones he knew. And then he saw one, then two shadows moving behind these different, almost tan, drab curtains. His smile disappeared, and he surprised himself by feeling more anger than fear. He walked into the building's front door behind a resident he didn't recognize and marched straight up the familiar marble stairs to his apartment.

Robert pressed his ear against the door of his apartment and, sure enough, he heard voices inside. Unsure what he would even do or say, he pounded the door firmly. He heard the voices go silent. He pounded again. After another moment or two, footsteps, then the door opened partially.

Still wearing the Jewish Star of David on his coat, he declared to a tall, portly man wearing a sweater: "I am Robert Holczer. My family owns this house. What are you doing here?"

The man, stunned, opened the door entirely for Robert. He turned back to a woman, presumably his wife, and Robert could now see three younger girls. Two of them were playing beside the couch, the other one, older, was apparently reading. Robert was incredulous. He could barely recognize his own house. Where was the dreaded piano? Where was the walnut cabinet … the table … whose couch was this?

"We fully expected this day would come, young man. My name is –"

"I don't care what your name is. You shouldn't be here. When my father—"

"Please, Mr. Holczer. We would have nowhere else to go. We were given this apartment when … when our own was destroyed early in the siege by Soviet shells."

"That's not my concern," Robert blurted, still surveying his now foreign surroundings. "And where is our furniture? Just one moment, you wait here," Robert suddenly thought. He remembered that they gave boxes of their belongings to their neighbors two doors down, the Slivacs, who were also supposed to look after the place when Robert and his mother, like all other Jews, were forced to move to yellow star houses … an eternity ago.

Robert stepped back into the hall and now pounded the door of the Slivacs. According to Madam Slivac, who barely recognized Robert either because he was almost a year older than when she saw him last or he was now so filthy and skinny, "the Soviets took everything, I'm sorry. There was nothing we could do, they would have killed us," she lied. Robert had seen the way Soviets looted places. They never took furniture or anything they couldn't easily transport. The Slivacs, or others must have sold the Holczers' possessions.

"You expect me to believe that, Mrs. Slivac? The Red Army took away my – my mother's grand piano? Everything?" She looked down at the ground, then remembered. She went into a closet and pulled out one small box and opened it. Indeed, it contained some of the Holczers' things … the things that the Slivacs probably couldn't sell or didn't yet get around to selling. "You are incredible, Mrs. Slivac. When my mother … when my father learns what you have done!"

From inside Mrs. Slivac's apartment, a man's voice called out. "Nazis didn't finish all of you off, eh? The Arrow Cross?" Laughter.

Robert's fists were clenched. He felt ready to explode. From behind him in the hallway, he felt a hand on his shoulder. It was the man who was now living in his house. "What do you—"

"Here, this is for you … and your mother. She's alive too? It's a message; it came for you two, three weeks ago. We had no idea what to do with it, only, like I said … I just expected your family would return one day."

Robert snatched it from the man's hand. It was a postcard from his father, dated December 29th. "My loving wife and Robi," it read, "I am better than expected and safe. I expect to be able to return when the war is over. Keep faith. I love and miss you beyond words. Robi, you take care of my lady, you hear? Be strong, be a man. Soon, your loving Lajos and *Apu*."

Robert felt his anger melt away like snow amidst a warm front. The man stood, looking at Robert. There was Robert, holding his father's words; his father's handwriting. He was alive. He would be home soon! Robert, softened, looked up at the man.

"What is your name," Robert finally asked.

"Berenyi, Miklos. And this is my family," he motioned, holding the door open with one hand. "We are good people. You may not think it, but I – we are all relieved that you and your mother are alive."

Robert was considering his next words. "I must do some things and will speak with my mother and family. You see," waving the postcard, "My father, also, will return. We will speak again soon."

"Of course. And here, why don't you take some bread?" Miklos motioned to his wife to bring bread from the table to Robert. "We have a bit of cheese, too. And some jam."

"No, thank you. I am on my way to get some now."

Robert's entire walk to the Dohany Street Synagogue felt like a dream. He arrived before he even knew it. He was conflicted. Feelings of anger that there were people living in his house and that the Slivacs had clearly sold off their property wrestled with news from his father – dated as it was – and the ostensible kindness of the Berenyis. His emotional tug of war lasted until he arrived, when he saw piles and piles of bodies alongside the synagogue. Men were somehow digging through the frozen ground, digging what appeared to be large pits; likely mass graves for the mountains of bodies all around. The smell, despite the cold, was overwhelming. The odor was in no way lessened by the fact he saw additional, almost infinite piles of what appeared to be … feces. Horse manure, human…. He had heard the synagogues in the ghetto had been used as stables, but he could not picture … imagine this. And then, over on the Wesselenyi utca, near the main entry to the synagogue, he saw long lines of starving, emaciated people. Robert had had no idea. It was not like the residents of 1 Zichy

Jeno were living or eating in luxury, by any means, but what he saw here made him feel almost embarrassed; he was truly fortunate.

Robert's emotions about what he saw and smelled almost obliterated his excitement to return to the building to share the news of his family's home and his father. Still, Robert was expected to bring back food from the relief organizations -- and so he would. As he stood in line for far longer than he wished, he did a double take as he came closer and saw one of the men passing out food supplies. The man was with some Jewish relief organization, right beside or with the "UNRRA," the United Nations Relief and Rehabilitation Administration. He was wearing quite a different uniform than the last time he saw him, but Robert was sure it was him. Robert stepped forward to the man when it was his turn.

The man did not look up, handing Robert several large packages of flour. He simply pointed to the next table over, where Robert was going to receive additional items. Robert placed the flour into one of his sacks.

"Thank you," Robert smiled.

"You're welcome," the man finally looked up. "Now move along to the next table please."

"I mean, thank you. You don't remember me? You saved me. Just a few days ago, you saved me, the Jewish boy you said was an idiot for being on the streets. You beat me up and sent me home, but I never had to pull down my pants," Robert beamed.

The man, blonder even than Robert remembered, did not smile. He seemed even more serious and distraught than he was the other early morning. "You, too?"

"What do you mean," Robert asked, puzzled.

"I saved you too? You don't know how many Jews as stupid as you that I saved. Now go on, be grateful and don't waste the chance I – the chance God gave you. Beat it, before I beat you up some more!"

Robert couldn't tell what was bothering this man. Perhaps it was the obvious: All one had to do was to look around and see the dead; the suffering … a realization of what life had amounted to for so many. Regardless, Robert smiled at the man. "I won't waste the chance. I intend to live a good, long life, thanks to you -- and a few others, too." He finally obliged the man's demand to move along.

It only occurred to Robert, hours later, that, once again, he had forgotten to ask for the man's name: The name of the latest person to save him.

***

Two days later, Robert and his mother brought their few belongings with them and returned to live at their home at 39 Rottenbiller *utca*. They had argued, only briefly, about what to do regarding the Berenyis, but Robert ultimately agreed with his mother's idea that they simply share the apartment with each other for as long as necessary. The Berenyis agreed that this was a gracious offer, and they were pleased to move their things and living space to one area. Robert and his mother, and soon his father, would occupy the other. They would share the kitchen and washroom. His mother had some very choice words for the woman she thought was her friend, Madam Slivac, but there was no longer anything that could be done. They simply stopped speaking with one another after the one and only confrontation, Robert by her side ready for whatever a short, skinny teenager could muster.

Now a free "man," out of his grisly job as limb transporter and his more dangerous job of siege building courier, Robert was bored waiting one day after another for his father to return. Not only that, he was angry. He had never been an angry person before the war had come to Hungary, but now he felt somehow that, for everything that had happened to him, his family, his friends … all Jews, society owed him. Someone, he thought, needed to pay for what they had done.

As it turned out, it wasn't someone, but rather anyone. Absent any clear idea of how to exact his revenge and against whom, he became enthralled with the relative riches the Red Army soldiers amassed every day from the stores and homes of Budapest citizens. Because his Aunt Aranka still lived at 1 Zichy Jeno in what was, after all, her apartment,

Robert continued to go back there nearly every day. His grandmother and several other relatives remained with Aranka, because their Kobanya house, very modest as it was, had been destroyed by the shelling. There was nothing left. On one of Robert's first visits to see them and check how they were doing, he asked one of the Soviets who spoke some Hungarian if he could tag along with them. The man smiled.

And so began Robert's career, brief as it was, as a street urchin. He brought with him a cart he had sometimes used as a courier at 1 Zichy Jeno. On this cart, he placed and brought home with him everything he looted from one shop after another. Of course, the Soviets would always get to choose first, but their interests – alcohol, sweaters, medicine, watches – did not typically conflict with those of Robert. In actuality, Robert was never really looking for anything in particular. The mere idea of taking things from shops in a Hungary that either wanted all its Jews dead or was at least willing to let them die was what preoccupied Robert. It was vengeance, pure and simple.

This went on for a couple of weeks, until the Soviet soldiers finally moved on. Robert would bring his stash back home, explaining to his mother, when asked, that he and some friends found the items. But his mother knew the truth, thanks to Aranka. His mother struggled more than ever to curb her teenage son's will, however, and resorted to warning: "Wait 'til your father gets home!" In addition, having emerged from the constant danger and preoccupation with survival allowed Robert's mother time to return to her thoughts; to the realization that she had no family whatsoever left in Vac. There would not even be remains … bodies to bury, from what she had been told. Still, she was preoccupied with just going there; taking account of things. *Soon*, she thought. But the thought that she and Robert were alive, and that her husband would soon return, gave her courage. One day at a time…. If only he would come back now.

***

Watching so many of those he had helped to save every day for the past few months leave in droves was difficult for Jeretzian. He had succeeded, as he seemed to always do, in gaining the trust and respect of the new Soviet authorities. He secured their recognition that 1 Zichy Jeno was the site of a functioning hospital and would provide excellent care for all wounded. Yet, it was now barely a functioning hospital. Too few of the non-original resident physicians and nurses had stayed. Jeretzian went out scavenging for medical personnel from any background and managed to bring in a few Hungarians worried about possible reprisals from the swiftly incoming Soviet leadership. But at this point, now that the siege was over -- at least in Pest -- very few people were interested in working for free. Apparently, that was alright only when their survival was in jeopardy, Jeretzian deduced.

Had so many forgotten what this building; this hospital, had meant for them over the last several months? Had they forgotten how not only over 400 Jews were saved here, but over 10,000 patients who came in and out their doors during the hospital's existence to this point? If it were not for the hospital, he wondered, how many more lives would have been lost – on both sides of the equation? But, to Jeretzian, his thoughts remained fixed on surviving. To him, the real dust had not yet settled for anyone. To him, the Soviets represented a new challenge that he would have to somehow "manage."

About a week after the Soviets arrived, Jeretzian saw Dr. Volgyesi speaking with a group of Soviet officers he did not recognize. Volgyesi had been continuing to demand the return of his apartment, and so Jeretzian, Dr. Zahler, and the others who remained, shrugged their shoulders and relented. Now, Volgyesi pointed in the direction of Jeretzian, who had been sorting through papers and writing instructions for his friend, Laszlo Nagy. In addition to trying to keep this hospital a going concern, Jeretzian knew he needed to also divert some of his attention to his own business affairs, which had stagnated to nothing since the Nazi occupation began last March.

The Soviet officers left Volgyesi where he stood near the stairwell and crossed the lobby to Jeretzian's new, modified workspace near Theo the super's desk. Great as it was that the hospital operations and residents were slowly moving back upstairs, it made for quite a mess everywhere.

"Jeretzian, Ara Gyorgy," one of the officers asked accusingly in Hungarian, standing over the kneeling Jeretzian with pen in hand.

"Yes, sir," Jeretzian slowly looked up, "what can I do for you?"

"No talking. Just come with us."

Jeretzian scanned around him. He stood up, trying to keep the smile he had strained to form. He saw Volgyesi turn and walk up the stairs to his apartment. Two men came on either side of Jeretzian and took him by each arm. They led him out the door, past a horrified Theo, who was, for the first time ever, speechless. They steered him toward a long black car in front of the building. One of the men opened the backseat door and pressed Jeretzian's head down, hastening him to enter. Once inside the car, another Soviet officer, already seated in the other rear passenger seat, hastily wrapped a blindfold over Jeretzian's eyes and tied it tightly.

Jeretzian had no idea what had happened, nor what was to come.

For almost eight months, Jeretzian was interrogated, tortured, and coerced to confess to having committed crimes with which he was never even charged. He was taken from dark cells in Budapest to darker places and holes deep inside the darkest parts of the Soviet Union before being transferred to a prison in Deva, Romania. Like Hungary, Romania, too, was under Soviet authority. Many around him confessed to similarly illusory charges and were killed or found dead under questionable circumstances. Jeretzian never did confess to anything. At one point, papers were thrown in front of him, papers he had allegedly forged or made up as an Arrow Cross party member on behalf of other Arrow Cross personnel and ministries. When Jeretzian tried to explain that these were documents necessary to the protection of over 400 Jews to spite the wishes and intentions of the Nazis and Arrow Cross, his captors went on to other charges, or worse, interminable silence and solitary time in dark pits. It was a nightmare, but he kept faith and hope that he would survive this. He did. While in Deva, he was given a brief opportunity to write to his mother that he was alive and in Deva, and that perhaps she could contact the police there and vouch for him. Anything.

Nearly eight months after he was taken captive by the Soviets for reasons never made clear to him, Jeretzian returned to Budapest a free man. It was now late summer, yet all he had to wear was the winter coat he had with him in January, ragged trousers, and a shirt whose color no longer resembled its original issue. These were all given back to him upon his release, which was granted with no more of an explanation than why he was ever imprisoned in the first place. The shoes on his feet were too big, fastened with wires tied together so that they would not fall apart and not fall off. These shoes never belonged to him. He didn't want to ask who owned them in the first place, or what happened to him. His hair and beard were filthy and long, reaching down practically to his waist on both sides.

When he stepped off the train at dusk from God knows where to Budapest, the first thing he did was to go to a stand to buy a pack of cigarettes. He dug deep into his pocket for the one 2-pengo coin he found on the train and he desperately set it on the stand. One sight of the downtrodden, bearded, Jesus-looking character in front of him, and the shop owner just slid the pack to "Jesus." Jeretzian offered the coin again, but the man made the sign of the cross and then motioned that he would not accept it. *A strange man.* Jeretzian thanked him, thought twice about saying, "God bless you" (he did), and turned around to smoke like his life depended on it.

Jeretzian proceeded from the train station and down Deak ter, a very short distance from his mother's apartment. A policeman stopped him, strangely dressed and presenting like a homeless person who did not belong in this neighborhood. Jeretzian explained where he was going and whom he was going to see. The officer escorted him there. Jeretzian rang the bell for his mother's apartment. Instead of his mother answering, however, it was the cleaning lady. He explained who he was, and she finally agreed to let him in. She screamed when she saw him, unable to recognize him.

"I assure you, I am Ara Jeretzian, my mother's son. Sophie's son. Is she here?"

"My God, you look—"

"Is she here, Madam? I have come a very long distance to see her."

"No, she is not," she composed herself. "I'm afraid she just left only an hour or two ago. She went to the train station. She was going to some place in Romania … to find her son – to find *you*!"

22

The Lucky Ones

Once Jeretzian was taken that one morning in late January, the hospital of 1 Zichy Jeno began to dissolve more rapidly. When that occurred, coupled with the slowing of incoming rations and other food supplies, Aranka and the other permanent building residents needed to start fending for themselves. Doctors returned to begin to restore their previous practices, the architects set about designing the reconstruction of Budapest, and Alfonzo and Hanna went, Alfonzo back to show business and Hanna to continue her education.

Shortly before Buda was liberated in the middle of February, Aranka rented a horse and cart and set out to the countryside. There she would sell what remaining valuables she possessed in exchange for lard, flour, fruit and vegetables. Robert accompanied her on most of these runs so that he could bring food back to his home. In this way, they were able to subsist during this time of great upheaval and uncertainty. Not only were Budapest and all Jewish families war-torn to one extent or another, but the city, and the country, was quickly coming under Soviet rule.

On one of their earlier excursions into the countryside, they were arrested by Soviet soldiers. Aranka and Robert were about 20 miles north of the city, returning from a small Danubian village. There was fighting against the Germans just across the river, and the Soviets were confiscating all horses for their war effort. When the Soviets saw Aranka and Robert with the horse and food, they took them and confiscated everything.

Sitting in a cell awaiting their fate, Robert started to fear the worst. He tried to calm himself but couldn't bear the prospect of being imprisoned or killed before he ever could be reunited with his father. He kept rocking back and forth, waiting, wondering. He reached into his pocket and took out the marble that looked like a planet graced with oceans, but purer than earth; the one he found that day in the small courtyard with Hanna. He twirled the marble anxiously between his fingers. He had brought it everywhere with him ever since he had found it. Aranka paced nervously.

After several hours, an officer finally called Aranka out of the cell and into another room. Robert was now alone, and even more afraid. Roughly two hours later, Aranka returned. She was disheveled, her dress askew, but she smiled. "Come, Robi. We are free to go."

"What? I don't understand."

"You don't need to understand anything. We are free, and that is all."

When they were released from their cell, they were led to the front of the small village house that now served as the base for this Soviet regiment. There, a soldier brought them their horse, and another man pulled the cart. It was still filled with all the food and supplies that were there in the first place. The men smiled sheepishly at Aranka.

"I don't understand, *Nagyneni* Aranka." He watched as Aranka walked briskly by, head down, face like stone. Wheels suddenly started to spin in Robert's mind and, then his stomach followed suit. He surmised....

***

One day in April, after the war was finally over in Hungary, Robert's father was permitted to keep his promise and return home. There was a knock on the door of the apartment at 39 Rottenbiller *utca*.

"Who is it?" Robert called.

"Delivery for Holczers," replied the voice behind the door.

Robert opened the door. All he could see in front of him were two arms enveloping bags containing loaves of bread, sausages and other items Robert could not easily see. His jaw dropped as his mouth watered. *Food,* he thought, excitedly. *Who…?*

The arms which encircled the bags lowered them, revealing the smiling face of … Robert's father! His mother dropped her cup of coffee on the table and jumped up. "*Apu,*" Robert shouted. His father did not even have time to enter, let alone set down his bags before first Robert, and then his mother pressed against the bags, against his chest and joined in a collective hug; the tightest, warmest hug Robert had felt in … as long as he could remember. For once, the tears they all shed were of joy, not sadness, fear or loss.

***

Catching up took until well into the morning of the following day, and Robert's father was transfixed by the long, winding stories of their survival. Certainly, there was still so much to say and learn – it had been roughly two years since they were all together. But his father learned how an Armenian Hungarian dressed in an Arrow Cross uniform saved them all, over 400 Jews. He heard how his sister, Aranka, had saved Robert time and again and kept Robert and his mother under her care, roof, and protection, always. He heard about how the Arrow Cross and Nazis could tell whether males were Jews, and how a blond Jew had beaten up Robert but saved his life. His father also heard of the deaths, so many: The Jews in the countryside who were sent to Auschwitz; his wife's entire family in Vac; the Jews shot and killed at the Danube; the Jews shot, and the starving Jews in the ghettos; the Jews marched to Mauthausen in Austria; a nephew caught on the street – his eyes pushed in….

Of course, Robert's father already knew all too well about the Jews sent for forced labor, for he was one of those Jews for far too long. While the Holczers' roommates, the Berenyis, did their best to give the reunited family privacy, they were simply incredible. They cooked some of the food that Robert's father brought, threw together additional items they had, and made a veritable feast to share. They even took out some Polish vodka, "but don't tell the Russians we have this," Mr. Berenyi joked. Robert's father was not up to talking about his own experiences in Bor. He only said: "I was one of the few lucky ones. Most -- almost everyone else -- was murdered." He changed the subject quickly. "My time after that was excellent, in comparison. I worked and was treated very well. I thought of you every single day, counting the days until this," he smiled widely. "Every single day."

Robert's father treated the Berenyis as though they belonged there. When he heard their circumstances, how they came to be in his home, and then how his wife and son handled the situation, he just smiled again. He was doing a lot of that. He did, however, miss his radio and phonograph immediately. He was so looking forward to seeing them again and resolved to find ways to get new ones second hand. Before finally going to sleep, he also learned what Robert had been up to for a few weeks with the Soviet soldiers. His wife opened the closet door to show him Robert's stash of jewelry, pottery and various odds and ends. Most were still unwrapped. His father listened, looked at the items that did not belong to them, then glared at Robert.

"Tomorrow morning, Robi ... in the morning."

***

"Wake up, Robi. Robi, wake up!"

Robert's eyes opened. He had absolutely no idea where he was. There was no way he trusted his inclination that this was the voice of his father; that his father was leaning over him in a bed at 39 Rottenbiller, their family home.

"Robi ... are you dreaming of a girl?" his father asked gently. "What was her name ... Hanna?"

Suddenly he felt a pillow hit his head. His mother.

"Get up, sleepy head! Your father's home," she teased, drawing out the word 'father' for emphasis.

When Robert managed to wipe the sleep from his eyes, he smiled. He didn't mind the pillow; didn't mind the abuse. At long last, his father was back. He looked over at him and saw him now standing by the door. He had two bags beside him.

"Come on, thief. We are returning what you stole from those shops, and we are doing it now." He was serious.

Robert would have objected but knew he did not have the higher ground on this issue. He could begin to explain why he thought he felt entitled to take what he wanted, but he knew he would get nowhere. He cleaned up, got on his things, and they left together. Before doing so, Robert's father kissed his wife goodbye and winked at her. "You're still the cutest thing in the world," he whispered. She smiled again. *God, how good it was to see her smiling again*, Robert thought.

Robert impressed himself by his memory of the stores from which he took the items in the two bags. Not only that, but apart from one or two mistakes out of over 50 items, he even remembered what he took from each of the 13 different stores that were his victims. What he dreaded, one by one, was the process of going into each of these stores, asking for the owner, then taking out what he took and explaining how and why he did what he did. Each time, the owner was dumbfounded; incredulous that a "thief" was returning what he had stolen. A couple of them scolded Robert, but most were so shocked, so awed or so grateful that anything was being returned at all, that they said nothing, or even muttered a thank you. Each time, there was Robert's father standing in the doorway, arms folded, a trace of a smile on his lips.

"How do you feel about what you have done today, Robi," asked his father after Robert had returned the last four items to the last store. "What have you learned from this?"

Robert didn't know whether to fight it; to assert his sense that he was now a man capable of making his own decisions. "It's just that … I don't know, *Apu*. You weren't there. I know, you also endured terrible things that I can't even begin to imagine or know, but you weren't here to see how Budapest – your Budapest changed so fast. It wasn't even the Germans, it was … regular Hungarians, -- people we worked with; went to school with -- they all hated us. They wanted us dead. And we were so scared, every day. I just wanted … revenge, I guess."

Robert's father suddenly looked over Robert's shoulder for just a moment, back into the shop from which they had just departed. He then looked at Robert again. "I'm sorry, Robi. You're right, I wasn't here. And I'm not here to compare our pain, our losses and suffering. But believe me, I saw the consequences of hate at Bor. I saw Germans … others. I saw the relatively few who survived with me, still hating and wanting to pay everyone back. But listen to me, Robi," he paused. "Hate gets you nowhere. Hate will eat you up, and you will never accomplish anything truly good. You cannot love, when you hate."

Robert nodded, warmly. He understood, but it is terribly difficult to dismiss an emotion that has been growing inside of you for such a long time. "I understand, *Apu* -- What do you keep looking at inside the store?"

"Come on," he said, motioning toward the store.

"Back in there? No thanks!"

Robert's father coaxed Robert back inside the store. The owner looked at them, perhaps wondering if Robert was either returning something else or worse, had second thoughts about returning the items. No, it was a phonograph on one of the shelves in which Robert's father was interested. After haggling with the owner over the price, the phonograph, wanting some varnish and a new needle, which the owner agreed to toss in for nothing, now belonged to Robert's father.

"You have no idea how long I've waited to play my Liszt; my Chopin and Beethoven … Brahms…!"

Robert smiled. "It's so good to have you back, *Apu*. I can't wait to listen with you -- just as long as *Anu* doesn't get any bright ideas of getting another piano for me to play!"

***

In time, Robert returned to school and completed his high school education. To his father's disappointment, Robert did not shed his anger for how too many of his so-called fellow Hungarians treated their Jews. He set his interests on Zionism, the ideal of developing and protecting the new Jewish state of Israel. He made friends with similarly passionate, idealistic people, and made plans to move and continue his education there.

His father took Robert and his mother to visit Vac and try to arrange his wife's family's belongings. It wasn't pretty. A gentile family was now living in her parents' home. The family shared nothing in common with the Berenyis. They were defiant; arguing at first that "the whole place and everything in it" now belonged to them. Robert's fists clenched. His father stepped squarely in front of his angry son. Apparently, there were so many gentile families now living in former Jewish homes, and so many of them were more like this family – and worse -- than the Berenyis. In the end, the family let Robert's mother take a few possessions that had not already been seized by the Nazis or Hungarian gendarmerie and other authorities. She managed to come home with some photographs, and she clung to them like life. Having already lost her argument that they buy Robert a new piano ("I'm a man now, and don't ever want to play again" and "I'll be moving to Israel soon"), she turned her attention to healing, to smiling more, and to finding work in offices as a secretary.

Robert's father was eternally grateful to his sister, Aranka, for her part in saving, well, everyone in the family. Robert got the impression that his father shared a great deal more about what happened in Bor with her, his mother, brothers and other sisters than he ever did with him or his mother. Robert's father visited his side of the family often, getting the chance to see 1 Zichy Jeno, well after the fact. He helped his mother acquire a home in Kobanya, near where she previously lived, and helped her finally begin to grieve her own loss – her husband, his father. Everything had been happening so fast….

Almost immediately, his father sought to reestablish ties with his old friends – those who survived and those who had not already left for Israel.

He frequented his favorite coffee house, the ornate New York *Kavehaz* on Erzsebet krt., where he read the newspapers, played cards, and talked and laughed, when he could. It was difficult to hear of those who perished and all the stories, all the destruction. Despite the imposition of Soviet rule, he tried to conform and stick to what he knew. He contacted his former employer and, of course, the sales job was always his. He also became a kind of community leader, elected by those who lived in the 5th District area where they lived. Despite his relative lack of formal education, he was a gifted listener and always so wise. People trusted him to lead, and so he did.

As the time for Robert to leave for Israel drew nearer, he went for a long walk with his father. At first, he figured it was an aimless walk for the sake of walking. But he should have known that his father never engaged in purposeless endeavors. They were walking toward his coffee house, the "New York." On the way, his father finally decided to share a small fact about his experience in Bor. Robert didn't know why now, nor why this fact.

"In Bor, I would always save some of the little water I was given so I could wash myself, as best as I could," he volunteered, out of the blue.

"Why, *Apu*? If there was so little water...."

"Because I never wanted to give the Germans the victory that I was ever less than a man. Less than human," he stated coldly. He looked at Robert, putting his hand on his shoulder before they sat down in the café at his customary table. Staff and others waved to him as he entered, familiar and revered as he was by everyone. "I would never let them take that away from me, my humanity. At least if I could clean up myself, I thought, then I had dignity. I was a man."

The two talked over coffee and cookies for nearly a half hour. Robert's father was posing myriad questions about Robert's intentions in Israel; where he would stay, where he would continue his studies, his safety, his friends.... Finally, Robert asked him again, for maybe the 15th time. Up until now, he had only gotten a shrug of the shoulders from him. Not this time.

"*Apu*, I must ask again. You know how much I love you and *Anu*. There is really no future for us in Hungary on account of the Soviets and everything that has happened here. Why don't you both just come there with me? It will be easy for you to find work there, and some of your friends are already there."

Robert's father took another sip of coffee from his cup, signaled to the waiter that he wished to have more, then set it down gently. He looked warmly at his son. "I will try and answer your question in this way, as a kind of story, or bad riddle, I suppose." He began. "Mr. Kohn sits in our New York coffee house alone. People who know him come up to him and say, 'Mr. Kohn, it is now the late 1940s. We are after the war, and all your friends are gone. They are dead or in America. What are you doing alone in the coffee house?'

And Mr. Kohn responded: 'Look, people. What would I be doing if I had also left for America? I would have arrived there the first day, and the next day I would have looked for my old surviving friends. I would have found them. Then, on the third day we would have sat down in an American coffee house to talk. About what? The good old days in *our* coffee house!'"

Robert's father scooted his chair closer to his son and placed his hand on his shoulder. "Look, son. I am already in the coffee house. My coffee house. I am where I belong, where I need to be. This is my home, my environment. And as long as you are happy and following your heart and head, then I am happy."

Robert shivered, despite the balmy spring day. He felt a tingling from his head down to his toes. He was now 18 years old. Inside his pocket was a marble that looked like a planet wondrously graced with oceans, but purer than earth. Better than earth. So much was already behind him; a lifetime lay ahead of him.

"Robi, *szeretlek*. I love you," he gushed, his brown eyes moistening, almost smiling. "*Szeretlek*. Never forget."

Cover and Back cover photos of "The Shoes on the Danube Bank" memorial in Budapest, Hungary, taken by the author, June 2018. The memorial, created by sculptor Gyula Pauer, is based on a concept by Can Togay, honoring the 20,000 Jews murdered by Arrow Cross members during the Holocaust.

Bibliography

Braham, Randolph L., and Scott Miller, eds. *The Nazis' Last Victims: The Holocaust in Hungary.* Detroit: Wayne State University Press, published in association with the United States Holocaust Memorial Museum, 1998.

Braham, Randolph L., *The Politics of Genocide: The Holocaust in Hungary, Volumes 1 & 2, Third Revised and Enlarged Editions.* Columbia University Press, New York, 2016.

Vagi, Zoltan, Csosz, Laszlo, and Gabor Kadar, *The Holocaust in Hungary: Evolution of a Genocide.* AltaMira Press, published in association with the United States Holocaust Memorial Museum, 2013.

Ungvary, Krisztian, *The Siege of Budapest: 100 Days in World War II.* Yale University Press, New Haven and London, 2005.

Goldberger, Tamas, *The History of the Budapest Ghetto 1944-1945.* Gabbiano Print Ltd and Publishing House, Budapest, 2016.

Nador, Eva, ed. *Yellow-Star Houses: People, Houses, Fates.* Nador and Partner Consulting Office, Budapest, 2015.

Kerenyi, Norbert. *Stories of a Survivor.* Xlibris Corporation, 2011.

Laszlo, Gabor, ed. *The Dohany Street Synagogue.* Simix Print Kft, Budapest.

Schmidt, Maria, ed. *Terror Haza, Andrassy Ut 60, House of Terror.* Public Endowment for Research in Central and East-European History and Society, Budapest, 2008.

Jeretzian, Ara. *A Vedett Haz.* Intermix Kiado, Budapest, 1993 *(translated into English, 2018, by Link Translations, Mr. Adam T. Bogar via Halil Yigit, courtesy of the United States Holocaust Memorial Museum)*

"Alfonzó." *Wikipedia*, Wikimedia Foundation, 23 July 2019, hu.wikipedia. org/wiki/Alfonz%C3%B3.

Interviews & Recorded Testimony

Holczer, Robert. Interview 35507. *Visual History Archive*, USC Shoah Foundation, November 16, 1997 (interviewer: Natalie Schneiderman). Accessed September 2017-August 2018.

Holczer, Robert. USHMM Archives (http://collections.ushmm.org) RG-50.030*0467 & RG-50.549.05*0001, January 10 & April 29, 1996; March 17, 1999 (interviewer: Arwen Donahue). Accessed August 2017-August 2018.

In addition to the above recorded testimony, this author conducted numerous interviews both in-person and telephonically with Robert Holczer in July and August, 2017, before Robert's death. This author additionally benefitted immensely from multiple conversations and exchanged messages with Robert's surviving wife, Jan, and stepdaughter, Mary de la Fontaine.

This author also interviewed, personally in Budapest (June 2018) and through many emails and messages, Ara Jeretzian, son of one of the two protagonists in this story. Mr. Jeretzian generously afforded this author the permission to refer to, and make full use of his father's memoir, *A Vedett Haz (The Protected House)*, cited above.

Frank, Ilby. https://www.youtube.com/watch?v=vKb35WDYZMc, courtesy of USC Shoah Foundation. Accessed August 2017.

This author additionally was privileged to see a video interview of Eva Berg (Kadar), the girl with laughing eyes, courtesy of her son, Dr. Danny Berg. This interview took place several years ago, conducted by Dr. Berg himself.

(Hungarian News Agency broadcast of Miklos Horthy's proclamation on the cease-fire, October 15, 1944, in Magda Adam et al., eds., Magyarorszag es a masodik vilaghaboru. Titkos diplomacial okmanyok a haboru elozmenyeihez es tortenetehez, 2nd ed. (Budapest: Kossuth, 1959), 479-80 (Vagi, Zoltan, Csosz, Laszlo, and Gabor Kadar, The Holocaust in Hungary: Evolution of a Genocide. AltaMira Press, published in association with the United States Holocaust Memorial Museum, 2013, 148-149).

Budapest and Hungary Maps WW II

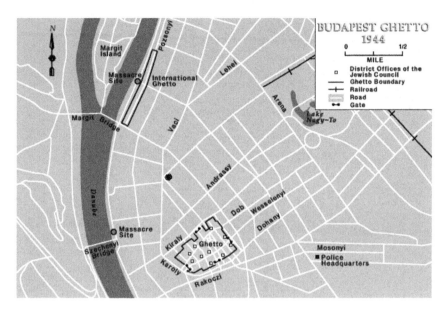

Figure 1: Budapest "Large" Ghetto marked near bottom, "International Ghetto" is long, rectangular shape north, near top of map. The rough location of 1 Zichy Jeno Utca, the "Yellow Star House," is drawn in as a square shape in block, north of Andrassy utca, the location of the Arrow Cross headquarters during the time in question.

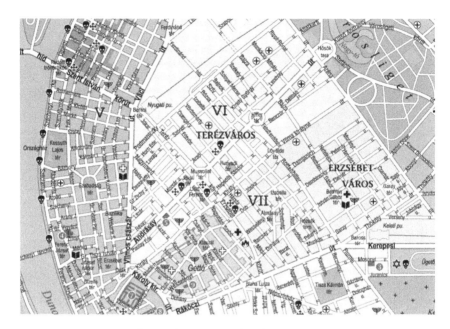

Figure 2: Street map of most relevant areas of Budapest, 1944. The Roman numerals represent the District numbers. 1 Zichy Jeno Utca was in District VI, it is located at Gr. Zichy Jeno's intersection with Vilmos Csaszar utca, where the building still stands today. Robert's father's family lived in Kobanya, District X, southeast of District VI. One can also see Rottenbiller utca, running northwest from the southeast in District VII. This was the street on which Robert and his family lived before Robert and his mother ultimately settled in with his Aunt Aranka at 1 Zichy Jeno utca. Varosliget Park, where Robert and his friend, Matyas, so often rode their bicycles is located in the northeast of this map.

Map credits: Figures 1 and 2 used by the kind permission of Jeno Marton, CEO of Hibernia Nova Kft. Contact: Jeno.Marton@hibernia.hu; http://www.hibernia.hu. These and other maps may be acquired at: https://www.map.hu/Catalogue/Hungary/2_HU_scientific_thematic_maps_/holocaust-budapest-hungary

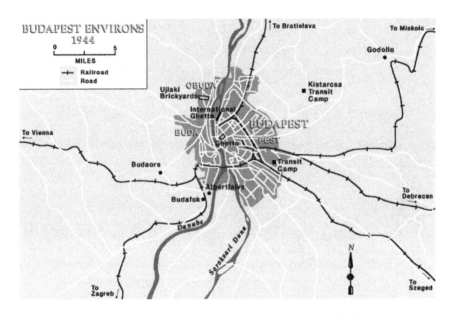

*Figure 3: Larger view map of Budapest environs during the relevant
time period. One can see more clearly how the Danube River splits
the Buda, western portion, from Pest, east of the Danube.*

219

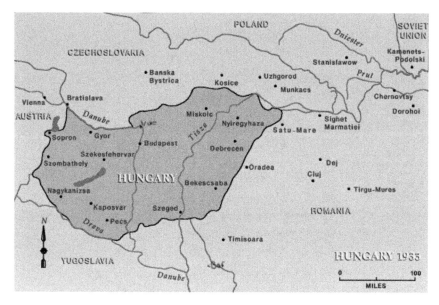

Figure 4: Map of Hungary and its surrounding neighbors before and during
World War II. Vac, where Robert's mother's family lived, is located north
of Budapest, a two-hour train trip at the time. Bor, the concentration camp
where Robert's father was sent and miraculously survived, is identified
approximately in Serbia, then Yugoslavia, southeast of Budapest.

Figures 3 and 4 are used by express permission and courtesy of the United
States Holocaust Memorial Museum encyclopedia, https://encyclopedia.
ushmm.org/content/en/map/budapest-environs-1944 https://encyclopedia.
ushmm.org/images/large/3c6752cc-f96d-405b-88e4-64a5549a38e8.gif

(sources: *The Holocaust in Hungary: Evolution of a Genocide*, Zoltan Vagi, Laszlo Csosz and Gabor Kadar (AltaMira Press, in association with the United States Holocaust Memorial Museum 2013); US Holocaust Memorial Museum encyclopedia; Wikipedia)

1914-1918: As part of the Austro-Hungarian Empire, Hungary participates in World War I as an ally of Germany.

October-November 1918: Following the collapse of the Austro-Hungarian Empire, a democratic revolution sweeps through Hungary, accompanied by anti-Jewish violence.

1919-1920: A counterrevolutionary regime is established; the National Assembly elects Admiral Miklos Horthy as regent. He holds the post from March 1, 1920, to October 16, 1944.

June 4, 1920: The Trianon Peace Treaty deprives Hungary of more than two-thirds of its territories and close to 60 percent of its population, including 3.2 million ethnic Hungarians.

1935: A Hungarian fascist party, the Arrow Cross Party, led by Ferenc Szalasi, was founded.

May 29, 1938: Hungary passes first Jewish Law, restricting the proportion of Jews in certain professions and white-collar positions at major industrial and commercial companies to 20 percent.

March 11, 1939: The Labor Service system is legally established.

May 4, 1939: Second Jewish Law passed. For the first time, Jews were defined racially. Jewish employment in government was forbidden, as were certain jobs (e.g. editors at newspapers). Numbers in certain professions and private companies were severely limited to 6 percent.

1940: Despite popularity in May 1939 elections, Arrow cross party is banned by Hungarian government under Admiral Horthy.

1940: Under pressure from Germany, Hungary joined the Tripartite Pact; the Axis powers, Germany, Italy and Japan.

1941: Hungarian forces join in the invasion of Yugoslavia and the Soviet Union. The attack on the Soviet Union on June 22nd is followed by the mass murder of Jews by the Wehrmacht and special killing squads of the SS and German police (*Einsatzgruppen*).

August 8, 1941: Third Jewish Law. Prohibits intermarriage and penalizes intercourse between Jews and non-Jews.

August 27-30, 1941: Einsatzgruppe C and Ukrainian militias slaughter some twenty-three thousand Jews at Kamenets-Podolski, including many thousands of deportees from Hungary.

1942-March 1944: Approximately 25-40,000 Hungarian labor servicemen die on occupied Soviet territory or in Soviet captivity.

March 1942: Miklos Kallay becomes prime minister (1942-1944).

September 6, 1942: Fourth Jewish Law, sets basis for confiscating land owned by Jews.

April 16-17, 1943: Hitler and Joachim von Ribbentrop confront Horthy about his government's peace negotiations and moderate Jewish policies.

March 19, 1944: German forces invade and occupy Hungary. Adolf Eichmann and his deportation experts arrive in Budapest.

March 21-23, 1944: The Nazis order the creation of a Jewish Council. The collaborationist government, headed by Dome Sztojay, is installed. The Arrow Cross Party is legalized.

March 31, 1944: By decree, Jews are forced to wear a yellow star, effective April 5th. A specific ghettoization plan is approved.

April 7, 1944: A confidential decree is issued on the concentration of Jews.

April 16, 1944: Ghettoization/concentration of Jews begins in Carpatho-Ruthenia (Deportation Zone I). A decree on the registration and confiscation of Jewish assets is issued.

April 22, 1944: A final decision is made on the comprehensive, total deportation of all Hungarian Jews to Auschwitz.

April 28, 1944: A government decree orders ghettoization of Jews.

May 15, 1944: Mass deportations to Auschwitz by the Hungarian authorities begin.

June 25, 1944: By this date, the Jews of Budapest are crowded into 1,948 designated buildings ("yellow star houses").

July 6, 1944: Horthy halts the deportations.

July 9, 1944: Deportations end. From May 15 until this date, more than 437,000 Jews have been deported from Hungary.

July 19, 24, 1944: Despite Horthy's decision, Eichmann's unit deports nearly 3,000 more detainees of internment camps to Auschwitz.

August 23, 1944: Romania withdraws from the Axis, turning against Hitler and his allies.

August 24-29, 1944: Horthy ousts Sztójay and the other Nazi-friendly ministers, replacing them with a new government under Geza Lakatos. Horthy refuses to hand over Budapest Jews to Germany.

October 15-16, 1944: Horthy announces a cease-fire with the Soviets and orders Hungarian troops to lay down their arms. Germany immediately deposes Horthy in a coup and installs Arrow Cross as government, under Ferenc Szalasi. Eichmann returns to Budapest for a short while. Deportations of Jews resume while possible. Arrow Cross Patrols begin shooting Jews in the streets and at the Danube.

October 26, 1944: Arrow Cross hands over 70 Labor Service companies to the Germans.

November 6, 1944: Forced marches of Budapest Jews to Hungary's western border begin.

November 12-December 10, 1944: Szalasi creates two ghettos in Budapest, the international ghetto and the "large ghetto."

November 21, 1944: Szalasi halts the "death marches."

November 7, 1944: Soviet and Romanian troops enter the eastern suburbs of Budapest.

December 24,1944: Soviets complete the encirclement of Budapest, laying siege on the city. Arrow Cross militiamen engage in anti-Jewish terror and massacres.

January 16-18,1945: The Soviet Red Army soldiers enter and liberate the Pest side of the city, containing 80-90,000 Jews, including the "Protected House" at 1 Zichy Jeno Utca.

February 13, 1945: The Soviet Red Army liberates the Jews in the Buda side of the city. Final surrender of Budapest to Soviet Forces.

April 13, 1945: Soviet occupation of Hungary is completed. More than 500,000 Hungarian Jews have been killed between 1941 and 1945.

April 30, 1945: Hitler is dead.

May 7, 1945. Germany surrenders. World War II in Europe is ended.

September 19, 1945: Father Andras Kun, Arrow Cross Party member and defrocked Roman Catholic priest, is convicted of war crimes and crimes against humanity and hanged.

March 12, 1946: Ferenc Szálasi is convicted of war crimes and crimes against humanity and is hanged in Budapest, along with ministers, Gabor Vajna, Karoly Beregfy and the party ideologist Jozsef Gera.

Afterwords....

Robert Holczer (1929-2017)

Robert escaped the then Communist-led Hungary for Israel, without his parents, in 1946. He cultivated his love and interest in Zionism there in a kibbutz before returning to Hungary two years later. He explained he did so because he was homesick for his parents and because he, admittedly naively, was intrigued by Communist ideals. Despite numerous hardships in a Communist State, he obtained a teacher's degree from the Teacher's Academy of Budapest, majoring in Geography, in 1954. He began teaching in various places, including 8th grade in Budapest as well as in Vac, where his mother's family had lived until they were killed, most in Auschwitz, in 1944.

In 1956, Robert fled the country following the Hungarian Revolution. He arrived in St. Louis, Missouri as a refugee, where a surviving cousin was living. From there, he moved to Aspen, Colorado working alongside folk and jazz musicians in a popular nightclub. Maintaining his dream to continue teaching, he knew he needed more money. He met a young group of men who sold Robert on the idea of going to Alaska to fight wildfires, which paid a great deal at the time. He did so in 1959 before finding a college willing to make sense of, and honor his Hungarian education and teaching credentials. He obtained United States citizenship in 1961, of which Robert was so proud because, as a Jew, he had never been afforded Hungarian citizenship. Robert earned a Masters Degree in

History from Fresno State College in Fresno, California in 1962. Shortly thereafter he began teaching history in the San Francisco Bay area, where he met the love of his life, Janice (Jan), a fellow teacher, whom he married in 1966. Robert's mother died in Budapest in 1971.

Robert became father to Jan's three children, Kevin, Mary and Shannon. From 1974-1993, Robert, Jan and Kevin lived in Frankfurt, Germany, where Robert and Jan taught Special Education at an American high school. Robert also taught U.S. Government and was the Advisor to a Model United Nations and Model U.S. Senate. This teaching experience was Robert's favorite. Back in Europe, Robert was able to visit his father much more frequently until he passed in 1980. They then moved to Paris, Kentucky before settling in Vancouver, Washington, just north of Portland, Oregon. While in Paris, he became affiliated with the Speakers Bureau of the United States Holocaust Memorial Museum.

One regret Robert always had was that he never had the opportunity to thank the savior of his family and so many others at 1 Zichy Jeno utca. In approximately 2008, however, he discovered that Jeretzian Ara was still alive, living in the Buda section of Budapest. Robert contacted him, flew out to meet him and they warmly embraced. Jeretzian, a wealthy, still chain-smoking businessman now in his 90s, permitted Robert to read his diaries of the era as they exchanged stories for hours.

Of his parents, Robert often stated that his mother had wished for many years to join Robert and Jan in America. Robert had no doubt whatsoever that his mother would likely have adapted to American life within days, whereas his father would never have coped. So rooted was he in Budapest life, and even more so, in his beloved New York Kavehaz.

Robert became increasingly involved in Holocaust education, culminating with his membership on Washington's Holocaust Center for Humanity's Speakers' Bureau. As a speaker, he would describe his experiences to captivated audiences of young students, families and teachers. He would encourage that nothing like the Holocaust could ever have happened if only people of all ages would have protested or otherwise voiced their opposition to hatred, prejudice and bullying, because this is how genocide begins. Robert died peacefully at home on August 28, 2017 at the age of 87. His grandchildren include, Allyson, John Robert, Angelina, Brandon, Andrew, Kate, Sara and Madeline, and great grandchildren Layne, Cooper, Felix, Desmond, Archer and Calvin..

Young Robi before the War, and playing his dreaded piano.

Top: Robert, as a child, with his mother. Top right: Robert after the war with his father. Class photo, 1936. Robert is in back (top) row, second from the far right.

Below: Robert's parents in Budapest, post-war.

Robert's mother's family in Vac. Robert's mother is at the far right. Her parents and sister were gassed at Auschwitz. Her brother, center, was killed in a forced labor camp.

Robert's Nagymama Julia, incredible cook and family matriarch.

Robert's father, Lajos Holczer, seated center in a
Budapest coffee house with his friends.

Robert, together with Mr. Regelbrugge's 6th grade students.
Finch Elementary School, Spokane, WA, 2012.

Robert and his parents, Lajos and Cornelia Holczer.

Robert with his wife, Jan

Robert at a bench honoring
him, Vancouver, Washington

*(all of the above photos courtesy of the Holczer family collection,
with the exception of the 2012 class photo – author's collection)*

Jeretzian, Ara. (1918-2010)

Following the war, Jeretzian remained in Hungary until 1958, when he relocated to Vienna, Austria for many years. Together with his wife after the war, Maria, they had two children, Ara and Sophie. The creativity he demonstrated time and again throughout World War II continued in all facets of his life, enabling him to run numerous successful businesses. Such businesses included fashion costume design, handcrafted small wool animals and advertising, among many others. He designed costumes and shows for the Moulin Rouge, the Maxim Variete and the Peace Orfeum. In 1993, he wrote a memoir of his experiences up to, and including World War II: *A Vedett Haz (The Protected House)* (Intermix Kiado, 1993). When Robert finally found Jeretzian to thank him in Budapest in 2008, Jeretzian presented him a business card that simply stated, "manager," after his name. At the age of 92, he wrote a book about orchids.

Many survivors who owed their lives to Jeretzian continued to keep in touch with and express their gratitude to him until the end of their respective days, and in 1981 he was honored by Yad Vashem as Righteous Among The Nations.

Jeretzian, with his wife, Maria, children Sophie and Ara, and his mother, Sophie Mechterian. (Ara Jeretzian family collection)

235

Figure 1: Ara Jeretzian (photo courtesy of Ara Jeretzian personal collection)

Jeretzian in his golden years, Budapest.

236

Photograph of a reunion of Jeretzian and survivors from 1 Zichy Jeno Utca, one
year after the war. Jeretzian is seated on the left, third from the bottom. Dr.
Emil Zahler is seated to his immediate left. (Ara Jeretzian family collection)

Jeretzian's Yad Vashem Righteous Among the Nations
certificate, 1981. (Jeretzian family collection)

Aranka Teply (nee Holczer)

Dubbed affectionately and admiringly by Robert's wife, Jan, as the "Hungarian Scarlett O'Hara" for her repeated cunning, intuitive, courageous but sometimes manipulative and conniving acts of heroism and selflessness, Aranka lived to the age of 85. She is survived by her one and only son, Tommy, born of her brief marriage to Tamas, who was killed during mine detection work as part of his forced labor during World War II. It was the photograph taken of Tamas, in a Hungarian military uniform despite being a Jew, that helped make it possible for Aranka to become a "Gentile" for citizenship purposes, enabling her to obtain an apartment at 1 Zichy Jeno Utca, and thus helping to save most of her family members, including Robert. An amazing cook, like her mother, she remained in Budapest until her death.

Aranka many years after the war, and Aranka in the kitchen, adapting one of her mother's recipes. (Holczer family collection)

Norbert Kohn (Kerenyi)

Following the war, Norbert Kohn changed his name to Kerenyi. He stayed in Hungary after the war, graduating first in his class at Semmelweiss

238

medical school in 1952, ultimately training as a pathologist. He escaped the communist dictatorship after the Hungarian uprising of 1956 and landed in Halifax, Canada in January 1957. He worked in Canada as a pathologist and, after a few years on the East Coast, moved to Toronto. He was married to his wife Eva for 60 years, also a Holocaust survivor, and raised a family in Canada. He wrote an autobiographical book about his life, including his experience in the war, *Stories of a Survivor*, by Norbert Kerenyi, Xlibris Corporation, 2011. Dr. Kerenyi died in 2017.

Alfonzo (1912-1987)

Alfonzo, also known as Alfonso, Jozsef Markos and Jozsef Markstein, resumed his career in comedy, art, theater and film after the war. He previously performed often at Moulin Rouge in Paris under the name, "Joe Stan," before he changed it to "Alfonzo" after the King of Spain, following a 1940 decree banning the performance of "English" artists. Some films include *Ket emelet boldogsag* (1960), *I Am Jerome* (1970), *En vagyok Jeromos* (1971) and *Nem er a Nevem* (1961). Alfonzo was considered a master of parody, infusing elements of pantomime. He wrote a memoir of his life, *Listen to People Here, But if Not, It Doesn't Matter to Me, Mosaics of a Genre*, in Modern Clown, NPL, Bp., 1975 (Szkeneteka), but he was silent about his experiences leading up to and including his time at 1 Zichy Jeno utca.

Dr. Ferenc Volgyesi (1895-1967)

Dr. Volgyesi enjoyed relative fame throughout his life, writing several books translated into different languages. Much of his work was devoted to the hypnosis of humans and animals. One of his best-known works, originally published in 1937, was *Hypnosis of Man and Animals*. It was published in English by Harcourt Publishing in 1966.

Dr. Emil Zahler (1875-1956)

A prominent Budapest pediatrician before the war and pillar of the Jewish community, Dr. Zahler's family were regulars at the seder table of the Chief Rabbi of Budapest. Dr Zahler remained in Budapest after the war where he ran a small clinic. He said farewell to his darling daughter and granddaughter Eva, who eventually made their way out of Hungary. He died at age 81 in 1956. He is buried at the Dohany synagogue in Budapest, where his name remains engraved.

Dr. Emil Zahler before the war

Dr. Zahler with his granddaughter, Eva   Dr. Zahler's mother before the war – she would be removed from the house by the Arrow Cross

Dr Zahler's second wife at his tombstone, Dohany Synagogue, Budapest
Foorvos = Head Doctor

Eva Berg (Kadar) (Girl with the laughing eyes)

Born in October 1928 to Erzsi Zahler and Istvan (Pista) Kadar, Eva
Kadar was 15 going on 16 years old during her time in the yellow star
house. After the war she and her mother returned to the hotel they had
owned on 12 Vaci Utca to find all of the property emptied out. As an
interesting historical footnote, Rudolph Kastner, who negotiated with
Eichmann and organized a train to save 1,600 Jews from deportation,
the so-called Kastner train, lived in and conducted business in the Zahler
hotel where he came to know Erzsi and Eva. The Kastner train consisted
of 35 cattle trucks that left Budapest on 30 June 1944, during the German
occupation of Hungary, carrying over 1,600 Jews to safety in Switzerland.
This amazing story is documented in the book by Anna Porter (2007),

Kastner's Train. Douglas & MacIntyre, for which Eva was interviewed and quoted (as Eva Zahler).

After the war, Eva was reunited as well with her father, who survived the war on the grounds of one of Raoul Wallenberg's safe houses in the "International Ghetto."

After a brief further time in Hungary, she reunited with her mother, in Foehrnwald, a Displaced Persons camp in Bavaria, Germany, one of the largest DP camps in post WWII Europe, and the last to close in 1957. On March 1st, 1947, Eva and her mother sailed on a refitted ship, the Abril, along with about 600 other Holocaust survivors from Port Du Bouc, France for Palestine. While at sea, the Abril was renamed the S.S. Ben Hecht, after the American playwright, Ben Hecht, whose Broadway play, "A flag is born" featuring a young Marlon Brando, raised funds for the financing of the ship. Seven days later, on March 8, British destroyers intercepted the Ben Hecht. She was boarded and towed to Haifa under British control. The refugees, including Eva and her mother, were sent to the prison camps in Cyprus. The American crew was arrested and sent to the infamous Acre Prison. Eva and her mother were released to Israel in 1948 and Eva would ultimately serve in the first military nursing class in the Israel Defense Forces, graduating in 1952. After some time in Israel, Eva would travel to live in South Africa where she would meet Joe Berg, a physician who would become her husband of 50 years. They moved to London, England, where their kids Danny and Kary were born, and ultimately to Toronto, Canada, where Eva still resides (2019). Eva, now a widow, celebrated her 90th birthday in Toronto on October 10, 2018. Her son, Danny, using videotape of Eva recounting tales of her life filmed thirty years before, tracked down Robert Holczer and, through him, Paul Regelbrugge, the author of this book. Although Eva suffered from dementia by the time of Robi's meeting with Danny, Robi and Eva -- after all the years -- were finally able to have a conversation on the phone nearly 60 years after they last saw each other in the protected, yellow star house.

Eva as a young girl with
her mother, Erzsi

Eva cycling streets of
Budapest before the war

School Photo. Eva is middle, back row

Eva in photos taken just after the war

In her nursing uniform, Israel   Eva, with her son, Danny, in Toronto,
circa approximately 1952 2000.

(all photos of Dr. Zahler and Eva Berg courtesy
of Dr. Danny Berg family collection)

1 Zichy Jeno utca today (author's photo)

*Interior small courtyard where Robert stacked limbs, 1
Zichy Jeno utca today. (author's photo)*

Made in the USA
Las Vegas, NV
26 February 2021